INTELLECTUAL EXPERIMENTS OF THE GREEK ENLIGHTENMENT

INTELLECTUAL EXPERIMENTS OF THE GREEK ENLIGHTENMENT

Friedrich Solmsen

PRINCETON UNIVERSITY PRESS
PRINCETON, NEW JERSEY

PUBLISHED BY PRINCETON UNIVERSITY PRESS,
PRINCETON AND LONDON

LIBRARY OF CONGRESS CATALOGING IN PUBLICATION DATA WILL
BE FOUND ON THE LAST PRINTED PAGE OF THIS BOOK
COMPOSED IN LINOTYPE ELECTRA
AND DESIGNED BY BRUCE CAMPBELL
PRINTED IN THE UNITED STATES OF AMERICA
BY PRINCETON UNIVERSITY PRESS,
PRINCETON, NEW JERSEY

CONTENTS

PREFACE

The origin of a book is of interest to the author, not to the readers. But in this case many debts have accumulated, which must at least be acknowledged in a Preface.

My wife, Lieselotte Solmsen, must be mentioned first. By right her name should be on the title page for there has been no stage in the process from first sketch to final proof in which her good sense, her advice, encouragement, and criticism have not helped me to move forward and take the hurdles.

At a critical juncture, when the unifying idea, instead of shaping the material, had become buried within it, Martin Ostwald of Swarthmore College, who had earlier read the manuscript, came to the rescue. In conversation with him, a way was found—neither remote nor difficult, yet it had eluded me—to organize the centrifugal chapters and give all of them the identical orientation. I am deeply grateful to him.

Mention of Swarthmore College turns my thoughts to a place very dear to me, where classical studies prosper to a degree quite unusual in these days, and where I was privileged to spend the Spring Semester of 1970 as a Visitor. Helen North, admired friend for thirty and more years, initiated our visit. She, with her sister Mary and with Lore and Martin Ostwald, made us at home, and soon we found ourselves living a life in which it was perfectly natural to write about utopian schemes and very easy to move from that chapter to others. New friendships provided additional incentive. I owe much to Mildred and Rudolf Hirsch, Gabriele and Henry Hoenigswald, and most assuredly also to Dorrice and Glenn Morrow. Glenn's stalwart personality remains alive for me; the warm interest with which he followed and encouraged my studies lives on in my memory, even though I can no longer place a dedication copy in his hands. For the book is dedicated to all who directly or indirectly have contributed toward its existence. I am merely returning to them what is theirs.

However, the list of my debts extends further. Loretta Freiling, paragon of secretaries, has dealt with not a few manuscripts on their way from author to publisher, but none yet, I am sure, has taxed her eyes and her power of intelligent divination as much as this. A succession of research assistants, Mary Xiroyanni, Henry Teloh, David Sansone, and Ellen Nonn, resourceful and invariably good-humored, turned chores into pleasures. The Graduate School of the University of Wisconsin financed this assistance in years of plenty and continued it in lean years. I greatly appreciate this support.

The completion of the book coincides with the end of my academic activity. During the last twelve years I have held an appointment at the Institute for Research in the Humanities at the University of Wisconsin. I could not have wished for a better combination of teaching and scholarly pursuits, more congenial friends and colleagues, or for a more inspiring exchange of information and thoughts between men and women at work in different fields.

To the Princeton University Press I am under deep obligation. Sanford G. Thatcher, the Social Science Editor, by his confidence and well timed encouragement helped me over the hurdles. Gail M. Filion, my reader, saved me from stylistic infelicities, from printers' errors and from most of the drudgery connected with the final stages of book-making.

BIBLIOGRAPHICAL NOTE

References to Presocratic philosophers follow *Fragmente der Vorsokratiker*, edd. Diels-Kranz (cited as D.-K.), 9th ed. (Berlin, 1960). Later editions of individual Presocratics use Diels-Kranz numbers or have concordances referring to them. For translations of the fragments see Kathleen Freeman, *Ancilla to the Presocratic Philosophers* (Oxford, 1948); for the Sophists and Antiphon (Orator and Sophist), R. K. Sprague, *The Older Sophists* (Columbia, S.C., 1972).

For fragments of tragedians, see *Tragicorum Graecorum Fragmenta* (*TGF*), ed. Augustus Nauck, with a supplement of new fragments of Euripides and anonymous tragedians edited by Bruno Snell (Hildesheim, 1964); see also Colin Austin, *Nova Fragmenta Euripidea, Kleine Texte für Vorlesungen und Übungen* 187 (Berlin, 1968), and the first volume of Bruno Snell's new *Tragicorum Graecorum Fragmenta* (Göttingen, 1970).

Editions and commentaries on Euripides mentioned frequently and as a rule only by author's name:

W. S. Barrett, *Euripides: Hippolytus* (Oxford, 1946)
A. M. Dale, *Euripides: Helen* (Oxford, 1967)
A. M. Dale, *Euripides: Alcestis* (Oxford, 1954)

Editions and commentaries on Thucydides mentioned frequently:

K. W. Krüger, Θουκυδίδου Ξυγγραφή (Berlin, 1858-1861)
E. F. Poppo and J. M. Stahl, *Thucydides de Bello Peloponnesiaco Libri Octo* (Leipzig 1875-1889)
J. Classen and J. Steup, *Thucydides* (Berlin, 1892-1922)

A. W. Gomme, *A Historical Commentary on Thucydides* I (Oxford, 1944; corr. repr. Oxford, 1950); II, III (Oxford, 1956; corr. repr. Oxford, 1962); IV, with A. Andrewes and K. J. Dover (Oxford, 1970). The responsible commentator will be cited.

Jacqueline de Romilly (Budé), *Thucydide: La Guerre du Péloponnèse* (Paris, 1953-1967)

For writers on rhetoric:

Ludwig Radermacher, "Artium Scriptores (Reste der voraristotelischen Rhetorik)," *SAWW* 227 (1951) Abhandlung 3

ABBREVIATIONS

Brunt	P. A. Brunt, "Thucydides and Alcibiades," *REG* 65 (1952) 59-96
Conacher	D. J. Conacher, *Euripidean Drama* (Toronto, 1967)
Delebecque	Edouard Delebecque, *Thucydide et Alcibiade* (Aix-en-Provence, 1965)
de Ste. Croix	G.E.M. de Ste. Croix, *The Origins of the Peloponnesian War* (London, 1972)
Dodds	E. R. Dodds, *The Greeks and the Irrational* (Berkeley, 1951)
Finley	John H. Finley, Jr., *Thucydides* (Cambridge, Mass., 1942)
Finley, *Essays*	*Three Essays on Thucydides* (Cambridge, Mass., 1967)
Fränkel	Hermann Fränkel, "Zeno of Elea's Attacks on Plurality," *AJPh* 63 (1942) 1-25; 193-206 = *Wege und Formen frühgriechischen Denkens* (Munich, 1955) 198-236
Gomme, *Essays*	A. W. Gomme, *Essays in Greek History and Literature* (Oxford, 1937)
GRBS	*Greek, Roman and Byzantine Stories*
Guthrie	W.K.C. Guthrie, A *History of Greek Philosophy* (Cambridge, 1962-)
Huart	Pierre Huart, *Le Vocabulaire de l'analyse psychologique dans l'oeuvre de Thucydide, Études et Commentaires* 69 (Paris, 1968)
Kagan	Donald Kagan, *The Outbreak of the Peloponnesian War* (Ithaca, N.Y., 1969)
Kennedy	George Kennedy, *The Art of Persuasion in Greece* (Princeton, 1963)
Kitto	H.D.F. Kitto, *Greek Tragedy* (London, 3rd ed., 1961)

Lesky	Albin Lesky, "Psychologie bei Euripides," in *Euripide, Entretiens sur l'antiquité classique* 6 (Vandoeuvres-Genève, 1960)
Murray	Robert L. Murray, "Persuasion in Euripides," unpublished diss. Cornell 1964
Parry	Adam Parry, "Thucydides' Historical Perspective," *YCS* 22 (1972) 47-61
Patzer	Harald Patzer, *Das Problem der Geschichtsschreibung des Thukydides und die thukydideische Frage* (Berlin, 1937)
Regenbogen	Otto Regenbogen, *Thukydides' politische Reden* (Leipzig, 1949)
de Romilly, *Imperialism*	Jacqueline de Romilly, *Thucydides and Athenian Imperialism*, trans. Philip Thody (Oxford, 1963)
de Romilly, *Histoire*	*Histoire et raison chez Thucydide* (Paris, 1956)
Ros	J.G.A. Ros, *Die* μεταβολή (*Variatio*) *als Stilprinzip des Thukydides* (Paderborn, 1959)
Schwartz	Eduard Schwartz, *Das Geschichtswerk des Thukydides*, 2nd ed. (Bonn, 1929)
Snell	Bruno Snell, *Scenes from Greek Drama* (Berkeley, 1964)
Kleine Schriften	Friedrich Solmsen, *Kleine Schriften* (Hildesheim, 1968)
Stahl	H. P. Stahl, *Thukydides. Die Stellung des Menschen im geschichtlichen Prozess, Zetemata* 40 (Munich, 1966)
Strasburger	Hermann Strasburger, "Thukydides und die politische Selbstdarstellung der Athener," *Hermes* 86 (1958) 17-40 = *WdF* 98, 498-530
von Fritz	Kurt von Fritz, *Die griechische Geschichtsschreibung* I (2 vols.) (Berlin, 1967)
Wassermann	Felix Wassermann, "Post-Periclean Democracy in Action: The Mytilenean Debate

	(Thuc. III 37-48)," *TAPhA* 87 (1956) 27-41 = *WdF* 98, 477-497
Webster	T.B.L. Webster, *The Tragedies of Euripides* (London, 1967)
WdF	*Wege der Forschung: Thukydides, Wege der Forschung* 98 (Darmstadt, 1968)
Westlake	H. D. Westlake, *Individuals in Thucydides* (Cambridge, 1968)
Wilamowitz	Ulrich von Wilamowitz-Moellendorff, "Thukydides VIII," *Hermes* 43 (1908) 576-618
Zuntz	Günther Zuntz, *The Political Plays of Euripides* (Manchester, 1955)

INTELLECTUAL
EXPERIMENTS
OF THE GREEK
ENLIGHTENMENT

INTRODUCTION

The Greek Enlightenment of the fifth century B.C., also known as the Rationalistic Movement or the Age of the Sophists, is generally associated with progressive or revolutionary ideas and even more, perhaps, with their negative correlate, the questioning of time-honored beliefs and values. In principle, nothing was any longer taken for granted, and the fact that something was commonly practiced did not in the least protect it from criticism. This criticism, not always original but skillfully employing whatever thought of the past could be drawn into its service, spared neither the official religion nor institutions, laws, or conceptions of justice on which the structure of the city-state was based. Although ideas as to the direction the reform should take diverged considerably, education was bound to be a key issue, since, for a more rational and successful life, instruction in subjects so far neglected was of primary importance.

These revolutionary theories have repeatedly been set forth by students of Greek philosophy or Greek thought. Some scholars confine their discussion to the sophists, who certainly provided a strong impulse and who in addition occupy a certain, if small and disputed, place in the history of Greek metaphysics, epistemology, and ethics. Yet even in such works it often becomes necessary to glance at some non-philosophical authors of the period. Their thoughts may convey the "environment" in which the moral doctrines flourished; conversely, the writings of such authors, and for obvious reasons especially of the historian Thucydides and the tragedian Euripides, may reflect the powerful impact of the new theories.

All the characteristics of the Enlightenment that we have mentioned relate to thought, in fact primarily to the content of thought. Yet since the movement we are discussing was adventurous and favored experiments, new departures would not necessarily take the form of doctrines, critical discussions, and programs of reform. Reason, exulting in a formerly unknown freedom and confidence, would also turn a searchlight upon itself and discover a potential of which it may have been dimly conscious but which it had not yet put to the test. If education and people's values were to change, arguments were needed to make the changes acceptable. The power of arguing resourcefully was a strong weapon. This power could be acquired; in the second half of the fifth century, it was treated as an art, a τέχνη to be taught, learned, and employed. Through arguments, one man's mind or reason would communicate with those of other men, trying to convince and influence them. Often, however, one could work more effectively upon the irrational tendencies of fellow human beings, upon their emotions. Pity, anger, indignation, and similar impulses could be manipulated, and we may study efforts of the kind and in some instances decide whether they sprang from honest intentions.

If reason was to be active in devising a better order of things, it could by a kind of compromise with reality confine itself to what was practical and possible. Yet it could also go to extremes and, ignoring all restraint, indulge in wishful thinking. If a reasonable world order would be very different from that actually existing, what form ought it to take? Such "ought to . . ." schemes, if worked out in detail, are apt to range into the realm of utopia, and, thoughts being free, nothing would stop them from crossing the borderline to the fantastic.

Reason is *logos*, but *logos* is a word of countless meanings. *Logos* in the sense of reason can hardly be divorced from *logos* in the sense of speech and language. These were and are the indispensable vehicle of all reasoning. Even prior to our period, the Greeks had consulted their language for a better understanding of the objective world. Scrutiny and experimentation showed that language could be employed far more thoroughly for this as well as for other purposes. Some of its possible uses had so far been neglected.

As we have seen, reason in this age of its triumph was far from ignoring the irrational aspects of human nature. Quite to the contrary, it endeavored to understand them. Their conflict with reason was studied, and so were the workings both of reason and of these irrational or emotional tendencies. The result was a psychology established on a purely secular basis, with no need for divine causation. As far as it was theory, this psychology ought to have a place among the revolutionary, new opinions advanced at this time. Our excuse for including it in a monograph not concerned with these opinions might be that it has failed to receive that place; more relevant, however, is that the practical psychology used to explain and understand human behavior reflects the new outlook. This closer understanding of both rational and irrational processes makes it possible to reconstruct human motives realistically and on the basis of experience (although speculation also plays a part). We shall see that such a reconstruction of motives combines readily with the reconstruction of events, most notably of recent political events. Reason is confident that it can synthesize individual, separately known events into a whole; the missing links are supplied in accordance with "probability." Again attempts of this kind are not entirely new, but in this period they are particularly bold.

The experiments here characterized may not be as significant as the proposition that "man is the measure," as the promulgation of "nature" (φύσις) against "convention" (νόμος), the pioneering ideas about education—in sum, as the new thoughts or doctrines put forward by the sophists or other advanced minds. Still they, too, are expressions of the freedom gained by reason, a precious yet at the same time dangerous acquisition, which could serve many purposes. Trial and error were needed to separate use from misuse.

The experiments of which we have given a rough description differ in kind, and there is relatively little connection between them. Essentially, what they have in common is that each in its own way is an adventure of reason. They are animated by the same spirit, but it is a restless spirit, moving in various directions. Beyond this identical basic impulse there are a number of limited contacts, some of them natural and almost inevitable, others more accidental. Reference has already been made to the ease with which the realistic new psychology could be employed to reconstruct historical developments. We also readily understand that someone wishing to argue effectively would like to avail himself of the previously unknown resources offered by the Greek language. On the other hand if psychology at the time was keenly aware of the human emotions and these emotions are what persuasion tries to guide and influence, we might expect to find links between these two ventures of reason into the territory of the irrational, but this expectation is not borne out. It remained for Plato (*Phaedrus*, 270b-272b) to postulate a scientific instead of the usual haphazard procedure in the orator's appeal to the emotions, and for Aristotle (*Rhet.*, B2-11) to implement this postulate by making psychology the basis of *psychagogia*.

Since each chapter treats one of the new devices, the chapters are parallel, not climactic, in relation to one another. No conclusion can synthesize them—unless it be a reaffirmation of the assertions made in these introductory remarks. If I have nevertheless written something in the nature of a "Conclusion," the reason is probably that dealing with so many adventures and experiments proved contagious and led me to speculate about the later fate of the devices here studied. A serious attempt of the kind would be premature, because the necessary spade work has not yet been done. True, some studies undertaken with quite different intentions may be used for this new purpose. Still, with or without the benefit of previous investigations, the sequel to the experiments whose early stages we explore would require a book of its own.

I have not aimed at a complete presentation of the relevant material, because it soon became clear that this was normally impossible (e.g., in Chapter I, where it seems beyond our power to identify all argumentative forms, and obviously also in Chapter VI). Where completeness might be possible, it would be pointless because the similarity of the material would become tedious and the comments inevitably repetitious. Since only material preserved verbatim could be of use, I have in a somewhat monotonous fashion drawn on two authors mentioned at the beginning, Thucydides and Euripides. Entire chapters are concerned with the one or with the other, and the reader may feel justifiably that, toward the end, the book becomes more and more concerned with facets of Thucydides' outlook and practice. The experiments of these two authors are not meant to be the only or "typical" manifestations of the Enlightenment; all we maintain is that this period and this movement rather than any other in Greek history would encourage their intellectual adventures. Aristophanes makes a few appearances, most of them to have his right of appearing questioned. Rather than Aristophanes it is Antiphon the orator who, after the principal authorities, comes *longo proximus intervallo*, whereas his namesake, the sophist—to my own astonishment—contributes nothing at all. Another absentee may cause surprise. "Hippocrates" might be expected in the discussion of some arguments or other uses of reasoning. That he does not appear is due not to negligence but to the lack of truly comparable items. The writings in the *Corpus Hippocraticum* may illuminate some aspects of Thucydides. In this monograph they could at most have been used for the generalizations discussed in Chapter V. Yet, even here, what they have in common with the Athenians is very "common" indeed; nothing specific or in any way illuminating was to be gained. We might have reached back into the past more often to trace antecedents or emphasize contrasts, but brief remarks to this effect proved in most cases unsatisfactory, and longish digressions are better reserved for publication elsewhere.

To repeat, I am conscious of, but not unduly discouraged by, the fragmentary nature of my attempt to deal with neglected facets of the Greek Enlightenment. Nothing could please me more than to see others take up some of the tasks I have left undone, especially in the area of Chapter I. The *reductio ad absurdum*, for instance, is a device whose history begins with Homer; yet there is no doubt in my mind that the fifth century developed new forms of it. The "calculus of advantages"—a phrase I permitted myself after the model of "calculus of pleasure"—is referred to a few times in this book, but I have not followed up its uses. Orators like to point out flagrant inconsistencies and conflicts between, say, one course of action and another, one of them usually still under consideration so that it may be abandoned. Demosthenes abounds in examples of this device, but it is also familiar to Antiphon, is used by speakers in Thucydides, and could doubtless be traced farther back. Finally, while I deal with the reconstruction of recent events and of the remote past in Thucydides, there are in his writings also instances of what might be called "pre-construction," the rational calculation of a probable course of events: Archidamus, Pericles, and the Corinthians use their minds—the Corinthians rather frivolously—to balance the prospects for and against victory in the coming war. We have lately been urged to distinguish this *pronoia* from the *prognosis* practiced by the Hippocratics (A. Rivier, *MH*, 26, 1969, 129ff.). It is well to heed this warning; yet *pronoia*, if absent in the Hippocratic writings, is used in Herodotus and indeed in Homer (not only by Odysseus). Mainly because of such antecedents, I excluded this application of reason from my monograph, but another student of *pronoia* in the sense of foresight may succeed in isolating the new features that appear in Thucydides and his contemporaries.

Enough has been said about the need to proceed selectively and about subjects we leave untouched. It is time to begin our analyses, and, as we turn to "Argumentation" as an important area for experiments with new forms, new techniques, and new uses, we shall no longer indicate what we leave to others but specify what we propose to study ourselves.

I

ARGUMENTATION

Central in importance as is argumentation for the vigorous new use of *logos*, an exhaustive account of its varieties seems impossible, and, even were it possible, would disturb the proportions of our study. On the following pages, we shall examine briefly one and, somewhat more fully, another type of argumentation. Instances of these types might be found in earlier days; but in the period of the Enlightenment they became appreciated and an object of conscious manipulation.

It seems expedient to start at a point where arguments run riot. Gorgias in his treatise *On Nature or Not-Being* uses arguments that are in content and form indebted to Parmenides and, among other Eleatic thinkers, probably most to Zeno. As is well known, he tries to prove three theses, and his method of reasoning changes as he moves from one to the other. The analysis of a relatively short passage taken from the proof for the first thesis will furnish samples of the two kinds of argumentation that we have selected as particularly rewarding for our study.[1]

The *demonstrandum* is "Nothing is" (or "exists," 66), but to demonstrate it, several other propositions must be established. "Neither Being nor Not-Being nor again Being as well as Not-Being can have existence." We may skip the reasons for Not-Being (67), but the arguments against Being (68-74) claim our attention because they exhibit the same

[1] I use 82B3 Diels-Kranz (D.-K.) as basis for my text. The arguments of Gigon for *De MXG* (*Hermes* 71, 1936, 186ff., esp. 192ff.) have a good deal of weight, but I continue to have more confidence in the version of Sextus, which includes fewer critical or other comments and preserves something of Gorgias' sprightly style. For our purpose the difference between the versions hardly matters.

pattern as the proof that Nothing exists. For here, first the one and then the other of two opposites is shown to be impossible, and, having shown this, Gorgias still examines the possibility of their simultaneous truth. If Being existed it would be eternal or temporal or eternal as well as temporal. If eternal, it would have to be without a beginning (*arche*), and having no beginning it would have to be infinite; yet if infinite, it would be nowhere (70). The last assertion is again supported by an argumentation moving both ways—we may as well now call it by its technical name *in utramque partem disputare*. Something infinite would be either in another entity or in itself; but the entity encompassing it would have to be larger than the infinite and thus render the infinite impossible; on the other hand, the infinite, if supposed to be in itself, would at once be the body and its place, which seems absurd. *Ergo* it is nowhere; and being nowhere it is *not* (70). This is the conclusion reached from the supposition that it is eternal. The *altera pars, scil.* the possibility that it is temporal and has come into being, still needs discussion. Here Parmenides had provided enough ammunition, especially if (as we prefer to think) he disproved genesis from Being as well as from Not-Being.[2] For this is in essence what Gorgias does, even if he does not follow Parmenides in every detail. Next, having disposed of Being as eternal and as temporal (70), he

[2] We are here touching on a much discussed crux in the text of Parmenides B8 D.-K. I refer for a discussion and bibliography to Leonardo Taran, *Parmenides* (Princeton, 1965); see his apparatus on B 8.12 as well as pp. 95ff. Uvo Hölscher, who shares with most the preference for the dichotomous approach, has recently (*Parmenides vom Wesen des Seienden*, Frankfurt, 1969) proposed οὔτε ποτ' ἐκ δὴ (for μὴ) ἐόντος, the smallest change; I wonder, however, whether δή is germane to this didactic style and would also set some store by the definite article. I prefer to read after αὐξηθέν (v. 7) ⟨οὔτ' ἐκ τοῦ ἐόντος ἔγεντ' ἄν⟩—not τεῦ ἐόντος (Diels)—and to continue, e.g., ⟨οὐ γὰρ ἐόν πω ἔην⟩. Alexander P. D. Mourelatos, *The Route of Parmenides* (New Haven and London, 1969) 123, defends the transmitted reading. I find difficulties in the meaning he extracts from it.

still turns against their combination by the simple argument that the one half of this proposition would invalidate the other (72). This should suffice to undermine Being; yet, Gorgias' resourcefulness having no limits, he adds an alternative procedure (*καὶ ἄλλως*, 73): Being might be either one or many. But if it is one, it would have to subsist as a body, a quantity, or something else that is divisible and thus would no longer be one; and if many, we must regard the many as a sum of ones, but as the one has been disproved, the many cannot exist either.

Even in paraphrasing Gorgias, we have had occasions for pointing out the care he takes to eliminate every conceivable possibility. In the section just studied, this device repeatedly takes the form of "neither the one nor the other nor a combination of both," but this pattern should not be regarded as a typical one. Gorgias evidently considered it appropriate to the thesis he here wished to establish,[3] yet in the *Helen* and in the *Palamedes* he uses basically the same method in entirely different ways. Helen may have left Menelaus and preferred Paris because she yielded either to the will of the gods (82B11.6), to force (7), to persuasion (8-14), or finally to love (15-19). One after another of these four causes is taken up, and Helen, cleared of each, emerges blameless.[4] Palamedes' defense carries this procedure even farther; there

[3] Guido Calogero aptly describes this treatise of Gorgias as "a highly ironical *reductio ad absurdum* of the Eleatics and especially of Zeno" (*JHS* 77, 1957, 16; see his more extended discussion of Gorgias in *Studi sull'Eleatismo*, Rome, 1932, 157ff.). In *De MXG* similarities with Zeno are noted *passim*. We cannot verify them; some are probably valid. See also Ernst Bux, *Hermes* 76 (1941) 403, and C.M.J. Sicking, *Mnemosyne* 4.17 (1964) 226ff., esp. 242ff. If G. B. Kerferd's acute analysis of the first section (*Phronesis* 1, 1955, 3ff.) is correct, my concentration on the form of Gorgias' arguments is open to criticism. Conversely, if the form is important, Kerferd's position is vulnerable. This is not the place to develop my objections (e.g. to the use of "it," of the "phenomenal" world, etc.).

[4] For literary interest in Helen during this period see below, p. 31.

are more conceivable motives to be refuted, and at times subdivisions are introduced. How, he asks (among other questions of the same type), could a desire for tyranny have prompted me to commit treason? Would I have wished to rule over the Greeks or over the barbarians, i.e. Trojans? If the latter, did I base my hopes on force or on persuasion? Or would they have voluntarily accepted me as their ruler (82B11a 13f.)?

Such presentations of possibilities followed immediately by their refutation recur in the orator Antiphon as well as in Euripides. Although this is never stated in so many words, we are left with the impression that all conceivable motives have been ruled out. In Antiphon's speech (*Or.* 5) "About the murder of Herodes," a Mytilenean must clear himself of the charge that he killed Herodes when traveling in the same boat. After pointing out inconsistencies in the accuser's strategy and having confirmed his own statements by witnesses, he asks, "For what reason would I have killed the man?" and proceeds to consider four possible reasons (57-60). They are hostility of long standing, the wish to oblige some third person, fear of suffering the fate that he is alleged to have inflicted, and finally the prospect of enriching himself. One of these motives, the wish to oblige someone else, had actually figured in the accusation. It might therefore seem imperative to give it the greatest attention and spare no effort to refute it. Rather surprisingly Antiphon does the opposite. He disposes of this point simply by asking: Who has ever committed this as a favor for someone else (τίς πώποτε χαριζόμενος ἑτέρῳ τοῦτο εἰργάσατο, 57)? Next, answering the question blandly, "No one, I think," he passes at once to another motive which, in principle, might carry conviction. This substituted motive is hostility. It had been the first on Antiphon's own list, and when dealing with it he thought it sufficient to declare that there was no hostility between himself and the victim. Coming back to it now, he repeats this peremptory declaration. At this critical point, the assertion gains strength from having been made once before. Still it is astonishing that a mere affirmation, unsupported by either argument or witnesses, should suffice.[5] And yet Antiphon must have been convinced of its effectiveness. For he resorts to it also in the celebrated defense of himself against the charge of plotting to overthrow Athenian democracy. Small as is the piece that has come to light on papyrus, we are yet able to discern here even more motives (coll. 1-3) brought up and refuted than in the speech for the Mytilenean. Again, sometimes a simple denial is considered sufficient, and there are even instances where the mere mentioning of the motive (in the form of a question: "or because you had deprived me of some property?") is all that Antiphon thinks necessary. Did he count on everybody's knowing that it had not happened? Or, on the contrary, would a closer examination have reminded the audience of something that had happened? I am inclined to think that he expected sheer bluff to carry him over the hurdle of an awkward situation. Still there also are motives that Antiphon refutes by showing them devoid of intrinsic probability.

Turning to Euripides, we see his characters use this type of argumentation in a number of the preserved plays, and we also find it in fragments. Perhaps the best illustration is Hippolytus' defense when he is confronted with Phaedra's dead body and finds himself accused of seduction. Proud of his exceptional purity, he thinks Theseus ought to show how he was corrupted (*δεῖ δή σε δεῖξαι τῷ τρόπῳ διεφθάρην*, v. 1008). Still, he immediately tries to satisfy this requirement himself

[5] After the four words *ἀλλ' οὐκ ἦν αὐτῷ* (*scil.* *χρήματα*), Antiphon suddenly turns the tables, declaring that the prospect of gain might rather have prompted the accuser to bring the charge (58). Slightly later when he defends Lycinus, alleged to be his accomplice, he adds another type of argument to what he has said in his own defense: On an occasion when it was far easier for this man to destroy Herodes, he did not do so (61f.).

(vv. 1009-1020). Three reasons why he could have so drastically departed from his normal chastity present themselves to his mind. Was Phaedra a woman of exceptional beauty? We have in our analysis of Antiphon learned to content ourselves with simple negations proffered without argument or evidence. This time we are given even less, yet Hippolytus has the best of excuses. To deny that Phaedra was beautiful while her body lies on the stage and Theseus is in a highly emotional state of mind would be the extreme of tactlessness, and even Hippolytus, hater of women and innocent in the ways of the world, has sense enough not to damage his case still further. He therefore turns at once to the second possible reason. Would a relationship with Phaedra have put him in the possession of Theseus' "house" (v. 1010)? This, he briefly but vigorously declares, would have been a most foolish hope. It would indeed, and an Athenian audience could be counted upon to realize this. A third reason would be the prospect of becoming the ruler or "tyrant." Here Hippolytus bursts into an emphatic declamation about the wrong-headedness of preferring such a life to being "second" in the city and enjoying some scope and freedom for action.[6] The reason why Hippolytus here waxes so eloquent may be Euripides' own delight in arguing for a rather unconventional point of view, but variation in the response to the three motives suggested would also have seemed to him worth his effort.

Elsewhere in Euripides the argument is cast in the same mold. Two passages in the *Hecuba* are less forensic than the self-defense of Hippolytus: "Why," Hecuba asks Odysseus,

[6] He would wish to be "first," but elsewhere, e.g. in the Panhellenic games. Despite difficulties in the text of v. 1012 (where Markland helps decisively) and of v. 1015, it is a mistake to suspect vv. 1012-1015. Each of these verses has its place and function in the pattern we are discussing. Three possible motives, each disproved in a different fashion, are most appropriate. Verses 960-970, where two are refuted by serious arguments, are different. Despite certain anomalies, these lines are close to the kind of argumentation which we study.

"should my daughter (Polyxene) be sacrificed at the tomb of Achilles?" None of the reasons that might be advanced could pass critical scrutiny (vv. 258-270). Toward the end of the play (vv. 1197, esp. 1201-1207) she similarly reduces *ad absurdum* any motive why Polymestor, when murdering her youngest son, should have had the interest of the Greeks at heart. Andromache, in the play bearing her name, employs the same pattern of reasoning to clear herself of a vicious accusation. The charge is that she, the concubine of Neoptolemus, tries to monopolize his favor and is plotting against his legitimate wife. This charge, from whatever point of view it may be considered, Andromache declares absurd; Hermione has only herself to blame if she no longer enjoys his love. Turning from the preserved plays to the fragments, we recognize this type of defense in the *Cretans*, where Pasiphae, having lain with the bull, declares her unnatural passion an "involuntary evil" (frg. 82.10-20); it lacks all probability (οὐδὲν εἰκός); point by point she makes clear that nothing conceivable could have induced her voluntarily to commit the crime.

Finally, lest Thucydides, whose work includes examples for many other types of argument, be considered a stranger to this, we may look at the words of warning spoken by Archidamus at the convention in Sparta, where pressure for war against Athens had become very strong (I 80.3-81.6): "On what would we base our confidence for victory?" is the question he urges the impatient convention to ponder. On our boats? We fall far short of the Athenians. On our financial resources? On our weapons? Our superior manpower? One after the other of these possible sources of confidence is shown either not to exist or to be of limited effectiveness (80.3-81.6).

The second form of argumentation, which the section in Gorgias' "On Nature" illustrates, will engage us longer. Neither Being nor Not-Being can exist; Being can be neither eternal nor temporal; something eternal and infinite could not exist in itself yet no more could it if enclosed in another body. This is one variety of the *in utramque partem disputare.* Both alternatives are disproved, and therefore the proposition that could be true in the one way or in the other is definitely refuted (in fact the *in utramque partem disputare* if used in this manner produces a *reductio ad absurdum,* but this is a type of argumentation we have excluded from our study). The consideration of alternative possibilities occurs as early as Homer, where it ends in a formula like ὧς ἄρα οἱ φρονέοντι δοάσσατο κέρδιον εἶναι.[7] But in Homer such passages call for a decision between two practical possibilities, and one of the two alternatives is eventually preferred. In other words, if the Homeric "form" has any place at all in the ancestry of the philosophical and sophistic *in utramque partem disputare,* the offspring has certainly gone its own, perfectly independent way. A safe pedigree based on genuine resemblances cannot be traced beyond Parmenides. Unfortunately we cannot say with confidence that the argument: Being cannot have originated from Being nor can it from Not-Being (both of these negative statements receiving further argumentative support) is common to Parmenides and Gorgias; for in Parmenides the crucial passage remains a problem and the text uncertain.[8] Still, where Parmenides upholds his thesis of Being as perfectly balanced, he argues both against the possibility of a "more" (higher degree) of Being and of a "less" (lower degree) of it. This passage and another of very similar argumentative complexion[9] should qualify as instances of *in utramque partem disputare,* although the precise description would be *ex utraque parte disputare.*

[7] *Il.* XIII 456-458; *Od.* V 464-474; VI 141-145 *al.*; but see also *Il.* XI 403-410; *Od.* V 408-423.

[8] See above n. 2.

[9] See 28B8.44-49; cf. *ibid.* 22-25.

In the history of strict and cogent argumentation, the Eleatic thinkers are epoch-making.[10] But, if in Parmenides progress in this sphere remains of secondary importance, overshadowed by his startling discovery of a new philosophical dimension, in Zeno the argumentative devices are no less intriguing than what he achieved by means of them. Again and again a student of Zeno has reason to wonder whether his chief interest was in his conclusions—which are provocative and puzzling enough—or whether the invention of new arguments interested him *per se*. Whatever the answer, our evidence, direct and indirect, agrees in associating his name with contradictory conclusions. Thus with Zeno conclusions frequently took the form that Parmenides at times had chosen for the arguments supporting his conclusions. Also, if in Parmenides such arguments disproved the opposite of his thesis, and thus formed a *reductio ad absurdum*, in Zeno the conclusion itself has this function and purpose.

According to Plato's *Parmenides* (127el ff.), Zeno arguing against the existence of "the many" proves that if there are "many" they are similar as well as dissimilar to one another. Elsewhere we find reports or actual quotations of his proofs that the many were limited and were unlimited in number, that they were large, in fact so large as to be infinite, yet also small and without any size at all.[11] In the *Phaedrus* Plato suggests a different purpose for Zeno's *in utramque partem disputare*. His audience, he reports, received the impression

[10] This is recognized by Guthrie, II, 44, whose admirable appreciation should be compared. So should G.E.R. Lloyd, *Polarity and Analogy* (Cambridge, 1966) 103ff., although our points of view are rather different. Cf. Eudemus, frg. 43 (29.12ff. Wehrli), about Parmenides as the first to employ ἀπόδειξις and about his use of ἀντιλογία. I know of no good reason why mathematical methods should have influenced Parmenides.

[11] I wonder why Pl. *Prm.* 127e is not included by Diels-Kranz, as it is by H.D.P. Lee, *Zeno of Elea* (Cambridge, 1936, repr. 1967) 20. The other passages are 29B1-3. About the correct sequence see Hermann Fränkel, *AJPh* 63 (1942) 15ff. = *Wege und Formen* 210.

that the same objects were similar and dissimilar, were one and many, at rest and moving (261d6). Against movement some specific contradictory statements and conclusions are attested: "The moving object can move neither in the place where it is nor in the place where it is not."[12] Moreover the famous paradoxes about movement, although not preserved in Zeno's authentic wording and the subject of much controversy,[13] *may* be cast in the form of an *in utramque partem disputare*, and one suggestion to this effect seems so congenial to Zeno's spirit that I cannot refrain from recording it: "Either motion will be stopped by the ever increasing fractions of the traversed space or it will wreck the continuum of space by splitting its units."[14] If this suggestion is close to the truth, Zeno may well have advanced these paradoxes with the intention of discrediting the common-sense belief in movement or, to put it somewhat differently, to perplex people by showing that this concept, although commonly taken for granted, bristled with difficulties. Whether he in addition pursued the ulterior object of defending the "unmoved" Being of Parmenides is another question. An improvised theory in Plato's *Parmenides,* welcome for this dialogue and duly parroted by Simplicius, turns Zeno into a dogged champion of the Parmenidean theories.[15] It is true that he operates with some concepts and develops—among others—some methods of Parmenides.

The same might be said of Gorgias, though with the difference that Zeno, however his philosophical intentions be

[12] 29B4. See Fränkel, 7 (= 204f.). Vlastos (*Phronesis* 11, 1966, 3ff.) thinks B4 was the basis for the arrow paradox.

[13] See 29A27; Lee, *op. cit.*, 17ff., 78ff.; Fränkel, 14 (= 210); Guthrie, II 91ff. W. D. Ross, *Aristotle's Physics* (Oxford, 1936) VI 9, 239b5-7, where the account of the paradoxes begins, holds that "Zeno did not argue disjunctively."

[14] Fränkel, 14 (= 212).

[15] Cf. my recent article: "The tradition about Zeno of Elea re-examined," *Phronesis* 16 (1971) 116ff.

defined, remains a constructive thinker of high rank. Resourceful and ingenious as Zeno is in his argumentative devices, he adjusts them to the demonstrandum and develops them with finesse; by comparison with Gorgias, he might also be considered economical. Gorgias has his position on the borderline between philosophy and rhetoric. Besides his obvious debt to the Eleatic thinkers, he was probably influenced by native Sicilian techniques of rhetorical argumentation.[16] To be sure there is uncertainty about the personal, the intellectual, and even the chronological relations between Gorgias of Leontini and the two Syracusans, Corax and Tisias. Moreover, to complicate matters still further, the teacher-pupil relationship between Corax and Tisias continues to be a problem. The testimonies allow the hypothesis that Tisias produced a *techne* incorporating the devices of Corax. Given the tendency of the ancient biographers to establish teacher-pupil relations, it was almost inevitable for Gorgias—as indeed also for Lysias—to be represented as taught by one of them.[17] We cannot isolate what, if any, historical kernel may be in these constructions. Still, reliable information suggests for the two Syracusans familiarity with the arguing "in both directions." If a weak man is on trial for assault, his defense is to be the intrinsic improbability of his daring anything of the kind. A strong man under the same accusation has to argue that the charge is improbable "because it would be considered probable" and he would therefore be careful not to incur it.[18] The Platonic *Phaedrus* (273b) gives us a slightly different version of these precepts, which, no matter how

[16] Cf. Guthrie, III 192ff., and others to whom he refers. For E. R. Dodds (*Plato's Gorgias*, Oxford, 1959, 8ff.) Gorgias is essentially a rhetorician.

[17] The evidence is meagre; see, however, 82A14 and Pl. *Phdr.* 267a.

[18] For testimonies see L. Radermacher, *Artium Scriptores* (*SAWW* 227.3, 1951) 11ff., esp. test. 6-9; 17-20; for the background W. Kroll, *RE* Suppl. 7, s.v. "Rhetorik" 1041f.

worded, are by far the best attested item of Tisias' or Corax's teaching. τὸ εἰκός is their legacy to rhetoric.

Tradition knows Gorgias too as a teacher of rhetoric, and we may readily admit his practicing this profession without denying his versatile personality other outlets. If he carried to self-defeating extremes the Eleatic technique in which Zeno had excelled, he may also have taught a rhetorical system embodying arguments like those associated with the names of Corax and Tisias.[19] However, these arguments represent a different variety of the *in utramque partem disputare*. They were not meant to be used on the same occasion and in the same speech; rather, if the one proved helpful in an accusation, the other would serve to defend the accused. Our evidence for attributing this kind of teaching to Gorgias is anything but abundant. The most valuable testimony is probably again a passage in the *Phaedrus* (267a), where Plato coupling the names of Tisias and Gorgias reports that both preferred the "probable" to the "true" and were masters in the art of "making small things appear large and large things small" (just as they knew to present new matters in an old and old in a new fashion). I should understand the quoted words as a description of αὔξησις (amplification), and μείωσις (diminution), yet again they would not both be used for the same subject, on the same occasion, and in the same speech.

Clearly, then, we must recognize two different forms of the *in utramque partem disputare*, even if an able man could sometimes ride the one horse and then again the other. When we read in Cicero's *Brutus* (46ff.), *scriptas fuisse et paratas a Protagora rerum illustrium disputationes qui nunc communes appellantur loci*, and immediately afterward Gorgias is men-

19 This does not mean that in rhetorical instruction Gorgias confined himself to the subject of argumentation. We shall discuss his theory of *psychagogia* in Ch. II. See George Kennedy, *The Art of Persuasion in Greece* (Princeton, 1963), 61ff.

tioned as author of *laudes* and *vituperationes* for a variety of subjects, we gladly believe that such commonplaces of contrary intent found themselves side by side in a rhetorical textbook. A practitioner, of course, would choose whichever could be of help on a given occasion.[20] In Antiphon's First Oration it suits the speaker to extol torture as the surest and fairest means of ascertaining the truth (8ff.); even those prepared to tell lies are forced by it to confess the truth (10 extr.). Quite different is the opinion, expressed in the Fifth Oration, that the statements made under torture are damaging for the speaker; here he dwells on the readiness of the tortured to say what is welcome to the torturers; therefore little trust should be put in their testimony (32ff.). In the *Tetralogies* that have come down under the same Antiphon's name, arguments of probability very similar in type to those attested for Corax and Tisias are used, but again they are appropriately distributed between accusation and defense.[21] Regardless what we believe about their author and date of composition, they are clearly intended as showpieces or models. If they originally belonged to a τέχνη (textbook), they may have been all that the τέχνη had to offer, may have been accompanied by specific instructions or finally have been illustrations attached to a substantial body of precepts and suggestions. On any of these views they are typical of the spirit in which early teachers of rhetoric practiced their métier.

[20] Cf., also for what immediately follows, my *Antiphonstudien* (Berlin, 1931) 14ff., 35f., 46, and *passim*. See further Wilamowitz, *SBBerlAk*. 1900, 398ff.; Kroll, *op. cit.*, 1044.

[21] See esp. *Tetr*. I β 6, γ 7. I still incline to regard the *Tetralogies* as spurious; cf. P. von der Mühll, *MH* 5 (1948) 1ff. yet also the counterarguments of G. Zuntz, *MH* 6 (1950) 100ff. J. S. Morrison (*PCPhS* 187, 1961, 49ff.) relies too heavily on the unsound theories of W. Aly. For *Δισσοὶ Λόγοι*, whose author von der Mühll (p. 5) calls a "Nachzügler"—I confess that, though unable to prove it, I have always felt that way myself—see R. K. Sprague, *Mind* 77 (1968) 155ff.

The *disputationes illustrium rerum* mentioned by Cicero as "made ready" by Protagoras are obviously to be connected with his assertion *de omni re in utramque partem disputari posse* and his much resented claim to turn the "weaker argument" into the "stronger." The pupils of the rhetoricians would in an actual speech incorporate one of these antagonistic *logoi* placed at their disposal (as we have just seen in the first Attic orator, Antiphon).

Since we have by now transferred our attention from the Greek outposts to the heart of Greece, to Ἑλλάδος Ἑλλὰς Ἀθῆναι, we shall presently study how some aristocratic genres of Greek literature, tragedy and history, employ the *in utramque partem disputare*. Before we become absorbed in them, a brief glance at comedy seems in order.

In the comedies of this period the outstanding ἀγών (contest) is that between the Just (or Stronger) and the Unjust (or Weaker) Arguments in the *Clouds*. After a good amount of bickering and after taunts that to the other party sound like delightful compliments (vv. 889ff., esp. 910ff.), the *agon* finally comes to a head (vv. 961-1082) in a comparison of the old and the new "education," the word being used broadly enough to include not only instruction of every kind but behavior in general, manners and mores. Each of the *Logoi* argues for the superiority of the life he advocates, yet their values are worlds apart; what for the one is attractive is for the other disgusting. As he speaks second, the Unjust *Logos* has an advantage that we shall find generally exploited by the second speaker. While himself extolling a life of profligacy and shameless disregard for all conventions, he also takes every opportunity to ridicule what the Just *Logos* has said; provoked by such unfair sniping, the latter interrupts him several times. We would never expect Aristophanes to conduct such a comparison between the good old and the wicked but profitable new style of life in a deadly serious spirit; with or without some naughty remarks in the Just

Logos and with or without a ludicrous defeat at the end, he would never allow us to forget that we are in the realm of comedy.[22]

Euripides

According to the Greek tradition—always prone to dramatize and personalize historical developments—rhetoric "entered" Athens to begin its flourishing career there in the year 427, when Gorgias appeared as one of the envoys sent from Leontini to ask the Athenians for help against Syracusan aggression.[23] There are good reasons for discounting such far-reaching effects of Gorgias' visit. While argumentative skill doubtless improved in the decade between 430 and 420, the capacity as such antedated these years. In tragedy, Euripides' *Alcestis, Medea,* and (the second) *Hippolytus,* all produced before 427, embody impressive samples of rhetorical technique including argumentations *in utramque partem.* And we may go even farther back. Although nobody would suspect Sophocles of partiality for rhetoric, in his *Aias* and *Antigone,* the earliest preserved plays and both of them prior to 440, we find speeches for and against a particular course of action. A comparison between these pairs of speeches—Teucer upholding his cause against Menelaus and Agamemnon, Haemon against his father Creon—and the contests of Admetus and Pheres or of Medea and Jason would show a clearer organization in Euripides but less integration

[22] Dover would probably agree; yet I fail to see his point when he collects errors, half-truths, omissions, anachronisms, and other inaccuracies of which the Δίκαιος Λόγος makes himself guilty (*Aristophanes: Clouds*, Oxford, 1968, LIX) and reconstructs what this Λόγος would say if he "were a real person" (LXI) or "more than ordinarily percipient" (LXII).

[23] For the impression made by Gorgias in Athens see D.S. XII 53.1ff. (A V 24 and B VII 32 Rad.). See also Pl. (?) *Hp.Ma.* 282b. In Paus. VI 17.9, Tisias even accompanies him!

of his contests (ἀγῶνες) into the action as a whole. Thus Medea's debate with Jason (vv. 465-575), far from advancing the action, retards it and forms a stumbling block that she later, when she needs his help, must remove by asking him to forgive unwise opinions expressed before she had given serious thought to the questions (vv. 869-893). However, a comparison of the two dramatists is hardly necessary for our present subject;[24] all we should bear in mind is that even before 427 Athens was familiar with the *in utramque partem disputare.*

We have emphasized the more deliberate organizations of speeches and speech contests in Euripides. Even in the *agon* between Admetus and Pheres, the articulation has attained a noteworthy degree. I should distinguish the following topics as more or less clearly set off from one another in Admetus' accusation:

vv. 629-32: introductory remarks, indicating a generally negative attitude;

vv. 633-35: you failed to show sympathy at the right time and in the right form;

vv. 636-41: you are not truly my father nor do I consider myself any longer your son;

vv. 642-47: how cowardly were you to let my wife sacrifice herself instead of offering up your own life;

vv. 648-50: (eliminating, as seems necessary vv. 651f.) it would have been glorious for you to die and save my life;

vv. 653-57: you have enjoyed whatever good things life has to offer;

[24] A comparison of the kind (better reserved for another occasion) should also point out how greatly Sophocles' own construction of *agones* changed after he had composed *Aias* and *Antigone*. His *Electra* in particular (516-609) may show it.

vv. 658-61: you cannot reproach me for unfilial conduct but you have not repaid my devotion;

vv. 662-68: I am no longer obliged to filial duties toward you.[25]

Pheres' retort may be similarly divided into a succession of clearly identifiable topics, even if on a few points there is room for doubt.

In the *Medea* Jason himself speaks of a ἅμιλλα λόγων ("a combat of speeches") (v. 546) forced upon him by the vehement accusations of his former wife. Both speeches show more emphasis on the disposition than any earlier play. With ἐκ τῶν δὲ πρώτων πρῶτον ἄρξομαι λέγειν (v. 475) Medea begins her enumeration of what she has done for Jason. After specifying three deeds, she continues καὶ ταῦθ' ὑφ' ἡμῶν, ὦ κάκιστ' ἀνδρῶν, παθὼν, προύδωκας ἡμᾶς (v. 488). Later after her νῦν ποι τράπωμαι; (v. 502) helped to convey the extent of her misery, one more ἀντὶ τῶνδε (v. 510) brings the contrast between her and his conduct to an end. Throughout her speech, despair and indignation are present, yet she has enough clearheaded, rational control to take up point after point. Jason's reply is less emotional and shows an even clearer organization—though the πρῶτον of v. 536 is not followed by a δεύτερον κτλ. and the disposition announced in vv. 548f.: . . . δείξω πρῶτα μὲν σοφὸς γεγώς, ἔπειτα σώφρων, εἶτα σοὶ μέγας φίλος is not so strictly adhered to that we could identify each of these *demonstranda* in the following thirteen lines. Instead another thought comes to the fore and requires its own

[25] There still follows a generalization (669-72) about the insincerity of old people when they profess to long for death, an allusion to a well-known fable; cf. Wilamowitz, *Griech. Tragödien übersetzt* III (Berlin, 1906) 81f., and A. M. Dale in her commentary on the play (Oxford, 1954), *ad* vv. 669ff. Jacqueline Duchemin, ΑΓΩΝ *dans la tragédie grecque* (Paris, 1945), attempts to analyze Euripides' speeches in accordance with the canonical *partes orationis* of the rhetorical systems. This seems possible only within very narrow limits.

proofs. I married the king's daughter, Jason declares, not (a) because I was truly in love with her, nor (b) because I wished to have many children, but (a) to be comfortably off, (b) to have children of noble standing, and (c) to secure in this manner a better status for the children of the first marriage. On the whole, then, the topics in Jason's speech are marked off. Also at the beginning, when he has to counter Medea's accusation of shameless ingratitude, Jason first insists that she saved him not by her own free decision but under the compulsion of Aphrodite, and then declares that she received more than she gave, for she exchanged a civilized life in Greece against her barbarian country and earned far greater fame than would have been possible in Colchis.

Yet it is not enough to study the intrinsic organization of the two speeches. The contest as such is something new, a previously unknown use of the *in utramque partem disputare*. It embodies the opposition of two fundamentally different temperaments, two irreconcilable outlooks and attitudes to life. Whether we think of Jason as insincere, as selfish, or as prudent is a minor question, and tempting as it may be to regard his speech as an instance of a "weaker argument" turned into a "stronger," we had better not go so far.[26] It suffices to realize that greater ingenuity was needed to build up Jason's defense than Medea's attack. In the conception of the play the contest, although retarding the plot, has its important function. The chief characters are face to face with one another and have an opportunity to state their motivations and justify their course of action. Not that without it we would have difficulties in understanding Medea's impulses; still less can there be a question of a "moral issue" here brought into focus. Yet we become better acquainted with

[26] Nor would I be as confident as H.D.F. Kitto, who believes (*Greek Tragedy*, London, 3rd ed., 1961, 266ff.) that "the utter baseness of Jason" is a conviction shared by Euripides himself with his Medea and modern readers.

Jason. Until his appearance, we have looked at the conflict exclusively from Medea's side, have seen Creon yielding to her entreaties, and found chorus and characters sympathizing with her. Jason's unabashed defense of his conduct takes us (like Pheres' denunciation of his son) by surprise.

The antagonism between the characters is more significant than the moral conflict (the conflict as such would not normally have caused a wife, even if gravely injured, to react as savagely as did Medea). After the contest in which the principal characters, besides stating their case, also reveal their temperament, the atmosphere is more highly charged than before it. At the stage of intellectual development where we find ourselves, it is appropriate that even in a character so ferociously passionate as Medea the power of reasoning should equal the dynamics of her emotion.[27]

Not all but most of the *agones* in Euripides remain without influence on the action. The *agon* between Theseus and Hippolytus, continued by briefer exchanges, ends with a sentence of exile for Hippolytus; yet Theseus' mind was made up even before Hippolytus tried to defend himself (vv. 983ff.); the prayer to Poseidon and the sentence of exile (vv. 887ff., 893ff.) precede Hippolytus' appearance on the stage. No change of heart comes about; both speakers remain as firm in their attitude, outlook, or determination as they had been.

The speeches in *Alcestis* and *Medea* may be considered as accusation and defense, though not in the legal sense of these words. Those in the *Hippolytus* (vv. 936-980, 982-1034) are close to the forensic sphere. Hippolytus' defense consists in the successive elimination of all conceivable motivations for the crime, a device familiar to us;[28] yet he also offers an oath;

[27] This may incidentally answer Kitto's strictures (*ibid.*). His analysis of Medea's speech is stimulating and so is his critical judgment. It seems a pity to question it by historical considerations.

[28] Vv. 1008-1020, but note also vv. 960-970. In this ἀγών, instances

and there are references to witnesses (μάρτυρες). Granted that these witnesses are of a somewhat unorthodox type, we cannot help recalling the important, often decisive function that witnesses and oaths had in the juridical procedure of the time.[29] On the other hand, common as defamation of character and protest against such defamation were in forensic proceedings, Theseus' indignant denunciation of what he considers his son's hypocrisy (vv. 946-959) would be too highflown for a lawsuit. Eloquence and vigor of language here attain a new height. His powerful and completely sincere indignation and Hippolytus' equally sincere and emphatic protestation of his innocence have little in common with the products of contemporary rhetoric.

We need not analyze all instances of the *in utramque partem disputare* in Euripides. If we did, our chief impression would be the variety of issues and, next in order perhaps, a certain amount of variety in the procedures employed. We find in Euripides innocence contending with wickedness, the injured with the offender, democracy with its detractors,[30] the heart with the head (even if Agamemnon's heart does not speak directly when he answers his brother, *IA* 378-401, we remember what he said and did earlier). Yet there are also arguments and counterarguments about ultimate responsibility[31] and about the value of the bow as compared with

---

of argument met head-on by counterargument are not easy to find, and I should not insist on considering it a good illustration of the *in utramque partem disputare*. Note however vv. 891f. where Hippolytus takes up the first point in his father's charge.

29 For ἄτεχνοι πίστεις see above, p. 22. References to oaths: *Hipp.* 960, 1025ff., 1037ff. (ὅρκους . οὐ σμικρὰν πίστιν), to μάρτυρες, v. 972 (Phaedra's dead body would probably not be called μάρτυς in a court), 1023. J. Duchemin, *op. cit.*, 198f., recognizes the ἄτεχνοι πίστεις and denies their provenance from rhetorical handbooks. Surely their employment in the courts antedated their inclusion in rhetorical systems.

30 See *Supp.* 426-455 as against vv. 409-425.

31 See below, p. 31 about the contest in *Tr.*

other weapons (*HF* 157ff., 188ff.). In the *Phoenissae,* Eteocles (vv. 479ff.), brutally frank about his love of tyranny, "greatest of gods," and his brother Polyneices (v. 469ff.), the exile, harassed and longing to return home, represent two βίοι familiar from contemporary experience, which is also true of Amphion and Zethus in the lost *Antiope.*[32]

Moreover, while it is true that the protest against injustice and the repudiation of such protest are represented more often than any of the other topics here listed, how many different forms does this contest take! The person considering himself aggrieved may to his surprise learn how reprehensible his own conduct is (Admetus); he may have brought his suffering upon himself and now build up a dishonest case (Polymestor in *Hec.*); the person accused may have a justification, sometimes convincing, sometimes less so, or he may like Jason turn the tables and charge the accuser with shortsighted misunderstandings.

Again, arguments may come naturally or be far-fetched and extraneous. What matters is sometimes just display, sometimes a masterly organization of relevant thoughts. Inventiveness may count, or vigor and vehemence. In the *Andromache* we are even treated to a goodly amount of vituperation (ὀνείδη and λοιδορεῖν are words used for it).[33] In the *Phoenissae,* Jocaste, after she has heard her sons champion opposite courses and fight for different values (cf. vv. 499-502), produces her own *in utramque partem disputare.* This time each of the opposite causes appears to have an additional intrinsic antinomy: Eteocles has the prospect of tyranny, a hollow name devoid of substance, but if he is defeated he will

[32] For the *Antiope* see B. Snell in his new edition of *TGF* (Hildesheim, 1964) p. 1030; D. L. Page, *Greek Literary Papyri* (Cambridge, Mass., 1942) I 1; see also Snell, *Scenes from Greek Drama* (Berkeley-Los Angeles, 1964) 82ff., and E. K. Borthwick, *CQ* 17 (1967) 41ff.

[33] *Andr.* 147-231 (as usual I ignore the stychomythia that follows the set speeches), 319-383, 590-690.

witness the miseries of a conquered Thebes (vv. 542-567); Polyneices on the other hand will either conquer his city by force (a disgrace!) and destroy it in the process or return to Argos after a shameful defeat and great loss of life (vv. 568-582). The debate between Hecuba and Helen in the *Trojan Women* (vv. 914-1032), an episode that as far as I can see has no bearing on the plot, would be particularly enjoyed by the audience because extraordinary skill was required to defend Helen in a democratic age, when Homer's values (οὐ νέμεσις Τρῶας κτλ. *Il.* III 151f.) were no longer recognized. Beginning with Gorgias, the vindication of her elopement was a challenge to human cleverness, and what Euripides offers is not only an ἀγών but an ἀγώνισμα.

The topics of the *agones* in the political plays are *sui generis*; some of them, like the unwritten laws that Athens is particularly proud to uphold and most of all the praise of democracy by no less a person than Theseus, must have produced great satisfaction in the audience,[34] even if its members were sensitive to dissonances and realized that the plays as such were anything rather than unalloyed patriotic propaganda.

Generally speaking, Euripides would hardly complain that the *in utramque partem disputare* could not be adapted to a large number of different purposes and experiments: ἐκ παντὸς ἄν τις πράγματος δισσῶν λόγων ἀγῶνα θεῖτ' ἄν, εἰ λέγειν εἴη σοφός (frg. 189). And yet, of the instruments that reason used in the realm of argumentation, this was only one, even if it was more conspicuous than others and may therefore with relative ease be traced through its metamorphoses.

[34] Cf. n. 30 and see *Heracl.* 191-201, 233f. (where however Iolaos' speech soon turns into an imploration), 242-249. Cf. G. Zuntz, *The Political Plays of Euripides* (Manchester, 1955) *passim*, esp. 17ff., 27 (yet note also p. 41 and many other wholesome warnings against the "conventional" interpretation). See below, Chapter V, esp. pp. 154ff.

Thucydides

In Thucydides, too, contests differ not a little in function as well as in subject matter. Yet an analysis of the political situation is the common purpose of most. Even the pre-battle speeches are in a sense political and, what is more remarkable, form contests, although we should perhaps put this word between quotation marks. As a rule the speeches influence the decision to be taken and thereby the action that follows; yet Thucydides is not primarily concerned with this influence but with the issues, especially the alternative analyses of one and the same issue. For almost every speech is analytical and thoroughly rational; the one exception—an appeal to pity by the Plataeans on surrendering their city—is so peculiar that we must reserve it for Chapter II. The "organization" of the speeches makes it easy to distinguish topics and subtopics. Not all speeches are equally "sincere" nor equally penetrating. Even without our advantage of knowing the outcome, we could sometimes recognize one of the two as saner, more perspicacious or more honest than the other. By means of his speeches Thucydides places a situation in a larger perspective, connecting the present with the past and the future but also relating specific decisions to overriding interests, general rules, or basic political principles.[35]

[35] Cf. for such an approach to the speeches, e.g., Hermann Strasburger, *Die Wesensbestimmung der Geschichte durch die Griechen* (Wiesbaden, 1965) 59, 95, and *passim*; also Eduard Schwartz, *Das Geschichtswerk des Thuk.*, 2nd ed. (Bonn, 1929) 27, or O. Regenbogen, *Thukydides Politische Reden* (Leipzig, 1949), where the "Einleitung" abounds in excellent formulations (e.g. pp. 20ff., 35f.). For the opposite viewpoint, I probably ought to cite A. W. Gomme, I 143ff. and *Essays in Greek History and Literature* (Oxford, 1937), 156ff., but he concedes far more than he seems to realize, and makes too much of extreme positions and inconsistencies in the works he attacks. I admit that some speeches are closer in content than others to those actually delivered. O. Luschnat in his recent *RE* article "Thukydides" (Suppl. 12) 1155ff., esp. 1171ff., is very sound.

The narrative presents events and connections between proximate causes and effects. The speeches disclose causes that are less immediately antecedent or considerations of far wider application. The spirit directing Athenian or Lacedaemonian politics, the prospects of the war, trends in the development of the Empire, the attitude of the allies toward Athens and the various possible ways of dealing with the allies, advantages and disadvantages inherent in a given political or military situation—these and similar topics that are debated in the speeches show what lies behind the actions or events and gives them their significance.

On some occasions Thucydides achieved his purpose with one speech. The reason why no Athenian answers Pericles, although at the time of his last appeal he had a strong opposition, is evident—or at any rate is meant to be so by Thucydides, in whose view there could be no answer. Again when four hundred twenty Lacedaemonians, including more than one hundred twenty Spartans, are cut off in Sphacteria, envoys set forth in Athens what unique opportunity this stroke of good fortune offers for a peace on favorable terms (IV 17-20, esp. 17.4). Here, too, one speech suffices, although theoretically it would be conceivable that Cleon had answered by "justifying" his unreasonable demands. Yet he operates by demagogic manoeuvres that appeal to the emotions. A speech would have implied that there was a rational answer to the Lacedaemonian argument.[36]

Still, when Thucydides sets speech against speech, must we necessarily look at this device in the perspective of the *in utramque partem disputare*? Thucydides had become familiar in actual life with the matching of wits in a political debate. We need not doubt that the Athenian Assembly was his

[36] Cf. on this "missed opportunity" Jacqueline de Romilly, *Imperialism*, pp. 40f., 172ff., who agrees with Eduard Meyer, *Forschungen zur alten Geschichte* II (Halle, 1899) 333ff. Gomme, III 458, takes a different view. See again Luschnat, *loc. cit.* 1098.

training ground where he learned lessons more substantial than Gorgias or Prodicus could teach him. Why then should the *in utramque partem disputare* of the rhetoricians matter for him at all? The obvious answer is that on his own testimony there were normally more than two speeches.[37] It is he who selects the most antagonistic and thus acquaints us with the opposite extremes of possible reactions. In addition, he concentrates on the essential, ignoring everything accidental; he must have excluded many smaller topics devoid of broader or typical interest.

The meaning the speeches (*logoi*) bestow on the events may as well be called by the appropriate Greek word: it is the *logos* behind them. However, it is in the nature of historical processes to allow more than one interpretation, both to the actively engaged politician and to the more distant student scrutinizing these developments. The antinomies or *antilogiai* have a basis in the ambivalence of the facts. There were, to take our illustration from the very first contest, reasons for accepting the Corcyrean offer of an alliance, and there were reasons for rejecting it and thus avoiding the conflict with the Peloponnesians latent in its acceptance. To explain why Athens took the decision that brought the war closer, Thucydides sees to it that the speeches of the Corcyreans as well as that of the Corinthians incidentally throw light on the Athenian situation before the war.[38] Of the decision itself, however, only a part is disclosed, and we may wonder why Thucydides, who in these speeches seeks to do justice to Corcyrean and Corinthian interests, keeps the information about Athenian responses to a minimum.[39] When we explore Thucydides' habits of reconstructing the course of historical

[37] See, e.g., III 36.6 (cf. 49.1). See also VI 35 in combination with 41. Plut. *v. Th.* 2 mentions a tradition of δεινότης πολιτική in Athens, which included the capacity for effective speech. Beginning with Solon it was in the end expanded—rather than transformed—by the Sophists.

[38] See esp. I 33.3f., 36, 40.4f., 41, 42.2.

[39] I 44. A fuller discussion will be found in Chapter VI.

events and understand some principles at work in this reconstruction (Chapter VI), we shall realize how he selects the occasions for *agones*. Not every situation that speeches *in utramque partem* might illuminate for us does receive such additional light.

In the contest (or *agon*) of the two cities, each has to justify its course of action and to make its cause and its friendship attractive to Athens. The Corcyreans in particular have to account for a good deal, most notably for their rather unusual attitude to the mother city and their radical change of policy from strict neutrality to a quest for allies.[40] Prior to the speeches, we have read about the development of their relations with Corinth during the preceding years.[41] Yet how thorough was the break with their traditions did not become clear and is only now pointed out in an act of historical synopsis. Conditions that formerly made it advisable for Corcyra to keep out of political entanglements no longer exist.[42]

Besides justifying themselves, the Corcyreans have to convince the Athenians of the advantage inherent in an alliance between the two cities. Here they have essentially one argument, but it is strong enough to appear again and again, suitably varied. An alliance would put the Corcyrean fleet on the side of the Athenian; two of the three largest navies in Greece would, if united, have an assured superiority over the third, which is the Corinthian (36.3; cf. 33.2). This point is driven home with special reference to the future war, and since it is in the Corcyrean interest to represent this war as certain to come, they support this prognosis by their own version of conditions and political plans in the Peloponnesian camp.[43]

[40] For the former point see ch. 34; for the latter ch. 32.

[41] Chs. 24-31; see esp. 31, yet also 28.3.

[42] See esp. 32.3f.; note the most concentrated formulation in 32.4.

[43] See the analysis of the prospects in 33.3 and the use made of it in ch. 36.

In short, to secure Corcyra as an ally will be an inestimable gain for Athens. To reject her will create a potentially dangerous enemy. Still, essential as considerations of expediency are, we have not yet reached the stage of the war where justice and morality are treated with contempt. The Corcyreans must prove that the war with their mother town is just and must convince Athens that she is not violating treaties by accepting the colony of another city as ally. In truth, they explain, Athens would give support to an injured party; it is Corinth which has flouted justice; and the treaty with the Lacedaemonians is not broken by helping Corcyra.[44] Still it is not easy for the Corcyrean envoys to maintain their stand on high moral grounds.

In their reply the Corinthians can make a better case for justice. Even the "advantageous" (*τὸ ξυμφέρον*) has nuances of justice for them, mainly no doubt because they could not offer advantages to match those of the Corcyreans. Athens ought to remember benefits received from Corinth in a former critical situation and should consider it advantageous —and even conducive to greater power—to refrain from injustice against a party of equal standing (42.4). Also, instead of looking at the war as bound to come, Athens would act wisely in removing frictions already in existence (42.2). To violate a treaty is always a mistake, and who accepts colonies that break away from their founding city sets up a new *νόμος* in Greece (40.4). The Corinthians also take issue with the account offered by the Corcyreans to justify their departure from neutrality. As they see it, past as well as present Corcyrean policy is dictated by selfish motives implying a cynical indifference to justice (37.2ff.; 39.2 etc.). Being intent on practicing injustice and wishing to keep

[44] For the relations to their mother town see ch. 34; for the injustice done to Corcyra 33.1, 34.2. An unfair advantage of Corinth is emphasized in 35.3.

the fruits of it to themselves,[45] they preferred political isolation as long as it proved feasible. We may find less political analysis and perspective in this speech than in the Corcyrean; yet perhaps in forming this impression we commit the same mistake against which the Corinthians warn Athens. Obligations resulting from favors incurred in the past as well as treaty obligations ought to have weight; to disregard them is not only morally wrong but also politically unwise.

In Thucydides, every political contest has its peculiarities, and instead of analyzing each of them and in this process recording much that is obvious or familiar, we prefer to give a brief account of these peculiarities and, when we have done so, to deal at greater length with the debate between Cleon and Diodotus, because there is something unique about the mutual relation of their speeches.

The *agon* between Nicias and Alcibiades in Book VI (9-14; 16-18) presents, like that between Cleon and Diodotus, two influential figures of Athenian political life arguing in support of opposite resolutions. At stake, however, is something far more momentous than on other occasions, namely the wisdom or folly of embarking on the Sicilian expedition. Very naturally a great deal is said about the prevailing conditions in Greece itself—is there really peace? (ch. 11, cf. 18.4)—and about the prospects of the expedition if the Assembly votes to undertake it; yet the peculiar feature of this oratorical duel is the importance attached to the speakers themselves.[46] Thucydides, though not present in Athens at the time, realized the crucial

[45] Chs. 37-39 are noteworthy for their extensive discussion of matters relating to justice. [If G.E.M. de Ste. Croix, 71, is right, the Corinthian references to "justice" are baseless, at least in a technical sense. Their δίκαιον has an ethical complexion, and there is a good deal of "theory."]

[46] See ch. 9, 12.2–13.1, 16–17.1; cf. H. D. Westlake, 171f., 219f.; von Fritz, I 729ff. (Alcibiades' speech is "die inviduellste Rede, die das Werk enthält"); A. Andrewes, *Phoenix* 16 (1962) 73 *al.*

role played by Alcibiades' ambition and recklessness; without giving proper weight to them and contrasting them with the cautious attitude of Nicias, the analysis of the situation would have been incomplete. The next *agon* (VI 33f.; 36-40) takes us to Syracuse and, besides dealing with the chances of a successful defense, assesses from a distance and thus from an entirely new perspective the improbability of the Athenian venture. Improbability, however, is in this instance tantamount to incredible folly. If here one of the speakers refuses to believe what we know to be true (chs. 36-38), we shortly afterward find one defending a thesis that he himself knows not to be true. For no matter how flexible the policies of Athenian imperialism and how persuasive a case Euphemus in wooing Camerina (chs. 82-87) makes for this flexible quality, to the desires and hopes that inspired the expedition this topic is irrelevant, and we must regard Hermocrates' account of Athens' foreign policy (chs. 76-80) as near to the truth (cf. VI 8.4; 18.4).[47]

We have reserved the contest of Cleon and Diodotus for a closer study. The debate about the treatment of the Mytileneans (III 37-40; 42-48) is unique not just because of the psychological theories about motives for secession and the effect of brutal punishment on other allies, especially on the *demos* in their cities.[48] Equally remarkable is the paradox

[47] In Book IV (59-64) Hermocrates addresses the Sicilian cities in a speech that remains unopposed and has a determining influence on the policies of these cities. If we discount the speech of Alcibiades in VI 89-92 as being only in part political, Hermocrates alone of all statesmen shares with Pericles the honor of remaining unanswered (see above p. 33), an indication how highly Thucydides thought of his political wisdom.

[48] Psychology: ch. 45; cf. 39.4. See H. P. Stahl, 119f. and *passim*. More will be said in Chapter V. Effect on the allies: 39.6ff.; 40.1, 5, 7; 47.1-3 (cf. J. de Romilly, *Imperialism* 158 f., 168; Felix Wassermann, 37f.). For other items of the large bibliography I refer to Wassermann's references updated by him in *WdF* 98, 496f. Add R. P. Winnington-Ingram, *BICS* 12 (1965) 70 (important).

that Cleon, who argues for a wholesale execution of the male population, claims to have expediency as well as justice on his side,[49] whereas Diodotus, the advocate of a more humane and discriminating punishment, professes to be indifferent to justice and to be guided solely by expediency.[50] His arguments against Cleon culminate in the statement: τὸ Κλέωνος τὸ αὐτὸ δίκαιον καὶ ξύμφορον τῆς τιμωρίας οὐχ εὑρίσκεται ἐν αὐτῷ δυνατὸν ὂν ἅμα γίγνεσθαι (47.5). We do not belittle the interest attaching to these aspects of the *agon*; yet what most calls for comment is the combination of two quite different and quite differently treated topics in each of the speeches. Only on the second of these topics, the action to be taken against Mytilene, are Cleon and Diodotus truly antagonistic; in the first, although different enough in their outlook, they complement one another, and, if understood in this sense, their strictures of the Athenian Assembly amount to a powerful indictment of all its deplorable habits.

Cleon, aroused because discussion has been re-opened on a topic he regarded as settled, blames speakers and audience alike. The speakers, if they are unscrupulous enough to argue for so irrational a cause as leniency toward Mytilene, must either have extraordinary confidence in their rhetorical skill or else be prompted by reasons of personal gain (38.2). The audience, he maintains, listens to the speakers in the same spirit in which they watch the performances of sophists displaying their rhetorical fireworks. They enjoy them and derive a particular amusement from trying to anticipate the next clever point a speaker will make. To quote Cleon's own words—more precisely, his own clever points—on this tend-

[49] See esp. ch. 40.1ff. for the concern with τὸ δίκαιον; but much in ch. 39 has a bearing on it. For justice and expediency combined see 40.4.

[50] See esp. chs. 44, 46 (esp. 4), 47.4f. The importance of expediency (τὸ ξυμφέρον) in the literature of the time is well brought out by John H. Finley, Jr., *Thucydides* (Cambridge, Mass., 1942) 51ff., 58ff., 209ff. and *passim*.

ency, the Athenians have turned into θεαταὶ μὲν τῶν λόγων, ἀκροαταὶ δὲ τῶν ἔργων ("spectators of the speeches"); they are judging even the past not on the basis of what has happened, but of what is said; they are δοῦλοι . . . τῶν ἀεὶ ἀτόπων, ὑπερόπται δὲ τῶν εἰωθότων.[51] Diodotus in turn protests the kind of calumny used by Cleon and his like to discredit honest men who offer good and sincere counsel. Intimations of dishonesty are vicious and have a demoralizing effect on the audience. They create an atmosphere of general suspicion so that even excellent opinions may not be accepted because the listeners wonder about concealed personal motives behind the words; and the speakers, knowing that a straightforward statement has little chance of being judged on its merits, must resort to deception. In fact the best and the worst advice alike must be supported by arguments that are insincere.[52]

Surely as long as Diodotus protests against the defamation of a speaker's character and motives (42.2ff.), he and Cleon are as far apart as later, when Mytilene itself becomes the subject. Yet his criticism of the audience as demoralized and Cleon's attack on its bad habits are in no way mutually exclusive. They converge to show how sadly tendencies of recent origin defeat the purpose for which the democratic assembly with its discussion and deliberation exists. Nor is there any reason why the modern reader should dismiss the one or the other criticism as sheer ranting. However great our admiration for Diodotus and however low our estimate of

[51] 38.4; see also 6: the Athenians tend when the speaker displays his brilliance, ὀξέως . . . προεπαινέσαι καὶ προαισθέσθαι τε πρόθυμοι εἶναι τὰ λεγόμενα, yet προνοῆσαι βραδεῖς τὰ . . . ἀποβησόμενα. The last προ- compound would of course be the one truly important for a wise decision. Cf. Wassermann, 32ff. (= *WdF* 484). Cleon's phrasing here is probably as much at variance with his own diction as Archidamus' is in I 84. What he says is too specific to be treated as a commonplace (J. de Romilly, *Imperialism* 168).

[52] 42.2–4, 43.1–3. In 42.4–6, suggestions possible as well as impossible are added for an amelioration of the regrettable habits. Note should be taken of Andrewes' comments, *Phoenix* 16 (1962) 73.

Cleon (though here if anywhere we should beware of blindly following Thucydides), to the open-minded student of Athenian democracy the strictures of Cleon, too, have a convincing ring. Yet while there may well have been criticism, and even sarcastic criticism, in the second assembly for reopening an issue settled on the previous day, the thoughts and the phrasing of Cleon are too intellectual for him. Thucydides must have lent him some sophistication. Of Diodotus, unknown as he is, the same may be said, since he too expresses himself in the idiom forged by Thucydides for these rational analyses.

Thucydides knew the weaknesses of the contemporary Athenian assemblies from personal experience. He knew the *aura popularis* and what it was capable of doing.[53] We here read his own bitter recollections of habits that he had observed or indeed experienced. Thucydides loved Athens but was not in love with Athenian democracy. Keen observation combined with an understanding of the deeper causes, and with the gift for the felicitous phrase has inspired this merciless diagnosis.[54] Just as the proposal gave him the excuse for expounding the new "secular" psychology, so the decision to reopen an issue already decided allowed him digressions scathingly critical of Athenian behavior in the deliberative assembly.[55] Yet despite the extent to which he indulges in

[53] See O. Regenbogen, *Kleine Schriften* (Munich, 1961) 235; Wassermann; also Andrewes, 75.

[54] Do these suggestions imply that Thucydides did not work out the two speeches before he was exiled? Not necessarily; the unsparing exposure of what was wrong may have originated as the immediate result of attending a meeting (much of the general criticism in both speeches has no connection with this particular occasion). Still the thought that he wrote from a distance has its attractions (pace J. de Romilly, *Imperialism* 167ff.). The alternative is less radical if we reckon with a good deal of recasting, rephrasing, etc.

[55] In an actual speech, a criticism as frank as we read in chs. 42 and 43 would hardly have served as a *captatio benevolentiae*, and I doubt whether Diodotus could afford to tell his audience such unpleasant truths.

these digressions, there are in this *agon* enough arguments germane to the issue as such; and of these arguments some relate specifically to the Mytileneans, whereas others connect the particular situation with principles of political action.

We have suggested that by means of such *logoi* Thucydides distilled the *logos* or rationale of the events. An alternative interpretation, by no means baseless, would be that he read a rationale into a welter of facts itself devoid of rational meaning. It may be safer to describe our own suggestion as what Thucydides *tried* to do. Moreover, besides such contests of two speakers and the few single speeches that we have mentioned, other devices serve the same end. At the convention of the Peloponnesian League in Book I (67-88), Thucydides needs four speeches to bring out the convictions and influences operative before the first move toward war was made. Envoys from Athens who are present seek to place Athenian policies in a favorable light (chs. 73-78). Thus they answer some of the Corinthian accusations. A fuller answer is given from a distance by Pericles in the "Funeral Oration," a speech that, besides correcting the Corinthians' description of the Athenian character (69.1-3; 70), also corrects the partly apologetic, partly laudatory account of Spartan habits offered by King Archidamus (I 84) at the convention of the League. Against this, Pericles sets a far more penetrating and exhaustive glorification of the Athenian way of life. Conceived in the same spirit is the version he here gives of Athenian "imperialism" (II 39, 41), doubtless the most glowing account of it in the entire *History*. As is well known, this subject, corresponding to its importance, is presented from many different viewpoints by Corinthian, Lacedaemonian, Mytilenean, Melian, Syracusan, as well as other Athenian speakers. As its problems have not long ago been treated in masterly fashion,[56] we need not once more show the gradual unfolding of its dialectic.

Almost equally important—and frequently interwoven with this subject—is the relation between justice and expediency. What view a speaker takes of it depends in large measure on the past or imminent experience of his community. We have had several occasions for touching on this subject and shall find others;[57] this would not be the place for a full treatment. Rather, as we are studying the variety of vehicles by which Thucydides conveys the *logos* of conditions or developments, the "Melian Dialogue" should still be added to our list. Unparalleled elsewhere, it shows most effectively the radical commitment of the Athenians to expediency. In coherent speeches it would not have been possible to dislodge the Melians so brutally from one position of hope to which they retreat after another (see V 88-110).[58]

Having dealt with the oratorical duels between political leaders and envoys, we may still glance at the speeches of military commanders. In Book II Brasidas and Cnemon on the one side and Phormio on the other address the sailors before the "Battle in the Gulf." In Book VII, when both parties are ready for the decisive sea battle in the harbor of Syracuse, Nicias makes an attempt to rouse the flagging spirit

[56] See the reference to J. de Romilly in n. 36 above. For Athens in the "Epitaphios" H. Strasburger is most illuminating. Hellmut Flashar's study, *SHAW* (1969) 1ff. does not convince me completely.

[57] See Chapters IV and V.

[58] For completeness, mention may also be made of the relatively few occasions (II 65.4-10 is the most significant) where the historian expresses his own opinion directly. In Book VIII, which includes no speeches, Thucydides comes forward with general conclusions of a type not found in any other Book (96.5 is a case in point), and here it even happens that, not having made up his mind, he presents to the reader several explanations of an event (87.2ff.).

of his Athenians, while Gylippus and the Syracusan commanders speak in a markedly different tone of high confidence.[59] Much that we have said about the political contents is equally true of pre-battle speeches; for oddly enough, they too are contests.

Again there is a historical substratum and a tradition; for even in Homer, and perhaps ever since Homer, commanders had been in the habit of appealing to the pride and courage of their soldiers before important battles. In giving us samples of such speeches Thucydides need not, as in political deliberations, select from a larger number that had been actually delivered.[60] Yet he does again select by concentrating on the essentials and conveying characteristic aspects of the situation. These aspects must however be propitious; for the intention is to raise the morale of the fighters.

Herodotus summarizes Themistocles' speech before the battle of Salamis (VIII 83.1) as "opposing the stronger factors to the weaker" (τὰ κρείσσω τοῖς ἥσσοσιν ἀντιτιθέμενα). This phrase, at first glance perhaps somewhat cryptic, is applicable to such speeches in Thucydides. It describes most adequately those preceding the "Battle in the Gulf" when there are "stronger" factors on both sides and the speeches make them even stronger. On the other hand if, with this formula in mind, we look at Nicias' exhortations in Book VII (61-64) and compare them with the speech of the enemy commanders, it becomes painfully apparent how poor and illusory the stronger factors on the Athenian side are. For obvious

59 The speeches: II 87-89; VII 61-63, 66-68 (note also 69.2). Speeches preceding Delion (IV 92-95) do not correspond to one another in the usual manner. Cf. for commanders' speeches O. Luschnat, *Die Feldherrnreden im Geschichtswerk des Th.* (*Philologus*, Suppl. 34, 1942), and F. E. Adcock, *Thucydides and His History* (Cambridge, 1963) 38ff.

60 He does however, where it seems appropriate, present one speech as delivered by two or even more persons (see II 86.6, VII 65.3).

reasons Nicias would not wish to create an atmosphere of gloom, but far from concealing the seriousness of the crisis he uses it as an incentive. He points out that at home, too, no hope would be left if the ships were to be lost in the battle.[61] We shall see later (in Chapter VI) why Thucydides decided to present a pair of speeches before this and no other battle of the Sicilian expedition.

Generally speaking, the moral and psychological as well as the purely strategic advantages are used to the full by such speakers. The address of the Peloponnesian commanders in Book II (87) is an exception since it includes nothing about strategic devices, whereas Phormio (II 89.8) gives some indication of his plans (his *pronoia*) and the results he expects.

Among the factors relevant to morale, the Athenian experience in naval matters occupies a prominent place. Cnemon and Brasidas assure the Spartan sailors that the much vaunted Athenian experience ("of which you are most afraid," II 87.4) is in itself no guarantee of courage. Superiority in the latter remains the Spartan prerogative. For Phormio in his "reply," Athens' truly superior experience in naval warfare entails a higher degree also of courage.[62] When "knowledge" makes a brief appearance in Nicias' speech before the battle in the harbor (VII 63.4), it seems to be a last sheet-anchor, yet finds itself in the company of weakness (ἀσθένεια) and chance (ξυμφοραί), items hardly conducive to a high morale. In the enemy's camp we hear: "You have defeated the Athenians in battles on the sea where they

[61] See esp. VII 64; see 71.2, 75.2. Cf. Luschnat, *Feldherrnreden* 91.

[62] By contrast the courage of the Spartans rests, according to him, on the mistaken belief that their experience in land battles will help them also in naval encounters (89.2f.). We may note Adcock's observation, *Thuc. and His History* 41: "In general, Greek battles depended more on morale than on tactics." For ἐμπειρία and related motifs in these speeches see Luschnat, *Feldherrnreden* 24ff., 108, 117, and *passim*.

pride themselves on having their greatest strength and at a time when you were still inexperienced (καὶ ἀνεπιστήμονες ἔτι ὄντες, 67.1). There is all the more reason for confidence now.[63]

What we have just called Phormio's reply deserves this designation; for not only does it "meet" the arguments and thoughts (*enthymemes*) of the enemy commanders but so close is the relation of the two speeches that we find in the second some thoughts of the first turned around and, as it were, put on their head. Semantic differentiations made in the first speech are by and large accepted in the second, but the relations between pivotal concepts are corrected or reversed. In our chapter on language (IV) we shall study these experiments more closely. Actually Phormio and his men could not know what had been said to the Peloponnesian sailors. In spite of this, the speeches are cast in the argument-and-counterargument mold; the *in utramque partem disputare* has determined their conception.

We have traced the history of this "form" through the latter part of the fifth century and hope that we were judicious in selecting it as particularly instructive from the numerous forms of argumentation that were in vogue during these decades. Through their number and variety these forms provided an outlet for the spirit of experimentation, but we have seen how many varieties even one form could develop.

[63] Compare II 87.4 with II 89.2f.; 87.5-7 with 89.5f. See below, pp. 100ff. Experiments with conceptual relations are, however, not typical of the pre-battle speeches, which Thucydides has kept on a less intellectual plane than the political debates.

II

PERSUASION

The third thesis that Gorgias defends in his treatise *On Not-Being* is that reality, even if it existed and could be grasped, could not be communicated.[1] This may well make us wonder why, with such pessimistic opinions, Gorgias devoted so much effort to *logos* in the sense of speech and what effect he expected of it. Some answer to this question is provided by his defense of Helen. Here we learn of great powers inherent in *logos*. They do not serve communication or clarification. Rather, they are the opposite or, if we prefer, the complement to the powers studied in the preceding chapter. The *logos* is able "to put an end to fear, to allay grief, to produce joy, and to increase pity."[2] We may take it for granted that the same emotions that may be aroused by speech may also be allayed by it and vice versa. Immediately afterward Gorgias refers to poetry as a kind of *logos* and as illustrating this effect, which in scholarly circles is frequently called *psychagogia*, the conscious guidance of another person's soul.

On Thrasymachus of Chalcedon, whose name the tradition about early rhetoric associates with Gorgias', Plato has this to say in the *Phaedrus*: τῶν . . . οἰκτρογόων ἐπὶ γῆρας καὶ πενίαν ἑλκομένων λόγων κεκρατηκέναι τέχνῃ μοι φαίνεται τὸ τοῦ Χαλκηδονίου σθένος, ὀργίσαι τε αὖ πολλοὺς ἅμα δεινὸς ἀνὴρ γέγονεν, καὶ πάλιν ὠργισμένοις ἐπᾴδων κηλεῖν, ὡς ἔφη . . . .[3] The humor of the de-

[1] 82B3.83-86.

[2] 82B11.8ff., 14 D.-K. Cf. also Pl. *Gorg.* 456b.

[3] Pl. *Phaedr.* 267c (= 85B6 D.-K.). His τέχνη may have provided for the arousing (and allaying) of other emotions as well. Aristotle's reference (*Rhet.* Γ 1,1404a 13 = 85B5) to Thrasymachus' Ἔλεοι combined with the testimony Athen. X 416A (= B4) about his προοίμια suggests to me a τέχνη composed primarily of model poems and epilogues, each designed to create an emotional condition in the audience

scription lies in the quasi-personification of the speeches. To the speeches themselves Plato attributes the kind of suffering—old age, poverty—that a person pleading in the court would envisage for the remainder of his life. We are here in the medium of the so-called ἔλεος, the appeal to the pity of the audience. This appeal had its normal and natural place in the epilogue of a speech, and as a rule it would be the defense, not the accusation, which found it expedient to resort to these devices. Like many other items of the early rhetorical *techne*, the theory of the epilogue formalized and canonized what practice had developed in pre-technical days. Plato almost seems to say as much; for one way, though not necessarily the only way, of interpreting the passage is to understand that laments about an old age to be spent in penury were common even before Thrasymachus appeared and organized them in a technical fashion.[4]

Some of the devices that were used to arouse pity are altogether "outside the *logos*." What Socrates says toward the end of the *Apology* is doubtless true: Very often someone on trial for smaller matters than he ἐδεήθη τε καὶ ἱκέτευσε τοὺς δικαστὰς μετὰ πολλῶν δακρύων, παιδία . . . ἑαυτοῦ ἀναβιβασάμενος . . . (34b). Tears must have flowed almost regularly on such occasions, and to "make the children go up" bids fair to have been a standard practice. In the mock trial of the *Wasps*, Philocleon's question "where are the children?" (v. 976) shows that it was expected at that particular juncture, after the arguments and the production of witnesses. "Go up" as addressed by the defendant to his small children or whoever could be of use to him in this final all-out effort, and "go

(cf. G. Kennedy, p. 69 on the Ἔλεοι), but including also explicitly formulated instructions. Cf. W. Kroll, *RE* Suppl. 7 s.v. "Rhetorik" 1046.

[4] Cf. Charles P. Segal, *HSCPh* 66 (1962) 116f., also for Gorgias' ψυχαγωγία.

down," the frantic reaction of the judge (or juror) in his struggle to keep matters in hand, are clearly marked in the *Wasps* as everyday occurrences in such lawsuits (vv. 979-981). Even earlier in this play Philocleon has dwelt on the boost to his ego derived from being fawned over ("have pity on me, father" v. 556) by otherwise mighty men and from the numerous devices used to humor him and to arouse his sympathy with the plight of the accused. "Poverty" and "troubles invented on top of what is true" (vv. 564f.) are familiar motifs that, as we have seen, survive into the technical provisions furnished by Thrasymachus.

An analysis of the earliest orator, Antiphon, whose three genuine speeches are dated between 430 and 420 shows no section of them oriented toward this emotional form of persuasion. The prologue of the speech (5) *On the Murder of Herodes* is calculated to secure the "good will" (εὔνοια) of the judges, a disposition which even if it has some affinity to the emotions (πάθη) does not truly qualify as one of them. And the epilogue of the same speech shows nothing quite corresponding to the words just quoted from the *Apology* or to Plato's description of Thrasymachus, but rather leaves us with the impression that Antiphon preferred to give the final section a somewhat more "intellectual" complexion.

For the *logos* as used in the service of *psychagogia* we find the best examples in Euripides. In him, it is possible to distinguish between speeches designed to uphold one side of an issue or more generally to prove an opinion and others intended to persuade a person by producing in him the necessary emotional condition. To use a distinction and concepts not yet known at the time—although the basis for them is laid in it—some speeches are addressed to the rational element of man's soul, others to the emotional parts of it.

Medea's triumph over Creon's resistance is the result of a particularly shrewd procedure. At v. 348f., Creon yields with the rueful words: ἥκιστα τοὐμὸν λῆμ' ἔφυ τυραννικόν, αἰδούμενος δὲ πολλὰ δὴ διέφθορα.[5] Thus he reacts to Medea's argument that she needs an additional day to make provisions for her children. Creon ought to pity them—"for you too are a father of children." But before Medea resorts to this final and intense appeal, the ground has been elaborately prepared. At the beginning of this episode she was faced with his stern command to leave Corinth at once (vv. 271-276). Creon is quite frank about his motives; he fears Medea's cleverness, knows her to be incensed by Jason's new marriage, and expects her to take terrible vengeance. Medea, realizing the importance of allaying his fear must first of all change his opinion of her. She is not as clever as her reputation makes her out to be. "Opinion" as well as "reputation" are in Greek expressed by the word δόξα. According to Gorgias the *logos* while working on the emotions proves able to change a person's opinion.[6]

To return to Medea, not only has her cleverness been exaggerated; she is also by now powerless, and, finally, as she endeavors to persuade Creon, she has no cause to resent anything that he has done (vv. 309ff.). Creon's reply (v. 316) shows that his fear persists, yet he must summon all his energy to stick to his decision. His increasing rudeness in the stichomythia (vv. 324-339) betrays his state of mind; at the end he threatens to have her removed by his bodyguard and calls her a nuisance. Rather suddenly she changes her tactic: It is not (as she correctly thinks he fears) her wish to have the sentence of exile revoked (v. 338); and, when he in astonishment asks why, then, she holds on to his hand, she implores him to grant her "one day" to make the necessary

[5] K. von Fritz (*Antike und Moderne Tragödie*, Berlin, 1962, 394ff.) vigorously protests attempts to discount this assertion. Creon may not be the "Klischée des harten Tyrannen"; he may be inwardly insecure, but it will scarcely be denied that his yielding is the result of Medea's tactics.

[6] 82B11.13 D.-K.

preparations for her departure and for her children (vv. 340ff.). It is probably important that at the moment when this request is made Creon is no longer as rational as he was, or tried to be, at the beginning of the episode. By now his emotions are a mixture of fear, annoyance, and I should say αἰδώς (αἰδούμενος), the decent regard due to a suppliant. For this, rather than pity, prompts him to change his attitude when Medea's request falls far short of what he was determined to refuse, and when it is reinforced by an appeal to his love for his own children. As soon as he has left, Medea discloses how much—indeed nothing less than the success of her plot—depended on his granting of her final request (vv. 368-375).[7] She has certainly directed his responses with extraordinary shrewdness.

In Medea's meeting with Aegeus (vv. 663-758), conditions are from the onset more propitious. Aegeus' disposition is friendly, and when he learns from Medea first of the wrong that Jason has committed against her and then of the further cruelty inflicted upon her by the decree of exile, his sympathy with her and indignation toward those treating her so shamefully develop as a perfectly normal reaction. The spectators had previously learned (vv. 387ff.) that uncertainty about her future, and specifically about a place of asylum, made Medea hesitant in her plans of vengeance. Yet it comes as a surprise when Medea (vv. 709ff.), as soon as she is assured of Aegeus' sympathy, touches his cheek and knees, falls at his feet, and implores him "have pity, have pity on my wretched condition . . . and take me into your country and your home." One line (v. 712) suffices to complete the picture of her hopeless condition; then she plays out the card held so far in reserve: She is able to cure him of his childlessness. Aegeus declares himself ready to assist her, yet considerations of

[7] For this and other episodes of ψυχαγωγία in Euripides, Robert L. Murray, "Persuasion in Euripides," unpublished diss., Cornell, 1964, should be consulted.

prudence make it inadvisable for himself to take her from Corinth. Still he promises her hospitality in Athens and, when she asks for it, is willing to bind himself by a strong oath.[8]

When Medea and Jason meet a second time (vv. 866-975), the audience cannot for a moment be in doubt about Medea's purpose and the deceptive quality of everything she says.[9] From the beginning, we see her establish a firm control over his mind and feelings. Her arguments, as becomes a speech of persuasion, are designed to be effective with a person of his particular character. After offering excuses for her earlier violent reproaches (vv. 863-871), she uses a reasoning very similar to his own to justify his new marriage.[10] She has reconsidered the state of her affairs, has come to accept his point of view, and in particular agrees with his claim to act "prudently" (*σωφρονεῖν*, v. 884). Preceded by her humble apology and a brief reminder of their previous tie (v. 871), such words might soften a person more capable of violent resentment than Jason. When she feels sure of having made sufficient progress, she calls the children (vv. 894ff.), bids them grasp the father's hand, and thereby completes the reconciliation; yet while the children by their mere presence and their behavior must arouse Jason's pity, this effect is heightened by her own tears (vv. 923f.)—tears which, natural as they are for more than one reason, still have an ulterior purpose. They prompt Jason to ask further questions and to console her by assurances that he has the children's future much at heart (vv. 914ff., 923ff., 929). His replies show him

[8] Vv. 719-755; see esp. vv. 731ff., 746ff.

[9] She has made this intention perfectly plain to the chorus shortly before this dialogue and has been assured of its discretion (vv. 774ff., 820ff.).

[10] Note esp. the *σύμφορον* motif (v. 876); compare vv. 551-567 with vv. 874-879, 884f. See Murray, "Persuasion in Euripides," 40ff., with whom I agree about this episode. In dealing with Medea and Aegeus, he underrates the effect of persuasion.

convinced by her arguments and touched by the pity which she evokes. Far from suspecting a scheme, he believes that security of the children is what she desires. Readily he promises it (vv. 925f.), and Medea, realizing how well her plan is working, moves on. She repeats that for herself she accepts exile as the best solution (vv. 934ff.) but, as Jason's heart is touched by the fate of the children, urges him to keep them in his own care and to gain permission for their stay in Corinth. Again ready to comply but unsure of the prospects (v. 941), he agrees with her that the better chance lies in the "indirect approach." Not he himself, but Creusa, his new wife and the King's daughter, is to intercede on their behalf (vv. 942-944). What remains for Medea is to press upon him the splendid and fatal presents that she says are certain to ensure Creusa's cooperation (vv. 945-958). Jason protests that these gifts are unnecessary; his own influence with Creusa should suffice (vv. 959ff.). But she easily overrides this protest: The persuasive power of gifts, especially gold, is greater than that of speeches.[11] An emphatic insistence on her readiness for the greatest sacrifice on behalf of the children completes her success, and the determination with which she sends her children into the palace to present the gifts forestalls any further objections on Jason's part.[12]

Here we see better than anywhere else how shrewdly in episodes of persuasion everything is oriented toward the desired end and how unerringly the responses of the interlocutor are manipulated. Before we proceed to some other

[11] This other form of πειθώ and its operation in the play are no part of our subject. Again different is the πειθώ of A. A. 385f., a passage and a conception that I hesitate to use for Euripides (see however Conacher, p. 162f.). Even less comparable is the divine πειθώ of *Eu.* 794ff., 824ff., 848ff., etc., where it operates through rational and sincere promises.

[12] Vv. 969-973 (975). The frantic intensity of vv. 964-973 shows her excitement, reminding us that simultaneously with overcoming Jason's resistance she has to stifle whatever hesitation about the fatal step may develop in herself.

plays of Euripides, it may be well briefly to look back at earlier Greek literature. How legitimate is it to speak of a new achievement? Speeches of persuasion and appeals to another person's emotions are by no means unknown in the earlier poetry. It suffices to remember the desperate implorations addressed by both Priam and Hecuba to Hector in *Iliad* XXII (vv. 33-78, 79-89), where they seek to keep Hector from meeting Achilles in single combat. In vivid grief and anxiety they are superior to any of Medea's three manoeuvres, for they are heartfelt and spontaneous, and the same would be true of the speech by which Lycaon in Book XXI (vv. 74-96) of the *Iliad* tries to move Achilles. With a certain hesitation I mention the appeal of Odysseus to Nausicaa (*Od.* VI 149-185) for, being Odysseus, he certainly knows throughout the speech what he is doing. Yet, returning once more to Hector, we certainly should add Andromache to those who by persuasion try to restrain his eagerness to fight. Her speech in Book VI (vv. 403-432) of the *Iliad* furnishes us with a welcome transition to tragedy before Euripides; for Sophocles must have had this episode in mind when he composed the speech of Tecmessa in his *Ajax* (vv. 465-524), and a comparison of the two speeches shows progress in the direction of tight and economic organization. For some of the subjects mentioned by Andromache (such as the honor paid by Achilles to her father and the trees planted by the nymphs around his grave), while contributing to the ethos and indirectly to the power of her entreaties, look like digressions when compared with the more concentrated efforts of Tecmessa. On the other hand there may be nothing as intense in her speech as Ἕκτορ, ἀτὰρ σύ μοι ἐσσι πατὴρ καὶ πότνια μήτηρ ἠδὲ κασίγνητος, σὺ δέ μοι θαλερὸς παρακοίτης (VI 429f.).[13]

[13] Some agreements are noted in the *scholia*. Most admirable is the discussion of similarities and differences by Karl Reinhardt, *Sophokles* (Frankfurt, 1933) 31f. As for disputed verses, vv. 433-439 are for me no part of the original text, whereas vv. 414-428 are an organic and

After this glance at earlier Greek literature, a few words should suffice to define the novel element in Euripides' handling of πειθώ. Only in his plays is it correct to speak of *psychagogia*, the cleverly calculated guidance of another mind toward the objective that the speaker desires but may not see fit to disclose. Euripides himself through his Medea gives us a welcome clue. After gaining from Creon the extension of her stay in Corinth, she triumphantly discloses her actual motive to the chorus: "Do you think that I would ever have played up to this man, if it had not been for the sake of some scheme or gain (εἰ μή τι κερδαίνουσαν ἢ τεχνωμένην)? I would not have spoken to him or touched his hands" (vv. 368-370). The Greek words in the parentheses may serve as a convenient epitome of the new orientation. To put it in the simplest, almost primitive way, Medea has not been honest—and who when dealing with the speeches of Priam, Andromache, and Tecmessa would not be appalled if the question of their sincerity were as much as raised? For Medea persuasion, whether predominantly argumentative or emotional, is a tool, a matter of strategy, one of the numerous resources available to her scheming mind.[14] She can turn it on and off at will. Medea is as capable as Priam or any other character in earlier poetry to expound everything that makes her condition desperate, yet the congenial medium for her is not an outburst but a rational exposé, in which she puts item after item in due order (vv. 252-258). It is true that on other occasions she

---

integral part of the entreaty. Their function is obvious even before the climax of vv. 429f., where it becomes poignantly acute. Note also in Sophocles the crescendo αἴδεσαι (v. 506), αἴδεσαι (v. 507), οἴκτιρε (v. 510).

[14] We learn of her abominable intention only vv. 790-793; cf. W. H. Friedrich, *Vorbild und Neugestaltung. Sechs Kapitel zur Gesch. d. Tragödie* (Göttingen, 1967) 19ff. Still there are ominous warnings earlier (vv. 89ff., 100ff., 112ff.).

strikes us as more emotional,[15] e.g. when she urges Aegeus: *οἴκτιρον, οἴκτιρόν με τὴν δυσδαίμονα καὶ μή μ' ἔρημον ἐκπεσοῦσαν εἰσίδῃς* (v. 711f.), but it does not take long before her calculation becomes patent again.[16] And yet her scheming *psychagogia* has more success than the sincere efforts at persuasion made by Andromache, Priam, and Tecmessa.

Calculation and deception are frequent in Euripides' plays, but *psychagogia* is not always used in their service. In the *Hecuba*, a condition of utmost misery, the experience of one heavy blow after another has not deprived the heroine of her capacity for cool and clear reasoning. Before deciding to fall at Agamemnon's feet, she considers with care whether to enlist his help is the right and advantageous course. Might she not rather aggravate her misfortune (*Hec.* 736-746)? Her hesitation does not last long. The hideous crime of Polymestor being at this point known to Agamemnon (vv. 760-784), a brief résumé with emphasis on its particularly revolting aspects (vv. 790-797) suffices to arouse his indignation. Her speech includes much that is truly felt, although even the sentence that begins with "have pity on me" continues in a less spontaneous vein, employing antitheses like *τύραννος ἦν ποτ', ἀλλὰ νῦν δούλη σέθεν κτλ.* (vv. 807ff.). Still, we should recognize genuine despair and deepest grief even behind what strikes us as self-conscious, as rationalistic, and indeed as speculative. For what, by normal criteria, could be less "natural" than Hecuba's reflection about *πειθώ* as a study more rewarding than the subjects commonly taught and learned (vv. 814-819)? The sentences that follow this call for educational reform are again profoundly moving (vv.

[15] Note also *ὄλωλα* (v. 704); but she probably leads up to these bursts of helplessness by drawing Aegeus' attention from his own problem to hers (see vv. 688f.) and then using stichomythia to acquaint him by degrees with the full extent of her plight.

[16] See her request for a *πίστις* (v. 731) and Aegeus' remark about her *προμηθία* (v. 741). Such precaution would not be necessary if she were an exile of the normal type.

820-823). Yet a new self-consciousness about persuasion is evident throughout this speech. The topics are set off from one another, one presumably very effective motif being introduced by the words: ἴσως μὲν τοῦ λόγου ξένον (?καινὸν?) τόδε,[17] another by ἑνός μοι μῦθος ἐνδεὴς ἔτι (vv. 824, 835). The former of these is designated as strange or new because it is unusual and daring to remind Agamemnon that Cassandra is now his mistress and that this ought to create a relationship of χάρις between Hecuba and himself.

Hecuba's speech also includes one of those utopian ideas hardly less strange and daring yet especially dear to Euripides' heart. For us they constitute another "experiment of reason." Not rarely—as we shall see in Chapter III—these "visions" take form when a character in a state of tension catches his breath, so to speak, for the real move. Thus Hecuba at vv. 836ff. goes off into speculations about a divine or human master craftsman endowing her entire body with voice to join in and support the implorations uttered by her tongue. And finally there is an exaltation of law (νόμος), basic rules and habits that govern civilized behavior and now depend for their preservation on Agamemnon (799-805). This invocation of a principle of universal validity is remotely—but indeed no more than remotely—comparable to what Tecmessa or Philoctetes say about the obligations of an εὐγενής.[18] Hecuba's reference to the νόμος has a somewhat abstract

[17] V. 824, where κενόν of the MSS. seems impossible. ξένον has been suggested by Nauck.

[18] *Aj.* 52-54; *Ph.* 475f. In *Hec.* there is an appeal to pity—very sustained, without any subtleties—also in the latter half of Hecuba's speech to Odysseus when he comes to fetch Polyxene to her death. Having in the former half dwelt on τὸ δίκαιον (vv. 251-270; note v. 271), she asks for his οἶκτος (vv. 272-295), pointing out how much she has suffered and how hard the additional loss of Polyxene would be for her. Interesting, if somewhat problematic connections between the Odysseus and the Agamemnon episode are suggested by Gordon M. Kirkwood, *TAPhA* 78 (1947) 64ff. For valuable observations see again Murray, "Persuasion in Euripides," 113ff., 125.

quality. In principle, it is not out of place. For inevitably, arguments are important also in speeches aimed at the emotions, and if one kind of argument may be singled out as most frequent and presumably most effective, it would be references to justice, whether it be endangered and in need of defense or actually violated so that the wrong, as in this instance, calls for an avenger.[19]

Euripides would not repeat the same pattern even where the situations were parallel. In his *Helen*, it is instructive to compare Helen's own appeal to Theonoe with that of Menelaus. Both know that their rescue depends on the silence of the mysterious Theonoe, and both turn to her with entreaties for help. But the contrast is striking. Helen has no hesitation about speaking as suppliant from the beginning to the end (ἱκέτις, v. 894; cf. v. 939); she does not conceal her misery and dire peril. After a long separation, she has just been reunited to her husband; and now he is in danger of being killed. "Save us, I implore you" (v. 900; cf. 925). True, she also resorts to arguments of an intellectual, even of a sophisticated complexion (vv. 912ff., 919ff.), but it is her own fate that is at stake and should move Theonoe. Menelaus refuses to speak in the same imploring tone "about his life" (vv. 945f.). He must conduct himself in a manner worthy of Troy and of his own nobility and honor.[20] Whatever may be said about a man of high aspirations as not disgracing himself if

[19] Of the former kind we shall presently find examples in *Hel.* and *Or.*; in addition, while I hesitate to use any of the final scenes of *Phoen.*, I might refer to the "political" plays (see below, Ch. V, esp. p. 154).

[20] After A. M. Dale's defense (*Euripides: Helen*), vv. 903-908 may confidently be regarded as genuine. Incidental remarks by her on v. 993 show a perfect grasp of the difference between the two speeches. See also K. Mathiesen, *Hermes* 96 (1969) 691ff. with references to Walther Ludwig, "Sapheneia," unpublished diss. Tübingen, 1954, 43 (to me not now available). See esp. for Menelaus also Murray, 239ff. Robert Schmiel, perceptive but at times over-subtle in his recent study on the *Helen* (*Hermes* 100, 1972, 274ff.), is unlucky in his treatment of this episode (pp. 289ff.).

he sheds tears in misfortune, he himself will not stoop to such conduct. Instead he insists on his "right" (vv. 959ff.), demands Helen back as his due, first from Theonoe, then even from Hades, who for her sake has received countless victims (vv. 962-974); in the end he even resorts to threats (vv. 975ff.). It would be futile to deny a tragicomic element in his conduct, but a discussion of it would not be appropriate here.

In the *Orestes*, the plea for help and pity, when it finally comes off, is thoroughly sincere; for Orestes, wretched in the extreme, harassed by the avenging deities, abandoned by almost everybody, and fearing that the Argives will pronounce his death sentence, is in urgent need of assistance. However he must endure two agonizing retardations. First Menelaus, of whom he expects help (vv. 380-384), having just learned about the catastrophes of his brother and of Clytemnestra, insists on receiving a very circumstantial account of all that has happened. His questions and Orestes' answers fill a stichomythia of no fewer than 63 verses (vv. 384-446). When, after this barrage of questions, Orestes is finally able to resume his imploration, something else happens that is even more disturbing and may prove fatal. All of a sudden Tyndareus appears on the stage, wrathful and determined to exact vengeance for the murder of his daughter Clytemnestra (vv. 456ff.). Instead of continuing to arouse Menelaus' sympathy, Orestes must engage in a contest (ἀγὼν λόγων) with a formidable opponent who marshals careful arguments in support of a just cause (vv. 491-604). In the event Tyndareus weakens Orestes' case as well as his prospects, for as he leaves he threatens to lend his authority to the accusation brought against Orestes (vv. 609ff., 622ff.); moreover his vigorous conduct intimidates Menelaus. Still, Orestes goes ahead with his plea (vv. 640-679). Its substance is the immense debt that Menelaus owes to Agamemnon; what he may now do in return is very small. This time there can be no question of calculated or deliberate behavior; everything that Orestes says comes straight from the heart. There still is more "argument" than Sophocles had used a year earlier in the plea of Philoctetes,[21] but, when he comes to the end, Orestes in acute despair bursts into tears and laments (δάκρυα καὶ γόους καὶ συμφοράς, v. 677). The emotional quality of this speech, so far barely concealed, is now fully apparent. When Orestes defended himself in his contest (ἀγών) with Tyndareus, his speech was rational; what counted was the variety and the skillful employment of arguments. The speech addressed to Menelaus is emotional; every word serves—directly or indirectly—the purpose of moving Menelaus, arousing his pity, and through pity securing his help. In both of his speeches there is much reference to justice; yet in the one it is an issue, discussed with restraint, hard as this is for Orestes—actually restraint is also hard for Tyndareus (see e.g. vv. 520f., 528ff., 534ff.); in the other it constitutes a claim, which is made ever more urgent. Euripides could hardly have provided better illustrations for two different yet, in a sense, complementary experiments of reason.

The calculation and deception characteristic of Medea's appeals are absent not only in the *Orestes* but also in the three episodes of the *Iphigeneia in Aulis,* where an appeal is made to pity. In tone, ethos, and sentiment, the appeals are utterly different, but a close analysis of the play would be needed—and despite valuable recent work much remains to be done—to appreciate the contrasts from the artistic side. Agamemnon, profoundly affected by the imminent sacrifice of his daughter, moves the chorus and finally even Menelaus as he expounds his misery (esp. vv. 442-505); Clytemnestra, upon suddenly learning of the true plan regarding Iphigeneia,

[21] See *Ph.* 468-506. The *Orestes* also includes a brief appeal by Electra for Hermione's sympathy and help (vv. 1337-1343; cf. the stichomythia, vv. 1326-1336). At vv. 1340ff., the plea rises to a remarkable pitch; and yet it is insincere, concealing the plot of vengeance in her mind.

falls at Achilles' knees and in despair urges him to help (vv. 888-916); finally Iphigeneia herself lovingly turns to her father and reminds him of the ties of affection and attachment between them in the past that were meant to last into the future (vv. 1211-1252).[22] In innocent frankness she expresses her desire to live (vv. 1218ff., 1250ff.). Our sympathy goes out to the anguish of her father and of her mother; yet her natural simplicity engages it more strongly than either of them. "Calculation" of the kind that we have found in the *Medea* is entirely absent in all three speeches. If anyone at all calculates, it is the poet, Euripides himself, who may be conscious of using the same instrument three times but who varies mode and ethos as he plays it.

We have so far confined ourselves to speeches aimed at arousing the pity of another character. However, in Euripides, not only speeches but also characters who find themselves in a lamentable condition produce pity, at any rate in the spectator, and such effects on him were doubtless a matter of the greatest importance for Euripides. We may remember Gorgias, who in exalting the powers of the *logos* over souls used poetry as proof and listed ἔλεος . πολύδακρυς (pity rich in tears) among the emotions experienced by the "hearers" (82B11.9 D.-K.). Some plays of Euripides, e.g. the *Troades*, present human misery unalloyed and unalleviated; others (*Heracles Furens*, *Orestes*) include episodes of profound despair. In the *Suppliants* the helplessness of the women crystallizes first in an appeal by Adrastus to Theseus (vv. 163-192), then after Theseus' refusal of help, in a heartrending chorus (263-285)

[22] Nothing that she says strikes us as artful or in the least premeditated. She can even invoke the arts of Orpheus (vv. 1211-1214) without producing a jarring note. Her intensely felt appeal differs strikingly from Clytemnestra's reproachful argument arguing and reasoning with her husband in a speech immediately preceding that of Iphigeneia (vv. 1146-1208). See however Kitto, 362ff., who takes a far less sympathetic view of Iphigeneia.

that prompts Aethra's tears and causes Theseus to change his mind. We are touching on a large subject. If we were dealing with it more fully, we should for instance have to contrast the Oedipus in Sophocles' last tragedy who has very few words of lament (e.g. vv. 199, 202, 847) with the Oedipus in the (almost contemporary) *Phoenissae* who has very few words that are not lament.[23] However the "pity (fear, etc.) produced by the action" that Aristotle (*Poet.* 19) distinguishes from that "produced by the spoken word" and the large question by what means Euripides achieves such emotional effects in the action call for treatment in a monograph; for us these matters are of minor interest because they do not serve any purpose of πειθώ.

In Thucydides, we do not look for a speech designed to influence the emotions but expect cool-headed rationality and a strictly pragmatic analysis of a given situation. However, the Plataeans, when left with no choice but to surrender their city, ask for "pity borne of moderation" (οἶκτος σώφρων, III 59.1) and describe themselves more than once as "suppliants."[24] Their speech is unique in Thucydides and invites a comparison with the appeals for pity and help that we have studied in Euripides, It, too, includes claims on gratitude (χάρις), which the Plataeans think is due them for their record in the past;[25] also, as e.g. in the appeal of Hecuba to

[23] The presence of interpolations stands in the way of a conclusive judgment. I should not recognize as many as Ed. Fraenkel (*SBAW*, 1963, 1, 88ff.); for in the final episodes there is more "weinerlicher Ton" and less "königliche Manneswürde" (pp. 93f.) than he admits; vv. 1622-1624, where the latter is present, are at variance with the emotional quality of the scene, in fact a striking exception.

[24] III 59.2, 4; cf. 58.3.

[25] III 54.3–5; 56.4; 57.1, 4; 58.4f.; 59.2. For εὐεργεσίαι as a χάρις which demands another in return see Soph. *Aj.* 520-24; 1266-1271; *Med.* 869-871; *Hec.* 829f.; *Or.* 647ff. The Plataeans have reason to fear that with the Lacedaemonians the χάρις felt toward Thebes may have more weight (53.4, 58.1). [Cf. J. C. Hagan, *Phoenix* 26, 1972, 241ff.]

Agamemnon, the "standard binding for all" (πᾶσι καθεστὼς νόμος, 56.2) is invoked, this time to justify the resistance of the Plataeans to the surprise attack by the Thebans.[26]

Emotional qualities are most conspicuous at the beginning and at the end of the speech. In the opening sentences, the speakers dwell on their helplessness, their apprehensions, and the unexpected and undeserved disadvantages under which they have to present their case (53). And in the final chapters (58f.), while again referring to their extreme peril, they call upon the Panhellenic gods (59.2, cf. 58.5) and remind the Lacedaemonians of the oaths sworn in the Persian War, of the graves containing the men killed in the great battle, of Plataea's historical merits culminating in the day of its most glorious (λαμπρότατα, 59.2) deeds, and of the old friendly relationship between Sparta and Plataea. These motifs in their favor have been used also in the central part of their speech but are reintroduced with a new emphasis, some of them even more than once (e.g. the graves 58.4f., 59.2; the fight for the freedom of Greece 58.5, 59.4).

The Theban reply invalidates both the Plataeans' rational arguments and their claims to pity, sympathy, and gratitude. Their merits of long ago, besides being less great than the Plataeans make them out to be (62.1f., 64.1f.), are overshadowed by their disgraceful conduct and policy in later years (63.3ff., 64).[27] It is rather the Thebans who deserve pity because some of their men were mercilessly slaughtered by the Plataeans, although they had surrendered on the promise that their lives would be spared (66.2, 67.3f.).[28] Fathers deprived of promising sons and the city deprived of

[26] 56.2 (see however also 58.3). On *Hec.* see above p. 57.

[27] See also 67.2, where they warn the Lacedaemonians: μὴ παλαιὰς ἀρετὰς . . . ἀκούοντες ἐπικλασθῆτε κτλ.

[28] Thus the νόμος invoked by the Plataeans would actually favor the Thebans who have suffered ἄνομα at their hands (67.5).

its youth are "suppliants" (67.3) on more just grounds than the Plataeans, who in their speech repeatedly applied this designation to themselves. On the whole, however, the Thebans counter the Plataean speech through reasoning and arguments. The passages where they deplore their own sufferings notwithstanding, their speech as a whole does not have the same emotional urgency as the Plataean. It hardly could, since their physical existence is not imperiled.

In Gorgias, pity is only one of four emotions that a speech is able to arouse or allay. Yet all the material we have found to illustrate *psychagogia* relates to pity. For the other three emotions, nothing analogous is available. Surely there are in Thucydides speeches of commanders assuring their soldiers or sailors that the enemy is not as formidable as they believe. The supposedly unrivaled experience of the Athenians in naval warfare need not prove decisive if, on the opposite side, other qualities are strong enough to outbalance it. The looks and the fighting habit of the northern tribes may be terrifying, but the men themselves are completely lacking in discipline; despite their threatening appearance, they will prove easy to deal with.[29] Speeches of this kind have the objective of "allaying fear," and the commanders while attempting to achieve this also try to build "confidence" (θάρσος).[30] However, these exhortations do not lend themselves to an analysis of the same type as the strategy of persuasion used by Medea, Hecuba, and other Euripidean characters to arouse somebody's pity. For whether the military leaders weigh advantages against disadvantages, showing the former to exceed the latter, or whether they proceed without such contrast simply by assessing the realities of a situation, their appeal is essentially

[29] See esp. Thuc. II 87, 89; IV 126. IV 10 and the encouraging speeches of Nicias in VII (61-68, 77) are peculiar owing to the precarious situations in which arguments of a very special complexion are necessary.

[30] See e.g. II 87.1; IV 89.2; 126.1, 3ff.

to reason, not to the emotions. What we have here tried to explore is the manipulation of the emotions through speeches constructed with this end in view. Reason so resourceful in devising and employing arguments is no less ingenious when it has to work on the "irrational" side of human nature.

III

UTOPIAN WISHES AND SCHEMES OF REFORM

As we have stated in the Introduction, we do not propose to deal with the content of radical and reformatory theories put forward in this period. Our concern is with forms rather than with subject matter. Sometimes the protest against tradition takes the form of a utopian wish or thought; in fact when criticism goes to extremes, it is apt to demand impossible changes, and the most radical ideas of the time are known to us only in the medium of utopian speculations. Speculations and wishes are free and can travel in any direction. To begin with a well-known instance, in the opening words of the *Medea* the nurse singles out three events of the past that "ought" not to have happened. The first is the expedition of the Argo to Colchis (here she mentions the greatest crisis of that journey, and her words sound as though she wished that ship and men had been smashed by the Symplegades); next comes the felling of the trees that provided timber for the shipbuilding; and finally the rowing of this ship by the outstanding heroes. If these events had not materialized, Medea would not have fallen in love with Jason, would not have accompanied him to Jolkos, not have plotted murder against the aged Pelias, and not have come to live in Corinth, where matters have now suddenly taken the worst turn (vv. 1-15). The correct chronological sequence is neglected in these initial wishes and was evidently considered immaterial by Euripides.[1] Still, there is a chain of causes, and the distress

[1] As is well known, this indifference was noticed by the philological commentators (Timachidas in the scholia *ad loc.*) and as a result avoided by Ennius in his *Medea* (frg. 246 Vahlen). Cf. Friedrich Leo, *Plautin. Forschungen* (2nd ed., Berlin, 1914) 87, and the very reasonable ex-

about the present misfortune is projected into the past, finding expression in the wish that the antecedents had not materialized.

The desire to find causes and even the tendency to carry the search back to the first "moving cause" are typically Greek. When this first event in the chain has been pinpointed, imagination may wipe out all that developed from it. In the standard conception of the Trojan War, the judgment of Paris was such a "first cause." Of the preserved plays, *Andromache* (vv. 274ff.) is the earliest to treat the judgment in this sense and with an amount of embroidery equal to that of the much later *Iphigeneia in Aulis*.[2] This may suggest that Euripides had used the motif even earlier and was in the habit of playing variations on it. From the ordeal of the captive Andromache in Thessaly, where Neoptolemus has taken her after the sack of Troy, it is a far cry to the judgment on Mount Ida. This time Euripides begins not with Paris himself but with Hermes as the "cause of great woe" (v. 274) when he took the chariot with the three goddesses to the wooded glen of Ida. Next we read of the goddesses washing themselves in the springs of that mountain so as to appear in their full beauty, and finally Euripides moves on to the persuasive words of Cypris "pleasant to hear but a bitter ruin" for Troy. In the second stanza the poet varies the first cause: "would that the mother had thrown him (Paris) over her head," paying heed to prophecies of Cassandra, before he came to live on Ida (vv. 293ff.). The

---

planation by D. L. Page, *Euripides: Medea* (Oxford, 1938) *ad loc.* As I am not aiming at completeness, I make it a point to refer to the full list of wishes, especially of the utopian kind in Schmid-Stahlin, *Geschichte d. griech. Literatur* III 1 (Munich, 1940) 709 n. 9.

[2] *IA* 1284ff., 1291. The entire aria dwells on the antecedents, visualizing them with a great amount of detail, as though by recapturing them in her imagination Iphigeneia could secure genuine relief from her anguish.

third and last stanza (vv. 301ff.) sets forth what would not have happened—to Troy as a whole, to Andromache, to the Greek warriors, to their wives who are now widows, and to their fathers who are now childless—if Paris had been killed at birth. The comparable passage in the second *Iphigeneia* begins by addressing Mount Ida and its scenery, for which a variety of details is supplied. However, it is hardly necessary and, given the uncertainties of the text, not even desirable to retrace the movement of thought in the entire aria.

The catastrophes that befall the house of Laius also have their first causes. In the *Phoenissae*, where we see the sons of Oedipus on the way to mutual destruction, a chorus (vv. 801-817) takes us back to these causes. The Cithaeron ought not to have kept Oedipus alive when he had been exposed there by his parents, and that Hades-sent monster, the Sphinx, ought not to have ravaged the population of Thebes.[3] Inevitably the reference to the Cithaeron brings another passage to mind. Ἰὼ Κιθαιρών, τί μ᾽ ἐδέχου we read in Sophocles' *King Oedipus* (v. 1391), and, as long as we look only at words, clauses, and sentences, the parallels to Euripides are indeed striking. In Sophocles, when the full truth has come to light, Oedipus himself turns to the crucial events of his life. Why had they to happen? Besides the Cithaeron, he mentions home and upbringing in Corinth, the fatal crossing of the three roads, and finally the marriage (1349ff., 1391ff.). All these stages of his life are now taking on an appalling new significance; he calls them to mind with desperate vividness and horror. They, too, are "beginnings" (ἀρχαί) and "causes" (αἰτίαι), and Oedipus is, even in the lyric passages, capable of reasoning out what would not have hap-

[3] See also the chorus vv. 1018-1065, where the antecedents of Menoeceus' heroic self-sacrifice are recorded, especially the misery caused by the Sphinx. The causal connection between her devastations and Menoeceus is tenuous (for what he expiates is the killing of the earth-born snake by Cadmus); but at this stage of tragedy, choruses and arias may wander off *ad libitum*.

pened if the fetters had never been taken off his feet—ὄλοιθ' ὅστις . . . did it (*OT* 1349). Yet even where he reasons, emotions break forth. With the cool, rational speculation in Euripides, these passages have only the most extrinsic similarity.

Passages in the *Helen* provide additional illustrations of this pattern. Both Helen and Menelaus wish the past undone. She, persuading herself that Hera and her own beauty have conspired to ruin her life, imagines how much better it would be if, washing off her beauty, she could acquire an ugly face and the Greeks were to forget all that is bad in her life (vv. 262ff.). Her husband, shipwrecked and looking back at a sequence of misfortunes, also wishes the past out of existence, but his desire expresses itself in a more radical way, familiar to us from other instances and the standard form in Euripides. In curiously solemn language he goes back to his ancestors. If Pelops' life had come to an end when he was slaughtered and offered to the gods (no doubt an ideal occasion), Atreus would not have been begotten, Menelaus would not have been born and experienced all his sufferings.[4] Euripides could easily have specified events in Menelaus' own life that ought not to have happened. He preferred the opposite course; as we have seen, he favors "remoter" causes.[5] We have emphasized the utopian quality of such wishes and shall find it also in the wishes and demands for reform put forward by characters and choruses in Euripides. Yet this quality though often present is by no means common to all passages of the kind. In the preceding chapter we have touched on Hecuba's criticism of mankind for studying various subjects but neglecting the "tyrant" Persuasion (*Hec.* 814ff.). If a sober comment on this out-

[4] Vv. 386-413. For the problems of text and tone, esp. in the first line, see the excellent comments of A. M. Dale, *Euripides: Helen*.

[5] Not invariably, however; *Med.* 1410ff., *Andr.* 1181ff., and *IA* 790ff. might be cited as instances to the contrary.

burst may be ventured, it would be that rhetoric can no longer have been unknown in Athens around 424 B.C. and that Hecuba herself has profited from it in her appeal to Agamemnon.[6] Far more difficult to change would be the custom that the chorus in *Hippolytus* (535ff.) describes as futile—without, however, actually specifying a reform. Again a "tyrant" is slighted by mankind. Eros, who holds the keys to the chambers of Aphrodite, receives no worship, while Zeus in Olympia and Apollo in Delphi are honored "in vain" (ἄλλως, ἄλλως) by large sacrifices.

In the *Andromache*, two passages critical of prevailing conditions might almost be considered as complementary. Andromache, revolting against the brutal and undignified conduct of Menelaus, bursts into a declamation (vv. 319ff.) against δόξα ("reputation") as apt to enhance the status of a man who has not deserved it, and Peleus somewhat later protests the Greek convention (νόμος . . . νομίζεται, vv. 693ff.) of giving the military commander credit for valorous deeds that have been performed by his men. In neither instance is a remedy suggested; all that the characters can do is to deal with the situation which faces them. In this respect a chorus of the *Helen* is more "constructive"; for after denouncing as foolish those who distinguish themselves in war and believe that bloodshed will ever produce a solution, the chorus refers to the possibility (1159) of settling by negotiations a discord like that created by Helen. The chorus hovers between generalizations and specific reflections about Helen's case. Still, since they envisage a different order and since this order, though often desired,[7] has never yet been realized, we may class this passage with utopian speculations.

[6] Perhaps the words ἐς τέλος bear the accent; rhetoric has not yet been studied sufficiently to the point of guaranteeing success.

[7] Cf. Hdt. VII 9 β 2 where χρῆν introduces a utopian postulate followed by a piece of armchair strategy.

We do not know what prompted a character in the *Cresphontes* (frg. 449) to recommend that, in view of all the suffering life has in store, we ought to engage in laments at the birth and rejoice at the death of a human being. Herodotus (V 4) reports about this custom as being actually practiced by a Thracian tribe. Euripides must have known Herodotus' account, and his mind, always in search of most thorough reform schemes, did this time not move freely but made use of a curious habit associated with another country.

From these samples of single wishes or isolated criticisms we proceed to a passage that presents three successive reform schemes. In the *Hippolytus* Theseus, after finding his wife dead and reading her charges against Hippolytus, is provoked beyond endurance when Hippolytus, upon appearing on the stage, shows the utmost surprise and ignorance. To Theseus this reaction must seem hypocrisy at its worst. Before he quiets down—relatively speaking, for his entire accusation (936-980) must have been uttered in a most vehement tone—his indignation expresses itself in three speculations, each of them more fantastic than the preceding. First he attacks mankind for teaching and inventing countless arts but having never devised a way of teaching sense to those who lack it (916-920). A person capable of achieving this would indeed have to be a δεινὸς σοφιστής, as Hippolytus observes in his reply, where he suggests that his father indulges in subtleties (λεπτουργεῖς) not appropriate to the occasion (921-923). The observation is correct enough and we are grateful for once to receive an authentic Greek expression for this curious feature of Euripidean drama; however Hippolytus does not yet know the reason for his father's astonishing behavior.

Theseus' second outburst produces a variation on a familiar theme, the demand for a criterion between true and false friends (vv. 925-931);[8] yet the variation must be original

[8] See *Scol.* 33 Diehl; Theognis 119ff., 419f. (Pi. *P.* 10.76); and in

with Euripides, since no one would yet have come forward with something so hyperbolically impossible as the demand for two voices in every individual, one disclosing the truth, the other expressing whatever the speaker wishes to say. Only Euripides himself could outdo this product of unbridled imagination. In the *Hercules Furens* he recommends a return to the sunlight and a second life as a distinguishing mark of good men (vv. 655ff.), evidently without considering how little help this would offer in the first life.[9] By its extravagance, the passage in the *Hippolytus* illustrates at once the degree of Theseus' indignation and of Euripides' indulgence in the fantastic and the grotesque.

Finally the third utopia (vv. 936-942) is neither an implied suggestion for reform nor, like the second, which begins with the typical χρῆν, a statement of what ought to be the case, but may be called a pessimistic prophecy of what will some day be necessary, impossible though it is. If human wickedness progresses at the rate it does, the gods will have to provide a second earth for the bad and unjust.

As we approach the discussion about the status of women, we may recall our preliminary remarks about the distance between the ideal and the possible. Looking first at the case for women, we note that some conceptions embodied in the *Medea* are without parallel in the serious literature of this period and that nowhere in the play is there an explicit demand for a world order in which women would no longer be kept in a position of inferiority. Surely there is a certain amount of reflection about their disadvantages, the most elaborate point by point account being Medea's first speech

---

Euripides himself also *El.* 367-379 (successfully defended by Denniston in his commentary, *Euripides: Electra*, Oxford 1939), where however no χαρακτήρ of a new kind is desired.

[9] Cf. Wilamowitz, *Euripides: Herakles* (Berlin, 1889) *ad loc.*: "ausmalen darf man sich diese Vorschläge . . . nicht; sonst gerät man ins absurde." Two lives are desired also *Supp.* 1080ff.

(vv. 214-265),[10] where she contrasts the physical and social conditions of women's existence with the freedom enjoyed by men. A complement to this account of present conditions is furnished by the confident vision in the first strophe and antistrophe of the next chorus. A turn is coming; the future will be better—but we may wonder in what respect. For we learn nothing specific beyond a change of reputation, of which, according to this as well as a later chorus (vv. 1081-1089), women themselves would be the guardians. If we wonder what inspires this confidence, only the daring action of Medea could be the answer, although to us it may seem exceptional rather than exemplary. Surely, neither Euripides' women nor anything in Aristophanes and Plato can attest to an actual movement aiming at emancipation.[11]

On the opposite side, there are if possible even more unrealistic demands for a worse treatment of women. Invectives against them are, after all, traditional in Greek poetry. Hippolytus, after listening to the suggestions of the nurse must—just like his father somewhat later—vent his indignation in utopian visions. The first and most extreme would dispense with women altogether. Zeus ought to have provided a different way of securing progeny (vv. 616-624).[12] Men might buy offspring in his temples, and, although Hippolytus fails to say this, he can have only male offspring in mind. His

[10] Her own condition is worse than that of most women; she has left her home, has no relatives to turn to, etc. (see vv. 252ff.).

[11] It is worth recalling that Ivo Bruns (*Frauenemanzipation in Athen*, Kiel, 1900 = *Vorträge und Aufsätze*, Munich, 1905, 154ff.), on the strength of passages in the *Medea* and similar ones elsewhere in Euripides, argued for the existence of an actual movement for the improvement of women's position. He failed to carry conviction, mainly because of Wilamowitz's protest (*Hermes* 35, 1900, 548ff. = *Kleine Schriften* IV 126ff.).

[12] For the meaning of the difficult words τοῦ τιμήματος τῆς ἀξίης (v. 623) cf. W. S. Barrett's careful disquisition (*Euripides: Hippolytus*). An amusing variation of the wish for a world not infested by women occurs *Cyc.* 187f.

second proposal (vv. 645-650) could, physically at least, be realized. It calls for a complete isolation of women from human company, especially servants, the worst type; only animals, harmless because they lack the use of language, ought to be with them.[13]

In a fragment attested for his *Theseus* (frg. 388) Euripides distinguishes between two kinds of *eros*, one more desirable than the other, suggesting that it ought to be a "law"—or norm of life—for reasonable people to have traffic only with the better, not with the emotional Cypris. Finally, to complete the variety of sexual reforms proposed in his plays, a stray line from the *Protesilaus* (frg. 653)—of all plays the least likely, we should think[14]—declares that women ought to be "common" (κοινόν) property.

The *Hippolytus* in particular is abundant in utopian flights, and a passage so peculiar that it can hardly find a place elsewhere may receive it here, since it after all concerns human relations. The nurse being deeply affected by Phaedra's "illness" wishes that human attachments might be less close. Now two persons suffer when one is hit by misfortune. Involvement in another person's experiences "ought" to be easily dissolved and easily restored (vv. 253-260). A first reading leaves the impression that she wishes human nature to be made over. But she herself thinks of moderation, and as she refers to traditional wisdom of the μηδὲν ἄγαν type she may not be asking for anything impossible.

It would have been desirable in principle to reserve all passages involving the gods for treatment in the same paragraph. But gods cannot be separated from divine dispensation, and this embraces a large part of human life. As we

[13] A thought quoted from the *Ino* (frg. 410.1) shows more restraint. The speaker merely wishes to see women limited to having servants who know what is right and are immune to baseness.

[14] The thought may, of course, be off the main lines of the plot. In the myth love proves stronger than death.

have seen, whoever asks for a world without women must address this demand to Zeus. In point of fact, only a few demands for reforms of the gods and their ways have not yet been recorded. The *Ion* offers many opportunities for criticism of their conduct, and we know by now how short is the way from criticism to suggestions for alternative arrangements. When Creusa, after her plot has failed, takes refuge at the altar of Apollo, the god is blamed for his unwise ordinance saving criminals from punishment (vv. 1312-1319). Unjust people "ought" to be expelled from an altar; only the just if threatened by arbitrary violence should find an asylum in a temple. Elsewhere (frg. 1049), a less inhibited speaker is willing to take justice into his own hands by removing the guilty person from the altar. Evidently, in a conflict between morality and established religion, the latter must give way. Ion seems to feel the same (esp. vv. 1275f.) yet contents himself with theorizing, and his most startling theory postulates a penalty to be paid by the gods for every rape of a mortal woman. This would empty their temples of the treasures. Ion knows that this will never become reality (οὐ γὰρ ἔσται · τῷ λόγῳ δὲ χρήσομαι, v. 444), but it would remedy the outrageous discrepancy, of which he has just become aware, between the morality sanctioned by the gods and their own conduct.

On the preceding pages we have included a few ideas that are utopian in conception and offer a blueprint for ideal conditions, even though no wish is uttered for the realization of these conditions. Still at times Euripides' imagination breaks through the boundaries between the possible and the impossible. Hecuba, in her desperate final attempt to sway Agamemnon would feel more confident if she could acquire voice in arms, hands, feet, and hair so that her whole body could join in her appeal. Here we should probably read the "if" (εἰ, v. 836), which introduces this grotesque thought as expression of a wish (= εἴθε); yet the wish would apply exclusively to herself and to her very specific emergency and anguish.[15] And there is certainly neither wish nor thought of reform in a passage of the *Melanippe* (frg. 506) where a character develops and simultaneously ridicules the idea that unjust actions have wings and fly to the gods where they will be recorded in the account books of Zeus for his inspection and judgment. The image of "divine bookkeeping" has antecedents in earlier poetry. In Aeschylus,[16] it was meant to be taken seriously, even if not literally. Here the speaker seeks to replace the idea of divine judgment by a justice near at hand.

The passages collected here must leave an impression of bewildering diversity.[17] Some are relevant only to their context and as an indication of the speaker's frame of mind. Others reflect a perfectly serious discontent. Still, whatever we think of individual passages, utopian speculations as such are germane to the Greek Enlightenment. Its demands for reform were inspired by conviction about what "ought to" be practiced and what "ought to" be valued. Programs mapping out a right, reasonable, and natural ordering of human

[15] We have commented earlier on Hecuba's demand for a more concentrated study of rhetoric, but should also, for the sake of contrast, note her desire (vv. 1187ff.) that an eloquent tongue should not have more power than the truth.

[16] See A. *Eum.* 272ff.; cf. my paper *CQ* 38 (1944) 27ff. = *Kleine Schriften* I 137ff.

[17] I repeat that completeness has not been my objective. Among topics altogether omitted from my purview are invectives against seers which may take the form of wishing their profession out of existence (see A. M. Dale in her commentary on *Hel.* 753ff.).—Ἔχρην or οὐ χρῆν in demands addressed to the gods strike us as alien to Sophocles. His authorship of frg. 103, where both occur, has therefore been questioned and the fragment assigned to Euripides (cf. Nauck, *TGF*, *ad loc.*). I myself find nothing Euripidean in the anemic lines; the thought is a commonplace. Utterly fantastic and in fact ψυχρόν is the idea (*Alc.* 348ff.) of Admetus' sharing his bed after the death of Alcestis with a δέμας of her worked by a master's hand so that he may believe that he is embracing Alcestis herself. (According to Hyg. *Fab.* 103f. a similar motif was used in the *Protesilaus.*)

life, of education, of government, etc., had little thought to spare for the question how far such thoroughgoing changes were possible. Whether it proved difficult or not, realities had to conform. If it was possible to "teach excellence" (ἀρετή), as the sophists offered and in fact undertook—producing results!—why should other startling ideas be dismissed as impossible?

If these observations are correct, a tendency toward the extreme and utopian is inherent in the new movement, and Euripides, close as he was to this movement, not surprisingly felt something attractive in this tendency. It gave wings to his own speculation. Satisfying at once his inclinations toward the fantastic and the theoretical, both of them strong, it provided a counterweight to his realism. And as his realism shows him a child of his age, so do his speculations. Utopian suggestions for reforms or a different world order are an intellectual experiment *sui generis*. There could not be much contact between them and the other experiments of the Greek Enlightenment.

Did emancipated reason, acting at times as though it had sole and unlimited control of the world,[18] encourage also the conception of Aristophanes' utopian plots? We may wonder, and it would not seem *a limine* unthinkable. To live in a city where man is free from all disturbance, where the greatest trouble is to be invited to a wedding banquet and where parents are distressed if nobody makes love to their boys[19] is the translation of a dream world into reality. Aristophanes

[18] This sovereign freedom may assert itself also elsewhere and in instances where we are not prepared to recognize it. Thuc. III 42.4–6; VI 11.2f.; 34.4–6 have been judged by wrong standards if they are largely a free play of reason. Mention may also be made here of the daring construction by which Critias (frg. 19 Snell) explains the origin of belief in a divine power. The "Old Oligarch" discusses constitutional and other political conditions in Athens *as though* everything had with remarkable consistency been planned for the greatest benefits of the *demos*.

[19] See *Av.* 128ff.; 137ff. and, e.g., *Pax* 292f., 302ff., 1316f.

enjoys following up fantastic conceptions into the details of their realization, but the connection between his amusing episodes and the idealistic reforms proposed in Euripides would be tenuous if all that it amounts to is the spirit of the time, reflected in both yet in widely differing fashions. Surely peace is desirable, and so is, from Aristophanes' point of view, the overthrow of Cleon. Both of these goals are possible, which is more than can be said of the proposals for a remaking of human nature, the reform of divine behavior, or a criterion for telling good men from bad. In devising ways toward his goals, Aristophanes shows as little regard for the possible as do Euripides' characters in their schemes for improvement. Even this falls short of truly significant resemblance. Perhaps another approach will take us farther. Euripides never produced a parody of the rationalistic speculation reveling in its newly won freedom; but when the women take over the Acropolis and organize a Panhellenic sex strike (*Lys.* 119ff.) to enforce peace; when Peisthetaerus cleverly argues why the gods will have to accept the empire of the birds (*Av.* 550ff.); or when Praxagora proves why and how Athens would profit if political affairs were handled by the women (*Ec.* 427ff.)—these inventions gain some of their comic effect from carrying familiar excesses of reason to new lengths. Here we may speak of parody; yet parody does not exclude affinity in the workings of the imagination.

Our judgment would rest on firmer ground if we could compare Aristophanes' plots with those of his predecessors or even his contemporaries. Our evidence concerning them offers not much more than variations on the "golden age" theme.[20] For a responsible conclusion it is utterly inadequate,

[20] With great reservations I mention Pherecrates' Μεταλλεῖς and Πέρσαι, Telecleides' Ἀμφικτύονες, and Cratinus' Χείρωνες. On their place in the chronology of Attic comedy see A. Körte, *RE* s.vv. "Pherecrates" and "Telekleides" as well as P. Geissler, *Die Chronologie d. altattischen Komödie* (Berlin, 1925) 15, 22, 81ff. Cf. also Gilbert Norwood, *Greek Comedy* (Toronto, 1932) *passim*.

and if we were rash enough to use it, we should yet credit the larger scope and freedom of Aristophanes' comic fantasies to his personal genius. If a change in the status of women is a topic common to Euripides, Aristophanes—*scil.* in his later period (*Ec.*)—and Plato's *Republic,* this may encourage us to look for bridges between the authors of these utopias. But it is hardly necessary to search for them. If Aristophanes did not know the content of the *Republic* before the work was completed and made public, he could nevertheless play with the idea of women as common property. Revolutionary theories about the rights and the position of women were in the air. More or less by accident we know that a demand for common ownership of women occurred in Euripides (see p. [74]), and it may again be a mere accident if, prior to the *Republic,* the common possession of material goods is not postulated anywhere in extant literature.[21]

The *Republic* itself lies outside the chronological orbit of our investigation. But here, if ever, it may be permissible to forget our self-imposed limits, since to ignore the question whether this work represents the continuation of the tendencies here studied would seem pedantic. To deny *a priori* such possibilities is arbitrary, even if we must make the largest allowance for the specific reasons that prompted Plato to his uncompromising rejection of Athenian democracy. Foremost among them is the impression of Socrates, his questioning and his fate in the contemporary city-state. As he himself

[21] Wilamowitz scorned the idea of a relation to the *Republic* (*Kleine Schriften* IV 126; *Platon* II, Berlin, 1919, 199f.). See also Karl Reinhardt, *Von Werken und Formen* (Godesberg, 1948, 307f.) on the *Ec.* and *Ploutos* as differing in plot and spirit from the earlier comedies of Aristophanes. For the *Lysistrata,* Ivo Bruns (*op. cit.,* 174), assuming a relation to the postulated movement of emancipation, does not fail to compare the heroine's *οὐ μεμούσωμαι κακῶς* (v. 1127) with *Med.* 1085ff. Noteworthy too is the opinion of a historian as eminent as W. S. Ferguson, *CAH* V 325, who finds "statesmanlike proposals" in the *Lysistrata.*

sets forth in the *Seventh Letter*,[22] it was such impressions that caused him to realize the need for philosopher kings if mankind was ever to live in a healthy condition. In the *Republic* this conclusion is the most formidable wave of the τρικυμία (V 472a) and the most paradoxical of all reforms that are considered essential (473aff.). Plato's scheme has in full measure what the utopian ideas in Greek tragedy lack; it is perfectly integrated and has a maximum of intrinsic consistency. It also is consistent in leaving nothing of the contemporary political institutions intact. Characteristically, where he entrusts the philosophers with the power of ruling the city and remolding it in conformity with the "divine exemplar" (θεῖον παράδειγμα), Plato makes them begin by "wiping the slate clean" (λαβόντες ὥσπερ πίνακα πόλιν τε καὶ ἤθη ἀνθρώπων, πρῶτον μὲν καθαρὰν ποιήσειαν ἄν, ὃ οὐ πάνυ ῥᾴδιον, VI 501a). From relatively few but all the more important propositions, e.g., that since human abilities differ, it would be better for everybody to devote himself to the one activity at which he is good rather than to many (II 370aff.), a large part of the ideal scheme is built up. Whenever necessary, an additional proposition is introduced and its truth briefly secured. In the Platonic city everything is indeed as it "ought" to be. The inexorable method of logical deduction is even more radical and rational than the premises; for the latter include certain traditional values such as ἀνδρεία, δικαιοσύνη, etc. The recent attack on all conventions had questioned their validity and made a new rational vindication of them necessary. Plato achieves this, incidentally, by defining them and giving them a place in his scheme where they are however no more than stepping stones.

Xenophon's *Cyropaedia* embodies a far less sustained intellectual effort. Still it, too, presents on a large canvas a vision

[22] *Ep.* VII 324b ff., esp. 326b f. I am familiar with the current fashion of questioning the authenticity of this letter (cf. *Gnomon* 41, 1969, 29ff.).

of things as they ought to be. It was Xenophon's bent of mind to prefer the concrete and to keep even such theoretical insights as he had closely related to the sphere of actions and events. The elder Cyrus had the unique reputation[23] of having brought about the voluntary, even the enthusiastic acquiescence of many diverse nations under his domination (I 1.3ff.). How did this come about? Endowment, education, and experience provide the answer. Nature implanted in him the right instincts, in particular an aversion to everything artificial and ceremonious.[24] His education combines the best in the Persian with the best in the Median traditions (both of them, needless to say, idealized). In addition, he continues to learn from experience and remains open to advice (e.g., I 6.9ff., 16ff.). Thus he emerges as a paragon of human and political virtues, far-sighted, generous, tactful, restrained and in complete control of his impulses or emotions, wise, humane (φιλάνθρωπος),[25] practically infallible in his actions and always proved right in his arguments. Many of the principles he follows are stated, often by himself, in the form of maxims or propositions of more or less general applicability. To compare these principles in originality or profundity with anything Platonic would be absurd. Besides being much closer to ordinary common sense, they are coordinated, if at all, only with those which relate to the same topic; to build up an edifice story by story would not occur to Xenophon. The only integration is provided by the personality of Cyrus. If Xenophon wrote this work in a spirit of rivalry with Plato's *Republic*,[26] he is likely to have regarded the realization of

[23] In all probability Xenophon had precursors, though we can name only Antisthenes, for whom Diogenes Laertius VI 16 lists a Κῦρος and a Κῦρος ἢ περὶ βασιλείας.

[24] See, e.g., I 3.4, 6.8; cf. V 2.14ff.

[25] See for this quality VII 5.73, VIII 4.6ff.; for tact and skill in difficult situations esp. IV 5.21; for farsighted planning VI 2.25. *Parcere subiectis* is illustrated IV 4.5ff.; restraint in ἐρωτικά V 1.4ff.

[26] Despite D.L. III 34, we should not rashly assume this. As Jaeger in

principles by deeds as a great advantage. Against the speculative freedom of Plato's philosophic construction, he sets an equally free manipulation of quasi-historical material. We shall see later (Chapter VI) that genuine historical material, when subjected to energetic organization, could be manipulated—but in the interest of truth, or of whatever the author, Thucydides, considered the profound historical truth. This is something utterly different from utopia as well as from philosophical truth.

The "ought to . . ." which establishes common ground between the *Republic* and Euripidean utopias is not so easy to find in the *Cyropaedia*. As we shall see in our chapter on the new psychology, the Enlightenment also knew ideal figures and ideal conduct. It hardly matters whether we classify Cyrus and his actions with the utopias or with the ideals. In either case they are a product of the Enlightenment with its penchant toward intellectual experiments.

---

his chapter on "The Prince's Education" (*Paideia*, tr. G. Highet, New York, 1944, III 84f.) reminds us, the *Cyropaedia* is a contribution to another favorite topic of the time (although *charta eadem*, he admits that only a small part actually treats education). See also Ed. Schwartz, *Fünf Vorträge über d. griech. Roman* (Berlin, 1896) 62, who finds a "Seitenhieb auf den platonischen Staat."

IV

EXPERIMENTS WITH THE GREEK LANGUAGE*

The principal instrument of reason is language, and if reason enjoyed new freedom and used it for experimentation, language was bound to be drawn into these experiments. In itself, a conscious attitude to language was nothing new. Even the early poets are likely to have known why they preferred one manner of phrasing to another. In the *Theogony* we observe the "invention" of names for deities and understand what the poet wishes to express through them. Aeschylus speaks of names given "truly" and names given "falsely."[1] Much more could be said about this subject, but our concern is with the developments in the later half of the fifth century, when treatment of the language attained a higher degree of consciousness.

Early Greek thought often had to deal with opposites.[2] Whether it asserted their identity or their mutual exclusiveness, it would almost inevitably employ antithetical forms of expression. Heraclitus offers excellent illustrations of this tendency and deserves a place in the history of "artistic

* My recent article "Thucydides' treatment of words and concepts," *Hermes* 99 (1971) 386ff. is written from a somewhat different point of view. Overlapping, especially in the material used, could not be completely avoided but has been kept at a minimum.

[1] For the epic poets cf. R. Pfeiffer, A *History of Classical Scholarship from the Beginning to the End of the Hellenistic* Age (Oxford, 1968). See also lists of names such as Hes. *Theog.* 243–262 (Nereids) or 349–360 (Oceanides). For Aeschylus cf. Ag. 681ff.; *Pr.* 85ff.; *al.* In M. L. West's *Hesiod: Theogony* (Oxford, 1966) the poet's originality in coining names is underrated.

[2] Cf. on the whole G.E.R. Lloyd, *Polarity and Analogy* (Cambridge, 1966) and for Heraclitus in particular Clemence Ramnoux, *Heraclite ou l'homme entre les choses et les mots* (Paris, 1959).

prose," even though the antitheses are invariably subservient to his thought and disclose conditions of reality. There could be no nobler purpose. In Parmenides it would be absurd to look for antitheses inspired by intentions other than philosophical. And when Melissus, approaching the conclusion of an argument, says: ἢν δὲ μεταπέσῃ, τὸ μὲν ἐὸν ἀπώλετο, τὸ δὲ οὐκ ἐὸν γέγονεν . . . (B8.6), he means to make his refutation more telling than it would otherwise have been. We may hesitate—briefly—before we commit ourselves to the same view about Zeno's remarkably striking antitheses. Still it is with his contemporaries, roughly speaking in the middle and second half of the fifth century, that formal ambitions begin to dominate and prevail over content.

The scanty material preserved verbatim from Thrasymachus barely conveys an idea of the extent to which he employed antithesis. As far as we can judge, he fell considerably short of Gorgias, and may not even have aimed at anything in the same order of accomplishment. From Gorgias we quote a passage of his *Epitaphios*: Τί γὰρ ἀπῆν τοῖς ἀνδράσι τούτοις ὧν δεῖ ἀνδράσι προσεῖναι; τί δὲ καὶ προσῆν ὧν οὐ δεῖ προσεῖναι; εἰπεῖν δυναίμην ἃ βούλομαι, βουλοίμην δ' ἃ δεῖ, λαθὼν μὲν τὴν θείαν νέμεσιν, φυγὼν δὲ τὸν ἀνθρώπινον φθόνον (82 B6 *init.*). For good measure we add an antithesis that is not yet as well known as it deserves to be χλωρὰ ⟨μὲν?⟩ καὶ ἔναιμα τὰ πράγματα, τρέμοντα ⟨δὲ⟩ καὶ ὠχρὰ τὰ γράμματα (*ibid.* 16).[3]

Despite his reservations about the showpieces of the sophists and about ἡδονὴ λόγων,[4] Thucydides was by no means above availing himself of novel stylistic devices. The speeches in his work afforded him almost limitless opportunities, and no Greek writer of whom we know has carried out more and

[3] The text in Diels-Kranz is incomplete (and incorrect); see my paper *Hermes* 66 (1931) 249 n. 2 = *Kleine Schriften* II 159 n. 2.

[4] See I 22.5 and 40.3. On the probability that such passages reflect Thucydides' own experience and feelings, cf. R. P. Winnington-Ingram, *BICS* 12 (1965) and above pp. 39ff.

bolder experiments with his language, straining it to the limit—or beyond the limit—of its potentialities and proving indefatigable in the variety of his startling innovations. It would be unjust, nevertheless, to think of Thucydides as competing with the new professional artists of speech. For he goes his own way and—very much as in his use of the *in utramque partem disputare*[5]—avails himself of the recently discovered forms and figures to bring out the complexity of a situation. This endeavor sets him apart from his contemporaries, and yet it would be futile to deny that he too succumbs to the fascination that form as such had for the Greeks.

We begin with "simple antitheses," even though in looking for samples we realize once more how rare simplicity is in Thucydides. Pericles' "Funeral Speech" mentions as one of the admirable traits of the Athenians that the same men plan a daring deed and carry it out. This contrasts with normal human behavior: ὃ τοῖς ἄλλοις ἀμαθία μὲν θράσος, λογισμὸς δὲ ὄκνον φέρει (II 40.3). While antithetical, the two clauses are at the same time complementary. Combined, they produce not so much a formal as an "intellectual" antithesis to the Athenian way; either half of the sentence includes one half of the distinctive Athenian quality, pointing up fatal aspects of its presence in isolation.[6]

Still in the category of "simple" antitheses, we may adduce some taunting comments made by the Athenian delegates in the "Melian Dialogue." Suggesting that the Melians put undue confidence in the possibility of Lacedaemonian help, they declare: μακαρίσαντες ὑμῶν τὸ ἀπειρόκακον οὐ ζηλοῦμεν τὸ ἄφρον (V 105.3).[7] Parrying this attack, the Melians speak of

[5] See Chapter I.

[6] See J. T. Kakridis, *Der Thukydideische Epitaphios. Ein stilistischer Kommentar, Zetemata* 26 (Munich, 1961) 54f.

[7] We shall discuss the passage from a different perspective below p. 117. Here not a δέ, as in the other instances, but οὐ produces the antithesis.

the Cretan sea as facilitating such help: δι' οὗ τῶν κρατούντων ἀπορώτερος ἡ λῆψις ἢ τῶν λαθεῖν βουλομένων ἡ σωτηρία (110.1).

Forgetting now about "simple" and not so simple, we may look at one more passage from the "Melian Dialogue." Again the Athenians are exposing illusions of their opponents: ὑμῶν τὰ μὲν ἰσχυρότατα ἐλπιζόμενα μέλλεται, τὰ δ' ὑπάρχοντα βραχέα πρὸς τὰ ἤδη ἀντιτεταγμένα περιγίγνεσθαι . . . (111.2). In thought, this antithesis leaves nothing to be desired; its formal structure is noteworthy for its inconcinnities. The predicate of the former clause (μέλλεται) is matched by the participle ὑπάρχοντα at the beginning of the latter where it functions grammatically as subject; correspondingly βραχέα, although a part of the predicate in the second clause, answers the grammatical subject (τὰ ἰσχυρότατα) in the first; moreover ἐλπιζόμενα on the one and τὰ ἤδη ἀντιτεταγμένα on the other side, while in some relationship of mutual correspondence, are strikingly different in form as well as in function. Decidedly, experimentation has here gone much farther.

In a speech of Book VI (76-80) Hermocrates tries to convert the citizens of Camerina to a realistic estimate of the Athenians and their political intentions. As on other occasions, the experiences of one-time "allies" are held up as warning examples. Under a variety of pretexts, one after another has changed from the status of an ally to a subject. This pattern of development suggests the conclusion: οὐ περὶ τῆς ἐλευθερίας ἄρα οὔτε οὗτοι (the Athenians) τῶν Ἑλλήνων οὔθ' οἱ Ἕλληνες τῆς ἑαυτῶν τῷ Μήδῳ ἀντέστησαν, περὶ δὲ οἱ μὲν σφίσιν ἀλλὰ μὴ ἐκείνῳ καταδουλώσεως, οἱ δ' ἐπὶ δεσπότου μεταβολῇ οὐκ ἀξυνετωτέρου, κακοξυνετωτέρου δέ (VI 76.4). Here antitheses are bursting upon us from all sides. Trying not to be submerged by them, we cling to the words τῷ Μήδῳ ἀντέστησαν. As from this rock we survey the scene, we see οἱ Ἕλλήνες holding its own to οὗτοι, and τῆς ἑαυτῶν to τῶν Ἑλλήνων; next, alerted by οὐ περὶ—περὶ δὲ we realize that καταδούλωσις and δεσπότου μεταβολή, while contrasting with one another, also cooperate in opposing ἐλευθερίας, which they negate; on a minor scale σφίσιν looks back to ἐκείνῳ and κακοξυνετωτέρου to ἀξυνετωτέρου.[8] Surely a *non plus ultra* of complexity but also a masterpiece of balanced construction; for, even if overloaded, it still does not confuse the reader; at the same time it is so replete with significant insights that the formal artifices may be considered a stimulus for the thought.

Cleon's speech about the Mytileneans includes simple antitheses side by side with others that should satisfy every definition of complexity[9] and may at the same time introduce us to the coincidence—rather frequent in Thucydides—of complexity and paradox. Here we quote his reproach of the Athenians for fostering the kind of oratorical demagogy of which he disapproves: οἵτινες εἰώθατε θεαταὶ μὲν τῶν λόγων γίγνεσθαι, ἀκροαταὶ δὲ τῶν ἔργων, τὰ μὲν μέλλοντα ἔργα ἀπὸ τῶν εὖ εἰπόντων σκοποῦντες ὡς δυνατὰ γίγνεσθαι, τὰ δὲ πεπραγμένα ἤδη οὐ τὸ δρασθὲν[10] πιστότερον ὄψει λαβόντες ἢ τὸ ἀκουσθὲν ἀπὸ τῶν λόγῳ καλῶς ἐπιτιμησάντων (III 38.4). We list the contrasts between θεαταί and ἀκροαταί, λόγων and ἔργων, μέλλοντα and πεπραγμένα, δρασθέν and ἀκουσθέν, ὄψει and λόγῳ; as for paradoxes, θεαταὶ

[8] See the complaints and criticisms of Dionysius, *de Thuc.* 48 (406.18ff. Us.-Rad.). Krüger *ad loc.* notes some instances of harshness, e.g. the shift to ἐπί with the dative in the midst of a clause introduced by περί and the use of καταδούλωσις as an Athenian activity not only with σφίσι but also with "Medes," although "for" these Athens would hardly enslave Greek cities.

[9] The same would be true of the well-known sentences about speeches and deeds in the "chapter on method" (I 22.1f.)—at least if we go all the way with G. Wille's most persisting analysis (*Synusia: Festgabe f. W. Schadewaldt*, Pfullingen, 1965, 53ff., esp. 66ff. = *WdF* 98, 683ff.).

[10] The alternative reading θεαθέν, although making excellent sense, is, apart from its poor standing in the MSS. tradition, excluded from consideration on morphological and lexicographical grounds. Another passage in Cleon's speeches, though far simpler than 38.4, is entertaining through its ingenious shift from the antithesis in the μέν clause to a quite differently organized δέ clause: (οἵ τε τέρποντες λόγῳ ῥήτορες ἕξουσι καὶ ἐν ἄλλοις ἐλάσσοσι ἀγῶνα) καὶ μὴ ἐν ᾧ ἡ μὲν πόλις βραχέα ἡσθεῖσα μεγάλα ζημιώσεται, αὐτοὶ δὲ ἐκ τοῦ εὖ εἰπεῖν τὸ παθεῖν εὖ ἀντιλήψονται (40.3).

λόγων used to balance ἀκροαταὶ ἔργων seems startling but is merely a prelude to the elaborate description of how the Athenians habitually judge the past by words rather than by the actual events, and put more trust in the elegantly phrased speeches than in the evidence before them.[11]

We know from Chapter I how much meaning Thucydides gives to the inherited *in utramque partem disputare.* Since this form brings out antagonistic points of view, it cannot surprise us if even individual sentences in such speeches formulate the antagonism. Examples abound in the speech delivered by the Corinthians at the convention in Sparta. The antitheses presently to be quoted are prefaced by a remark that the Lacedaemonians do not even realize the difference between the restless Athenian spirit of enterprise and expansion and their own conservative habits.[12] This difference is spelled out: οἱ μέν γε νεωτεροποιοὶ καὶ ἐπινοῆσαι ὀξεῖς καὶ ἐπιτελέσαι ἔργῳ ἃ ἂν γνῶσιν· ὑμεῖς δὲ τὰ ὑπάρχοντά τε σῴζειν καὶ ἐπιγνῶναι μηδὲν καὶ ἔργῳ οὐδὲ τἀναγκαῖα ἐξικέσθαι (70.2) . . . καὶ μὴν καὶ ἄοκνοι πρὸς ὑμᾶς μελλητὰς καὶ ἀποδημηταὶ πρὸς ἐνδημοτάτους . . . (70.4). Other matters apart, these samples show how cleverly Thucydides avoids the pitfalls of monotony even in a succession of antithetical statements. Immediately afterward, the speakers with a slight change of subject concentrate on the Athenian way, without any longer using the Lacedaemonians as foil. Still the versatility of the rival power, the ease with which it combines opposite patterns of conduct is meant to stir Sparta into action: κρατοῦντές τε τῶν ἐχθρῶν ἐπὶ πλεῖστον ἐξέρχονται καὶ νικώμενοι ἐπ' ἐλάχιστον ἀναπίπτουσιν. ἔτι δὲ τοῖς μὲν σώμασιν ἀλλοτριωτάτοις ὑπὲρ τῆς πόλεως χρῶνται, τῇ δὲ γνώμῃ οἰκειοτάτῃ ἐς τὸ πράσσειν τι ὑπὲρ αὐτῆς (70.5f.).

[11] G. Wille, *Synusia* 61ff. (= 692f.), rightly speaks of an "Oxymoron parallel formulierter Wendungen."

[12] For the significance of these passages see H. Gundert, "Athen und Sparta in den Reden des Thukydides," *Antike* 16 (1940) 103ff. (= *WdF* 98, 121).

There is no comparable resort to antithesis in either the Athenian or the Spartan reply. Intellectual and stylistic subtlety, while by no means absent, is used for different ends in both and favors different vehicles for their expression. The ephor, who by his brief and energetic intervention puts an end to the deliberations, does employ antitheses like the following: *καὶ ὡς ἡμᾶς πρέπει βουλεύεσθαι ἀδικουμένους μηδεὶς διδασκέτω, ἀλλὰ τοὺς μέλλοντας ἀδικεῖν μᾶλλον πρέπει πολὺν χρόνον βουλεύεσθαι* (86.4). Does the barely concealed impatience of the speaker prevent this antithesis from attaining the formal perfection of others?

In yielding to his delight in antitheses, Thucydides employs them also for thoughts that would not normally or naturally take this form. Themistocles, he tells us, owed his extraordinary power of improvisation to *φύσεως μὲν δυνάμει, μελέτης δὲ βραχύτητι* (I 138.3). We accept the first half of this explanation more readily than the second. Was "short practice" really a help in the development of his priceless endowment? A concessive phrasing ("despite . . .") would carry more immediate conviction. The second dative owes its presence to the first. Thucydides was determined to cast the explanation in antithetical form.

In the Funeral Oration, Pericles' assertion that Athens *καὶ μόνη οὔτε τῷ πολεμίῳ ἐπελθόντι ἀγανάκτησιν ἔχει ὑφ' οἵων κακοπαθεῖ, οὔτε τῷ ὑπηκόῳ κατάμεμψιν ὡς οὐχ ὑπ' ἀξίων ἄρχεται* (II 41.3) combines two claims antithetical in form yet at the same time (as antitheses frequently are) complementary in meaning. The former *οὔτε* clause would, if true, be a rather out-of-the-way truth; as for the latter, Pericles could hardly expect many one-time allies (or "subjects") to endorse it with genuine enthusiasm. Slightly later in the same eulogy (42.4)[13] we

[13] In 42.2 the difficulties created by *δηλοῦν*, which is used for the first manifestation as well as for the final confirmation, are perhaps minor. However conscientious commentators (e.g. Krüger, E. F. Poppo-J. M. Stahl, and Gomme) struggle with the passage.

understand and accept the clause τῶνδε δὲ οὔτε πλούτου τις τὴν ἔτι ἀπόλαυσιν προτιμήσας ἐμαλακίσθη without reservation, but for the sequel: οὔτε πενίας ἐλπίδι ὡς κἂν ἔτι διαφυγὼν αὐτὴν πλουτήσειεν ἀναβολὴν τοῦ δεινοῦ ἐποιήσατο, a far greater mental effort is required, even though the puzzling words πενίας ἐλπίδι are explained by the ὡς clause. Without some intellectual contortion, poverty could not figure as a motivation ranking on a par with wealth. Other antitheses—in the neighborhood of these and elsewhere—can hardly be said to reproduce an unquestionably true or inescapable antinomy in a realm of facts, but, after the samples studied, little would be gained by scrutinizing them.[14]

Clearly, the relation between form and content in Thucydides' antitheses is subject to great variations. Each instance must be interpreted and appreciated on its own merits. A well-known passage of Pericles' last speech describes the Athenian empire as a tyranny ἣν λαβεῖν μὲν ἄδικον δοκεῖ εἶναι, ἀφεῖναι δ' ἐπικίνδυνον (II 63.2). Both halves of the antithesis are valid and illuminating. The generalization immediately following: τὸ γὰρ ἄπραγμον οὐ σῴζεται μὴ μετὰ τοῦ δραστηρίου τεταγμένον could profitably have been expressed in a less ambitious form, and, for its complement οὐδὲ ἐν ἀρχούσῃ πόλει ξυμφέρει ἀλλ' ἐν ὑπηκόῳ ἀσφαλῶς δουλεύειν, A. W. Gomme's comment that "no one would suggest that τὸ δουλεύειν is advantageous for an imperial city and there is no need to contradict it" is perfectly correct. We need not, however, follow him in looking for an alternative (and as it turns out, equally problematic) interpretation;[15] knowing Thucydides' addic-

[14] II 42.4 *extr.* is desperate. If following the *scholia* and some modern commentators (e.g. Krüger, who pertinently quotes Arr. *An.* 7, 6.17, to all appearance a restrained imitation of the passage) we connect the genitives δόξης and δέους with ἀκμῇ, the former yields a good and pertinent meaning, while the other is, euphemistically put, gratuitous.

[15] See Gomme *ad loc.*, also for the meaning of ἄπραγμον. Attempts made by Hobbes and others to use ἄπραγμον as grammatical subject also in the sentence οὔτε ἐν κτλ. are "hart und nicht nötig" (Krüger *ad loc.*).

tion to antithesis and to experiments involving this figure, we are prepared to find him balance two possibilities of which only one may be seriously entertained.

Hermocrates explains to the Sicilian representatives who have gathered in Gela how much their cities have to gain from settling their differences without the Athenians, who in this case would have to go home: *καὶ οὕτως . . . οἵ τ' ἐπίκλητοι εὐπρεπῶς ἄδικοι ἐλθόντες εὐλόγως ἄπρακτοι ἀπίασιν* (IV 61.7). In both instances the conjunction of an adverb characterized by *εὐ* with an adjective negative in form and import may be elegant, but it is also labored; we may feel uncertain whether the "pretext" under which the Athenians arrived in Sicily did not make their coming speciously just rather than "speciously unjust." Unlike some other facets of this antithesis that are "real" enough, this probably belongs to the "dubious" class. Dubious or more than dubious I should also call what Cleon says in his denunciation of the Mytileneans: *ἐλπίσαντες μακρότερα μὲν τῆς δυνάμεως, ἐλάσσω δὲ τῆς βουλήσεως* (III 39.3). Since, as we shall see (Chapter V), Thucydides is interested in the psychological effects of *ἐλπίς*, we try to discover a genuine meaning in the latter clause, but it is not easy.[16]

For adventures in language, many further opportunities were at hand. The "sophistic movement," to use this broad and inadequate term, had created a more professional interest in the Greek language. One of its representatives, Prodicus, chose "the correct use of words" for his special province. As strictly logical definition was not yet known, his favorite method was to compare words of closely related meaning and to explain their difference. In the best known testimony, his preoccupation with such distinctions appears

[16] The antithesis by which Alcibiades recommends himself to the authorities in Sparta: *φυγὰς γάρ εἰμι τῆς τῶν ἐξελασάντων πονηρίας καὶ οὐ τῆς ὑμετέρας . . . ὠφελίας* (VI 92.3) is effective, but Greek usage is strained by the first and mishandled by the second genitive. Poppo-Stahl *ad loc.* call this phrasing a *lusus verborum satis frigidus.*

almost obsessive. During a crisis in Plato's *Protagoras*, when the debate threatens to break down, Prodicus pleads for its continuation, urging Socrates and Protagoras ἀμφισβητεῖν μέν, ἐρίζειν δὲ μή and as a result of it εὐδοκιμεῖν but not ἐπαινεῖσθαι, while the others present should consider themselves κοινοί but not ἴσοι and expect εὐφραίνεσθαι but not ἥδεσθαι.[17]

What the *Vita Marcellini* (35f.) has to say about Gorgias and Prodicus as objects of Thucydides' imitation (ζῆλος) would have little authority even if Homer and Pindar did not figure in the same role. But Thucydides did accept devices that had recently gained currency, and Prodicus' differentiation between words almost but not quite synonymous was one of them. He need not have attended Prodicus' famous fifty-drachmai lecture to produce samples of his technique.[18]

A passage close to this technique is I 69.6, where the Corinthians after their trenchant criticism of Sparta's temperament and political traditions try to take the sting out of their reproaches: καὶ μηδεὶς ὑμῶν ἐπ' ἔχθρᾳ τὸ πλέον ἢ αἰτίᾳ νομίσῃ τάδε λέγεσθαι· αἰτία μὲν γὰρ φίλων ἀνδρῶν ἐστὶν ἁμαρτανόντων, κατηγορία δὲ ἐχθρῶν ἀδικησάντων. The latter sentence is very much in Prodicus' manner; [19] but we cannot fail to note that, in the

[17] *Prt.* 337a. Other Platonic testimonies (*Chrm.* 163a ff. etc.) are collected in 84 A 14-18 D.-K. For the most recent accounts of Prodicus see Guthrie, III 274ff., 276ff., where due emphasis is given to this special interest in "semantics," and R. Pfeiffer, *op. cit.*, 39ff., who has sent me back to F. G. Welcker, *Kleine Schriften zur Griech. Literaturgesch.* (Bonn, 1845) II 452f. Regarding Socrates' connection with him, I should make more allowance for the ironic tone or undertone of the Platonic passages than Guthrie. See, however, Vlastos as cited in n. 40, below.

[18] See 84 A 11 D.-K.

[19] For comments on the passage see e.g. Hermann Mayer, *Prodikos von Keos und die Anfänge der Synonymik* (Paderborn, 1913) 66; Jan Ros, *Die μεταβολή (variatio) als Stilprinzip* (Paderborn, 1959) 97 n. 5; Walter Wössner, "Die Synonymische Unterscheidung bei Thukydides . . ." (unpublished diss., Berlin, 1937), 12, as well as the commentaries (esp. Poppo-Stahl) and some translations, e.g. Marchant's. As might be

former, not *αἰτία* and *κατηγορία* but *αἰτία* and *ἔχθρα* are set apart from one another. There are reasons for considering this departure from the pattern (if it is legitimate to speak of a Prodicean pattern) characteristic of Thucydides. For the present, another comment may suffice: Thucydides does not observe this distinction throughout his work. It may be intentional that Archidamus in his defense of Sparta's habit, which is after all a reply to the Corinthian criticism, affirms *καὶ ἤν τις ἄρα ξὺν κατηγορίᾳ παροξύνῃ, οὐδὲν δὴ μᾶλλον ἀχθεσθέντες ἀνεπείσθημεν* (I 84.2); for this *κατηγορία* must be what the Corinthians define as *αἰτία*. Moreover the *αἰτία* that the Lacedaemonians, according to Brasidas (IV 86.5), are anxious not to incur among newly won allies would be inspired by strong resentment and almost certainly qualify as *κατηγορία*.

The closest parallel to I 69.6 is a distinction made by Pericles in his third speech. Here he urges the Athenians *ἰέναι δὲ τοῖς ἐχθροῖς ὁμόσε μὴ φρονήματι μόνον, ἀλλὰ καὶ καταφρονήματι· αὔχημα μὲν γὰρ καὶ ἀπὸ ἀμαθίας εὐτυχοῦς καὶ δειλῷ τινι ἐγγίγνεται, καταφρόνησις δ' ὃς ἂν καὶ γνώμῃ πιστεύῃ τῶν ἐναντίων ὑπερέχειν . . .* (II 62, 3f.). As in I 69, the sentence embodying two definitions takes up only one of the concepts juxtaposed in the preceding; the other, *φρόνημα*, is replaced by *αὔχημα*, just as, in I 69, not *ἔχθρα* is defined but *κατηγορία*. Thucydides must have been aware in how whimsical a spirit he handled the new method. He prefers to surprise the reader, and we may regard these passages as samples of a shock tactic for which the speeches offer more illustrations.[20] In some respects, the change to *αὔχημα* may have been advantageous. Although for the ear *φρόνημα* makes an excellent contrast with *καταφρόνημα*, it has at the same time a wider range of meaning than *αὔχημα*.

---

expected, they often differ in interpretation and judgment. On the following pages I have limited bibliographical references to occasions where more than a simple indication of agreement or disagreement seemed to be called for.

20 See e.g. below pp. 122ff.

Still a reader puzzled by *φρόνημα* may wonder whether *αὔχημα* is fair to Pericles' thought in the former sentence.

Slightly less close to I 69.6 is a passage incidental in Cleon's violent denunciation of the Mytileneans. Having dwelt on the preferential treatment they enjoyed in the past, he asks (III 39.2) *τί ἄλλο οὗτοι ἢ ἐπεβούλευσάν τε καὶ ἐπανέστησαν μᾶλλον ἢ ἀπέστησαν (ἀπόστασις μέν γε τῶν βίαιόν τι πασχόντων ἐστίν).* Having learned that Thucydides does not "conform" to a pattern, we shall resist the impulse to add to the definition of *ἀπόστασις* the complementary of *ἐπανάστασις*, even if at first glance form as well as content would appear to gain from this operation.[21]

Did Prodicus, in addition to studying words similar but not synonymous in meaning, deal also with true synonyms? In the absence of positive testimonies we have no right to assume that he did. In Thucydides, however, there seem to be more instances of genuine synonyms than of discrimination between near- or pseudo-synonyms.[22] To begin once more with a relatively simple case (II 39.3), the strategic powers of Athens need not be concentrated in one area but may be divided for the simultaneous pursuit of several objectives. As a result, Pericles points out, no enemy has ever encountered the entire Athenian force, although boasts to that effect are common: *ἤν δέ που μορίῳ τινὶ προσμείξωσι, κρατήσαντές τέ τινας ἡμῶν πάντας αὐχοῦσιν ἀπεῶσθαι καὶ νικηθέντες ὑφ' ἁπάντων ἡσσῆσθαι.* Is there a difference between *νικᾶν* and *κρατεῖν*? Did Thucydides keep the stronger term in reserve for the enemy's adverse experience? I doubt whether *κρατεῖν* really qualifies as an euphemism and should not think that I 70.5, where the Corinthians employ the same *variatio*, would support this

[21] On "solitary" *μέν* in such constructions see J. D. Denniston, *Greek Particles* (Oxford, 2nd ed., 1954) 159ff., cf. also 380ff.

[22] Instances of the kind are most frequently treated—with or without reference to Prodicus—under the heading of *variatio* (see e.g. Ros, p. 322, whose reservations I cannot share).

view: *κρατοῦντές τε* (*scil.* *οἱ Ἀθηναῖοι*) *τῶν ἐχθρῶν ἐπὶ πλεῖστον ἐξέρχονται καὶ νικώμενοι ἐπ' ἐλάχιστον ἀναπίπτουσιν.*

In another Corinthian speech (I 124.2), we read: *ἐκ πολέμου μὲν γὰρ εἰρήνη μᾶλλον βεβαιοῦται, ἀφ' ἡσυχίας δὲ μὴ πολεμῆσαι οὐχ ὁμοίως ἀκίνδυνον.* Interest in *variatio*[23] rather than any material reason explains the substitution of *ἡσυχία* in the second clause for *εἰρήνη* in the first. On breaking up their conference with the Melians, the Athenian representatives volunteer a final piece of advice: *ἐνθυμεῖσθε πολλάκις ὅτι περὶ πατρίδος βουλεύεσθε, ἧς μιᾶς πέρι καὶ ἐς μίαν βουλὴν τυχοῦσάν τε καὶ μὴ κατορθώσασαν ἔσται* (V 111.5).[24] The sentence seems to have been thus phrased in the confidence that *κατορθοῦν*—whether generally or in this specific context—could serve as equivalent of *τυγχάνειν.*

Examples of this idiosyncrasy could be multiplied, but a few more instances will suffice: In Cleon's speech on the punishment of the Mytileneans, his warning against misplaced clemency (III 40.2) is peculiarly intriguing. He urges the Assembly not to rescind the brutal decision of the previous day, *μηδὲ τρισὶ τοῖς ἀξυμφορωτάτοις τῇ ἀρχῇ, οἴκτῳ καὶ ἡδονῇ λόγων καὶ ἐπιεικείᾳ ἁμαρτάνειν. ἔλεός τε γὰρ πρὸς τοὺς ὁμοίους δίκαιος ἀντιδίδοσθαι καὶ μὴ πρὸς τοὺς οὔτ' ἀντοικτιοῦντας ἐξ ἀνάγκης τε καθεστῶτας αἰεὶ πολεμίους* (arguments against the two other *ἀξυμφορώτατα* follow). Even without the help of *ἀντοικτιοῦντας* in the second sentence, we would recognize *ἔλεος* as *variatio* of *οἶκτος*; however the return of *οἶκτος* in a compound adds piquancy to the experiment.[25] At I 33.1, the Corcyrean envoys

[23] The change between the two nouns recurs in III 12.1, where *ἡσυχία* is once more the antonym of *πόλεμος* and to all appearance a synonym of *εἰρήνη* (see 13.1).

[24] The syntax presents difficulties. Classen-Steup *ad loc.* suspect corruption. *ἧς* which the scholiast seems to have read is better than *ἥν* of the MSS. There is no disagreement about the meaning of the relative clause but none about the obscurity of the phrasing either, and even if we knew what subject, if any, is to be understood with *ἔσται*, the problem of *ἐς* would remain.

[25] Note *οἶκτος* also 37.2; 44.1.

call Athens particularly fortunate since it may secure a great political advantage and yet act justly at the same time: *καλὴ ἡ ξυντυχία κατὰ πολλὰ τῆς ἡμετέρας χρείας, πρῶτον μὲν ὅτι ἀδικουμένοις καὶ οὐχ ἑτέρους βλάπτουσι τὴν ἐπικουρίαν ποιήσεσθε. . . .* Is there a slight nuance between *βλάπτειν* and *ἀδικεῖν*? The harder we try to find it, the more we realize the futility of such efforts.[26] The Plataeans, on surrendering their city, fear that the Lacedaemonians will listen to their implacable enemies, the Thebans. To prevent this, they urge them not to yield to the lure of *τὸ ξυμφέρον* (III 56.3), arguing *εἰ τῷ αὐτίκα χρησίμῳ ὑμῶν τε καὶ ἐκείνων πολεμίῳ τὸ δίκαιον λήψεσθε, τοῦ μὲν ὀρθοῦ φανεῖσθε οὐκ ἀληθεῖς κριταὶ ὄντες, τὸ δὲ ξυμφέρον μᾶλλον θεραπεύοντες.* *ὀρθόν* and *δίκαιον* need not be synonyms, yet *χρήσιμον* and *συμφέρον* almost certainly are, at least on this occasion. A passage in the "Funeral Speech" (I 141.5) remains puzzling: *σώμασί τε ἑτοιμότεροι οἱ αὐτουργοὶ τῶν ἀνθρώπων* (i.e. people like the Lacedaemonians) *ἢ χρήμασι πολεμεῖν, τὸ μὲν πιστὸν ἔχοντες ἐκ τῶν κινδύνων κἂν περιγενέσθαι, τὸ δὲ οὐ βέβαιον οὐ προαναλώσειν* (especially if the war lasts a long time). Are the adjectives almost but not entirely synonymous? Is Thucydides teasing his readers? If we make the experiment of exchanging *πιστόν* and *βέβαιον*, we begin to wonder whether the former is not after all more in place for *σώματα*, the latter for *χρήματα*.[27]

It is embarrassing to touch briefly on a passage for whose explanation a maximum of ammunition has been expended. Still, from our present perspective I should, in the famous statement about the "causes" of the War (I 23.5f.), regard *αἰτία* and *πρόφασις* as synonyms *for the occasion*. The qualifying appositions, *ἐς τὸ φανερὸν λεγόμεναι* (*αἰτίαι*) on the one side, *ἀληθεστάτην* and *ἀφανεστάτην δὲ λόγῳ* (*πρόφασιν*) on the other, bear the burden of producing the contrast. Stylistically the

[26] In IV 98.1, where *ἀδικῆσαι* is followed by *ἑκόντες βλάψειν* the addition of *ἑκόντες* makes a difference. Cf. Gomme *ad loc.*

[27] *Variatio* however does remain and it even extends farther; cf. Ros, p. 379.

contrast of ἀφανεστάτην δὲ λόγῳ with ἐς τὸ φανερὸν λεγόμεναι is the most effective, yet, for the meaning, the opposition between the one word ἀληθεστάτην and either of the phrases just quoted has greater importance because ἀληθεστάτην is the word that conveys the historian's insight and final verdict. If, as good arguments suggest, πρόφασις usually denotes an "expressed reason," its combination with ἀφανεστάτην δὲ λόγῳ must be a deliberate paradox. Once more Thucydides strains the Greek language almost to the breaking point.[28]

There is no reason that variations of this type should be confined to single words and not also occur in larger syntactical units. Brasidas, about to lead his Peloponnesians against a barbarian army, assures them that they have no cause for fearing large crowds on the other side (IV 126.2). Think of yourselves, he says in effect, as men οἵ γε μηδὲ ἀπὸ πολιτειῶν τοιούτων ἥκετε ἐν αἷς οὐ (οἱ conj. Stephanus) πολλοὶ ὀλίγων ἄρχουσιν, ἀλλὰ πλειόνων μᾶλλον ἐλάσσους. Although opinions differ on οὐ πολλοί and other points of detail,[29] on almost every interpretation πολλοὶ ὀλίγων and πλειόνων ἐλάσσους are distinctions without a difference, i.e. a purely stylistic device.[30]

[28] Besides Gomme *ad loc.*, I am here particularly indebted to Gordon M. Kirkwood (*AJPh* 73, 1952, 37ff.), some of whose conclusions I have incorporated. Kirkwood's persuasive diagnosis of VI 6.1 (the Athenians ἐφιέμενοι τῇ ἀληθεστάτῃ προφάσει τῆς πάσης ἄρξαι, *scil.* Σικελίας) as "reusing a felicitous and forceful phrase" (p. 51) shows once more how pleased Thucydides was with his experiments. He feels no obligation to abide by the synonymity produced in a special context and for a special effect (see Gomme *ibid.* and Kirkwood p. 46 on III 13.1; cf. above p. 93). A partly new interpretation of I 23.6 is advanced by de Ste. Croix, pp. 53ff.; he makes some good points but reads too much of his own view about the "origins" into the passage. The net effect is a question mark on some statements in my text, but I see no need to withdraw my interpretation.

[29] Cf. J. de Romilly's "note complémentaire" in her translation p. 184f.

[30] An even larger number of words is involved at III 43.2: A speaker must disguise his intention, whether arguing for a good or for the most wicked cause. ἀπάτῃ προσάγεσθαι τὸ πλῆθος and ψευσάμενον πιστὸν γενέσθαι convey the same idea. Cf. Gomme *ad loc.*

To go deeper into this subject,[31] to classify the diversity of forms in which synonyms are used, and finally perhaps to examine passages in which *variatio* may or may not be present, would be a fascinating task; but the gain for our immediate purpose would be slight,[32] and it seems more rewarding to unravel, with the help of what we have so far learned, a passage so bristling with subtle devices that even in Thucydides there is nothing to match it.

Archidamus' defense of the much maligned Spartan habits has claimed our attention in other contexts; our present concern is with his explanation of military virtue: πολεμικοί τε καὶ εὔβουλοι διὰ τὸ εὔκοσμον γιγνόμεθα, τὸ μὲν ὅτι αἰδὼς σωφροσύνης πλεῖστον μετέχει, αἰσχύνης δὲ εὐψυχία (εὔβουλοι δὲ . . .) (I 84.3). These words include certainly one, perhaps several synonyms; for the causal connection that Archidamus tries to establish between σωφροσύνη and εὐψυχία (i.e. warlike attitude) would not work out unless αἰσχύνη could in the second part of the explanation replace αἰδώς as its synonym. Once this is understood, we have found the clue to the very tight and at first glance hopelessly obscure reasoning of the king.[33] Beginning at the end, because this is more convenient, we may paraphrase: Courage rests to the largest extent upon a sense of shame—we would probably say, of honor—and the sense of shame rests to the largest extent upon balance of mind. This paraphrase leaves open which of the two concepts linked to one another is "to the largest extent" present in the other,

[31] The danger of missing nuances is considerable. In III 43.2 (see n. 30) I considered the possibility that προσάγεσθαι might suggest a dishonorable procedure, but found no evidence to this effect.

[32] The categories employed by Ros are one such attempt. Others would be conceivable. Examples of variation in the widest sense of the word are to be found in Norden, *Antike Kunstprosa* (Leipzig-Berlin, 1898) I 98 and n. 1.

[33] O. Regenbogen in his translation missed this clue, which did not escape others; cf. Gomme *ad loc.* and his references. There is an illuminating disquisition about the two nouns in W. S. Barrett, p. 207 on v. 244.

more specifically whether most of courage consists in a sense of shame or most of this sense takes the form of courage. If we have to commit ourselves, the former alternative would seem more attractive;[34] yet on either assumption the king would prove his point as soon as αἰδώς and its equivalent αἰσχύνη are recognized as the link between his two "premises," and what technical logic calls a *quaternio terminorum* is thereby avoided. Taken as a whole, the argument approximates the classical form of the syllogism sufficiently to excuse our use of these technical terms. The temptation is strong to consider εὔκοσμον and σωφροσύνη likewise as synonyms because on this view the initial thesis πολεμικοὶ . . . διὰ τὸ εὔκοσμον γιγνόμεθα would be completely proved.[35] However, to treat πολεμικοί as an equivalent of εὐψυχία strains our feeling for the Greek language; for Archidamus to make good his assertion, it should suffice if εὐψυχία is necessary for πολεμικοί. This is easy to believe, and we had better not demand more of the king for whom this unfamiliar excursion into logic must in any event have been an exhausting effort. We may imagine the relief with which he turned to the explanation of Spartan εὐβουλία as resting on ἀμαθία. Here he is on familiar ground, and, taking pride in his countrymen's closed minds, says that they are not τὰ ἀχρεῖα ξυνετοὶ ἄγαν. We should have thought so, and since we readily identify the king with their ingrained conservatism, we are amazed at finding him immediately

[34] This is the interpretation chosen by Gomme and as far as I can make out, for the problem is not always squarely faced, Classen-Steup *ad loc.* Regenbogen's rendering seems to imply the alternative view. For the verb μετέχειν, noteworthy even if no Platonic connotations should be assumed, cf. III 83.1.

[35] See J. E. Powell's sweeping identifications in *CR* 53 (1939) 13 and *contra* Gomme *ad loc.* For εὐψυχία and concepts akin to it see below pp. 100ff. Despite the extreme artificiality and the unmistakable experimenting with language and "logic," Thucydides does in this sentence make a serious attempt to understand traits of the Spartan character by finding his way to their root (αἰτία); and there is also—if only intermittently—ἠθοποιία.

before this declaration try his hands at so modernistic a form of reasoning—certainly an ἀχρεῖον if there ever was one—until we remember that not he, but Thucydides is responsible for the phrasing. In this instance Thucydides seems not to have been troubled by the incongruity between form and content.

From the impressions so far gathered, we should have a rough idea of the length to which Thucydides carries his experimentation with the Greek language. Our main difficulty in dealing with this aspect of his style is to distinguish where he uses synonyms in the strict sense of the term and where he plays with words not strictly synonymous, yet approximately identical in meaning. Archidamus made us wonder about the relation of εὐψυχία and πολεμικοί. Elsewhere, εὐψυχία occurs in conjunction with other words that may be comprehended under the general denominator of "courage." The passage including the largest number of such "conceptual" relations is II 87.3f., a part of the exhortation addressed by Brasidas and other Lacedaemonian commanders to their sailors before the battle in the Gulf.[36] Since the sailors are, understandably enough, apprehensive about the Athenians and their long familiarity with naval matters, the Lacedaemonian commanders weigh the importance of "knowledge" against that of bravery, the latter being represented by a cluster of words presumably similar in meaning.[37] It is reassuring, before we become entangled in the network of conceptual relations, to learn ταῖς γνώμαις τοὺς αὐτοὺς ἀεὶ ὀρθῶς ἀνδρείους εἶναι (87.3). Immediately after this, the sailors are urged not to use ἀπειρία as an excuse for failing in their customary ἀνδρεῖον. We must quote the reason: ὑμῶν οὐδ' ἡ ἀπειρία τοσοῦτον λείπεται ὅσον τόλμῃ προύχετε· τῶνδε δὲ ἡ ἐπιστήμη, ἣν μάλιστα φοβεῖσθε, ἀνδρείαν μὲν ἔχουσα καὶ μνήμην ἕξει ἐν τῷ δεινῷ

[36] Not only Phormio's "reply" (see below) but also passages in VI 72.2–4, where Hermocrates addresses men discouraged by a defeat, invite comparison with these passages.

[37] See Gomme for comments on the thought and style.

ἐπιτελεῖν ἃ ἔμαθεν, ἄνευ δὲ εὐψυχίας οὐδεμία τέχνη πρὸς τοὺς κινδύνους ἰσχύει. φόβος γὰρ μνήμην ἐκπλήσσει, τέχνη δ' ἄνευ ἀλκῆς οὐδὲν ὠφελεῖ. πρὸς μὲν οὖν τὸ ἐμπειρότερον αὐτῶν τὸ τολμηρότερον ἀντιτάξασθέ . . . (4f.).

A satisfactory definition of all logical relationships here displayed[38] is impossible. To make some headway, we may place on one side ἀνδρεία, τόλμη, and εὐψυχία on the other ἐμπειρία, ἐπιστήμη, and τέχνη. To what extent are those in the same group interchangeable and employed solely for *variatio*, and where does Thucydides produce his effect through nuances of closely related concepts? Μνήμη is certainly different from the other intellectual concepts. To judge by the two passages where it occurs (4), it should be the condition under which ἐπιστήμη functions. Simultaneously we learn that φόβος is detrimental to μνήμη; going farther but remaining deliberately vague, we may regard it as opposed to ἀνδρεία and its alternates. But where are we to place ἀλκή (4 extr.)?[39] We tend to think of it as something more physical than either ἀνδρεία or εὐψυχία. Two clauses including ἄνευ (ἄνευ δὲ εὐψυχίας 4, τέχνη δὲ ἄνευ . . . , 4) describe the disadvantage of fighters who have experience but lack courage.

More difficult problems remain. Tempting as it may be to regard ἐπιστήμη as the ingredient of ἀνδρεία which sets it apart from τόλμη, we do better not to yield to this "Socratic" inclination. Without a Prodicus to assist us, we must leave open how far Thucydides knew and observed differences between the words denoting bravery[40] (having in 87.3 called

[38] In passing we may note *variatio* also between τὸ δεινόν and οἱ κίνδυνοι, ἰσχύειν and ὠφελεῖν, even though they are not "synonyms."

[39] J. Classen's conjecture αὐτῆς for ἀλκῆς reflects indifference to a peculiarity of Thucydides' style.

[40] Gomme (*ad* 87.4) finds only μεταβολή and "repetition." J. de Romilly (in a note to her translation) groups εὐψυχία with ἀλκή as "innée," an attractive proposal, for the relation between φύσις and experience is clearly an issue between the commanders (see also I 121.4; VII 64.2). But would not ἀνδρεία according to 87.3 be innate too? How

the sailors' ἀνδρεῖον an abiding quality, should he immediately afterward refer to their τόλμη as something distinct from ἀνδρεία?). Nor do we get farther with the "intellectual" terms. Before Plato there was nothing to prevent an equation of ἐμπειρία and ἐπιστήμη;[41] as for τέχνη and ἐπιστήμη, it is possible —but indeed no more than possible—that the former word denotes the latter as put into practice.

Shortly afterward in chapter 88, where Phormio addresses the Athenian sailors, his speech is *more Thucydideo* a reply, in a sense even a refutation, and we have seen in Chapter I that some propositions of the former speech are reversed. As befits samples of the *in utramque partem disputare*, antagonistic viewpoints suggest opposite relations of the pivotal concepts. The more important condition for victory becomes the less important and vice versa. Still, what would please us most, a clarification of the "semantic" problems, can hardly be extracted from the new relationships between experience and courage. The words τέχνη and ἐπιστήμη do not recur. As far as we can tell, both enemies are credited, seriously or *ex hypothesi*, with ἐμπειρία. Ἀνδρεῖον, εὐψυχία, and τόλμη do reappear, and there is even a new word for bravery, θαρσεῖν (89.2; cf. θρασύτεροι, 3). Yet again, if there are nuances, they must be of the slightest, and we may as well refrain from adventurous theories.

The one net result of comparing the thought of "corresponding" passages in the two speeches is that ἀνδρεία does not depend on knowledge, but may be present with or with-

---

consistent is Thucydides in the use of these key words? For some clarification in Plato's *Protagoras* (and *Laches*) see G. Vlastos in the "Introduction" to *Plato's Protagoras* (New York, 1956) xlviff.; note his references to Prodicus *ibid.*

41 See in this connection S. *Tr.* 588-91, where πεῖρα is treated as guarantee of knowledge (εἰδέναι). J. C. Kamerbeek's explanation (*The Plays of Sophocles*, II, Leiden, 1969, *ad loc.*) is better than Jebb's; however εἰδέναι δεῖ δρῶσαν means "it is necessary to know when you act," not "pour être sûr il faut agir."

out it; nor on the other hand is the possession of knowledge a guarantee for ἀνδρεία. The clusters of concepts surrounding ἐπιστήμη and ἀνδρεία remain impenetrable. Pathways into the thickets are found in Plato's *Laches* (192a ff.) and *Protagoras* (349a ff.), where the relationship of ἀνδρεία, θράσος, καρτερεῖν, τὸ ἄφοβον etc. with ἐπιστήμη, τέχνη, φρόνιμος, σοφία is no longer a matter for experiment but for investigation. A close comparison of these dialogues with Thucydides' contributions should prove rewarding.

It should be emphasized that all statements considered here have a basis in reality. However artificial their phrasing, they never take us into the realm of "pure theory." Still, while true to the facts, they are not on the level of facts but above them, in an intellectual stratosphere—here as well as later I avoid speaking of a νοητὸς τόπος. For anyone delighting in the manipulation of concepts, the situation in its strategic, its moral, and its psychological aspects allowed a considerable variety of combinations. Thucydides is determined to exploit them. Some assertions, e.g., ὑμῶν οὐδ' ἡ ἀπειρία τοσοῦτον λείπεται ὅσον τόλμῃ προύχετε, apply only to the men addressed and to the situations in which they find themselves. Others such as φόβος μνήμην ἐκπλήσσει have a far wider range but there is nothing anywhere to indicate a transition from the specific to the general (or the reverse). Finally, although we find Thucydides, like some of his contemporaries, eager to discover new, empirically verifiable generalizations, he shows no intention to coordinate these discoveries into, say, the core of a moral or psychological system. However, psychological discoveries and generalizations are experiments *sui generis* that demand a separate treatment (see Chapter V). To communicate them adequately, language had to display its maximum of flexibility; at times we may wonder whether more was demanded than could be achieved.

So far we have studied passages whose phrasing in some way or other betrays Thucydides' particular interest in words, their meaning, and their mutual semantic relations. The frankest avowal of such interest is probably found where he provides an actual definition for one or two words he considers in need of clarification. To the examples presented earlier in this chapter, we may add another, which differs from them in that it does not relate to a word just used. Accused by the Thebans of violating the sacred rules obtaining in a temple of Apollo, the Athenians adduce "necessity" as one of their excuses (IV 98.6): *παρανομίαν τε ἐπὶ τοῖς μὴ ἀνάγκῃ κακοῖς ὀνομασθῆναι καὶ οὐκ ἐπὶ τοῖς ἀπὸ τῶν ξυμφορῶν τι τολμήσασιν.* We should note *ὀνομασθῆναι* as an appeal to "usage." In fact Thucydides by his definitions never tries to "legislate" about language in the sense of correcting the practice of his time or introducing something at variance with it. No more did Prodicus (as far as we can judge) try to promulgate new meanings.[42] Rather, what both of them did was to record and if necessary to clarify the prevailing usage.

Truly different in conception from all samples of Thucydides' mannerisms that we have so far studied is an argument of the Corcyrean envoys. Pleading in Athens for an alliance, they must justify the departure from their traditional policy of keeping aloof (I 32). In the past aloofness seemed wise policy; now the threat of a powerful Corinthian expedition forces them to change their political orientation: *καὶ περιέστηκεν ἡ δοκοῦσα ἡμῶν πρότερον σωφροσύνη . . . νῦν ἀβουλία καὶ ἀσθένεια φαινομένη* (32.4). Here no distinction is made between words close to being synonyms. Rather a designation formerly and for a long time correct must now be considered false and replaced by one or two others of opposite meaning. Countless alternative ways of conveying this insight were available, and most authors would have chosen a less intellectual or conceptual phrasing. What fascinates Thucydides is that a new political constellation suggests a revaluation that may be

[42] Cf. Guthrie III 205ff., 223ff., 275f.; R. Pfeiffer (*supra*, n. 1) 39ff.

presented as a change of name. The participles δοκοῦσα and φαινομένη add spice to this change: formerly the Corcyrean policy could be considered "good sense"; now it is patently "bad counsel" and "weakness." Comparable to this passage is I 122.4, where the Corinthians deprecate καταφρόνησις, which often causes men to commit serious mistakes, and therefore τὸ ἐναντίον ὄνομα ἀφροσύνη μετωνόμασται.

At I 32.4 unexpected political developments necessitate a new appellation. But at V 105.4, where the Athenian negotiators summarize Lacedaemonian foreign policy as follows: ἐπιφανέστατα ὧν ἴσμεν τὰ μὲν ἡδέα καλὰ νομίζουσι, τὰ δὲ ξυμφέροντα δίκαια, no change of external circumstances accounts for the replacement of two words by two others. What the Athenians describe here is simply and clearly a habitual wrong attitude to moral values. How true to the facts this definition of the enemy's outlook is need not concern us;[43] again, however, assuming it to be correct, there would have been many other—and in fact more obvious—ways to describe this Lacedaemonian tendency. The form chosen by Thucydides reflects his personal taste in matters of style and his curiosity about the uses to which the language might lend itself. He charges the Lacedaemonians not so much with a confusion of names as with a misuse of concepts. And if their actions correspond to his description, their thinking does not; for it is Thucydides himself who thus interprets their political behavior, translating time-honored habits into concepts and expressing relations between concepts by a provocative play with words.

We still wonder about the status of the ἡδέα and ξυμφέροντα.

[43] I incline to the opinion which, I know, cannot be proved, that, after the equation of δίκαια and ξυμφέροντα had suggested itself to Thucydides' mind, that of ἡδέα and καλά was added for good measure, i.e. fuller stylistic effect. What kind of actions were at the time καλά in Sparta we can hardly say; an earlier testimony (Tyrt. 10.1ff. West; cf. 10.21ff. on αἰσχρόν) would certainly not bear out the equation.

Are they for Thucydides entities of unquestionable reality and clearly defined content? Are they, in other words, φύσει, and their names fixed, stable, truly representative of them, so as to be likewise φύσει? Or are they θέσει (i.e. νόμῳ), in which case the Lacedaemonians might have slightly more excuse for adopting whatever words suit them in preference to the conventional ἡδύ, δίκαιον, etc.? Thucydides never tells us where he stands on this issue.[44]

Since he is a historian, not a philosopher, his silence on this point is justified. And yet it was precisely as historian that Thucydides made contributions or even discoveries about language of which no theorist had dreamed. Being alert to historical developments and at the same time sensitized to linguistic phenomena, he would (to state it rather pointedly) find some of the former reflected in the medium of the latter. What I have in mind are the well-known chapters about the deterioration of Greek morals (III 82f.).[45] Manifesting themselves for the first time in the outrages perpetrated in Corcyra, brutality, cynicism, and the disregard of all ties and moral standards were soon to become characteristic of the war in every part of Greece.

Would this increasing barbarization have escaped Thucydides if it had not been accompanied by the semantic innovations that we are about to consider more closely? Very prob-

[44] Besides Guthrie III 204ff. and others to whom he refers, see especially F. Heinimann, *Nomos und Physis* (Basel, 1945, repr. 1965) 44f., an illuminating and comprehensive treatment of the question. Thucydides likes to exploit discrepancies between ἔργον and λόγος (or ὄνομα); see e.g. I 69.5, 84.3; II 35.1; V 111.3; VI 78.3. Cf. *Hermes* 99 (1971) 379ff. The subject has been treated by Adam Parry in his dissertation which (to judge by the summary in *HSPh* 63, 1958, 522ff.) should be rich in new ideas.

[45] Like the majority of scholars I consider III 84 as spurious. Even if its author tried to imitate more than the surface characteristics of Thucydides' style, his failure is glaring. The most prominent defender of the chapter's authenticity is Eduard Schwartz, pp. 284ff.; the most determined advocate of "interpolation" G. Jachmann, *Klio* 33 (1940).

ably not; but the question need not distract us from matters more pertinent to our subject. We must first of all determine as precisely as possible the nature of his observations.

Superficially speaking, what Thucydides discovered was a new type of synonym: καὶ τὴν εἰωθυῖαν ἀξίωσιν τῶν ὀνομάτων ἐς τὰ ἔργα ἀντήλλαξαν τῇ δικαιώσει (82.4).[46] Illustrations follow immediately: τόλμα μὲν γὰρ ἀλόγιστος ἀνδρεία φιλέταιρος ἐνομίσθη, μέλλησις δὲ προμηθὴς δειλία εὐπρεπής, τὸ δὲ σῶφρον τοῦ ἀνάνδρου πρόσχημα, καὶ τὸ πρὸς ἅπαν ξυνετὸν ἐπὶ πᾶν ἀργόν· τὸ δ' ἐμπλήκτως ὀξὺ ἀνδρὸς μοίρᾳ προσετέθη, ἀσφαλείᾳ δὲ τὸ ἐπιβουλεύσασθαι, ἀποτροπῆς πρόφασις εὔλογος.[47] Some of these sentences clearly embody statements about "words" (ὀνόματα), but if we here find "synonyms" we do not imply that they are of the same type as, e.g., ἔλεος and οἶκτος, κρατεῖν and νικᾶν. For one thing, Thucydides does not endorse the use of ἀνδρεία (with or without a qualifying adjective) for τόλμα, of δειλία for μέλλησις, or of ἀργόν for ξυνετόν. Nor is he in sympathy with the new tendency of treating someone προβουλεύσας . . . τυχών as ξυνετός, a χαλεπαίνων as πιστός, or a man on his guard against involvement in plots as τῆς ἑταιρίας διαλυτής. These innovations are a misuse of words; the deterioration of language corresponds to the deterioration of morals that it parallels and reveals. They are, in short, false or pseudo-synonyms. Yet regardless of sympathy or lack of it, Thucydides' interest in legitimate synonyms, and, more broadly, his sensitivity to language as such, was a prior condition for these observations.

[46] If ἀξίωσις is defined as "meaning" (as some current renderings suggest), δικαίωσις would have to take care of the moral valuation, but the notion of value cannot be entirely absent from a word pertaining to the root of ἄξιος. It was a mistake in *LSJ* to list this passage under a special heading. Dion. Hal., *de Thuc.* 29 (375.3ff. Us.-Rad.) is content to understand: ἄλλως ἠξίουν καλεῖν. In chs. 29ff. he transposes many sentences of III 82f. into "normal" Attic.

[47] Note the sequence ἀνδρεία . . . ἄνανδρον . . . ἀνδρὸς μοῖρα. In the last example, I definitely prefer the dative ἀσφαλείᾳ to the nominative but am uncertain about the meaning of ἀποτροπή.

Would any other historian have put so much emphasis on what might well be considered a secondary or surface aspect of the new habits, a mere symptom? (I do not suggest that Thucydides' own view of its significance is utterly different.)

Still, whether right or wrong, legitimate or not, here are synonyms new and representative of a new type. Fragmentary as our knowledge of Prodicus' and other current theories about words happens to be, there is every probability that they considered language to be static. When explaining the difference between ἀμφισβητεῖν and ἐρίζειν, κοινός and ἴσος, Prodicus accepts language as something "given," a *datum*. Not even the awareness of, for example, items in the Homeric vocabulary that were no longer in use and needed explanation led anyone to question this static conception. Thucydides, we should repeat, does not introduce a new theory of language, yet the changes of usage and the new synonyms recorded in these chapters imply that language develops. They are the first intimations of a "historical" approach.[48]

Moreover these shifts and changes of meaning have their causes, and Thucydides' primary concern is with the causes. All innovations here listed pertain to the realm of human conduct. In fact the semantic developments reflect moral developments (καινοῦσθαι τὰς διανοίας, 82.3), and the moral developments in turn are causally related to the war, i.e. to political developments (cf. 82.1f.). To state it briefly, what happens to language does not take place in a vacuum. Here again Thucydides' observations contain the germs of an entirely new understanding of human language. It was not

[48] I am anxious not to overstate my observation. Thucydides did not discover a "law" concerning the development of language. On the other hand it is not sheer accident that, of all Greek authors known to us, it was Thucydides who noticed these changes and treated them as reflecting other developments. Pl. *Prt* 341c and 346d (on which see Pfeiffer, *History of Classical Scholarship*, 41) suggest that Prodicus and his contemporaries used dialects and even environment to explain departures from the norm. This does not impair the originality of Thucydides' contributions.

his way to develop this insight into a new theory. A long time had to pass before sociological aspects of language, or whatever we may call it, could become a subject of wider interest.

Actually, the relation between language and the underlying facts is in this instance particularly complex. We have treated semantic changes as a seismograph for moral valuations; yet as we look at a sentence such as καὶ ὁ μὲν χαλεπαίνων πιστὸς ἀεί, ὁ δὲ ἀντιλέγων αὐτῷ ὕποπτος (5), we may wonder whether the missing verb is ὠνομάσθη, ἐνομίσθη or simply the auxiliary ἦν.[49] Very shortly afterward we read of praise (ἐπῃνεῖτο) bestowed upon men of special temperament, but there is no reference to a designation, whether old or new. The sentence immediately following (82.6) reports that people felt closer to friends (τὸ ἑταιρικόν) than to kinsmen; it adds rather elaborate explanations but includes no word about new appellations. While we read of men's changed habits in dealing with one another (82.5–8) we have much opportunity to admire Thucydides' shrewd psychology; we also may notice his skill in avoiding monotony, even though he continues to record symptoms of one and the same disease; still observations on new meanings of words are conspicuous by their absence. The very pointed—and for us somewhat troublesome—statement: ῥᾷον δ' οἱ πολλοὶ κακοῦργοι ὄντες δεξιοὶ κέκληνται ἢ ἀμαθεῖς ἀγαθοί, καὶ τῷ μὲν αἰσχύνονται, ἐπὶ δὲ τῷ ἀγάλλονται (82.7)[50] has appellations for its subject, but does it deal with changes? Outwardly at least this is a generalization about human nature and should as such be valid at any time. If Thucydides saw this tendency of human nature come into the open dur-

[49] The best answer is probably given by Gomme and de Romilly, who in their rendering while using the auxiliary convey that it "was" a matter of reputation.

[50] Since Thucydides employs *variatio* also in the word order, I here recognize the figure called "chiasmus" and understand: ῥᾷον δ' οἱ πολλοὶ κακοῦργοι ὄντες δεξιοὶ κέκληνται ἢ ἀμαθεῖς (κέκληνται) ἀγαθοὶ (ὄντες). Cf. J. de Romilly's translation and note. Dionysius (*de Thuc.* 32; 378.27ff. Us.-Rad.) struggles and stumbles.

ing the war, he must have counted on the context rather than on his own phrasing to convey this thought. He certainly did not write the latter part of III 82 and the whole of III 83 for the sole purpose of illustrating changes in the use or in the connotations of ὀνόματα.[51]

Finally (as though the complications so far noticed did not suffice) the longer we look at the sentences purporting to acquaint us with new meanings of words, the more we are bound to wonder whether people really developed the habit of praising a man for ἀνδρεία φιλέταιρος or blaming him for δειλία εὐπρεπής. Had they ever, when discussing ruthless daring, spoken of ἀλόγιστος τόλμα? Another look at Thucydides' actual wording shows that he does not even maintain this himself. A phrase such as ἀποτροπῆς πρόφασις εὔλογος (82.4), however we decide to understand it, has the earmarks of Thucydides' own delight in experimentation, which when carried to excess baffles the reader by the resulting obscurity. Throughout these chapters, whether Thucydides professes to deal with semantic, moral, political changes, or still other topics, we must make allowance for his own stylistic ambitions. Some innovations in the use of words may with due caution be accepted as correct, but we have to dig them out, as it were, under the top stratum formed by his own language, and by no method of counting can they be as numerous as the examples of Thucydides' stylistic idiosyncrasies.

One more manifestation of this new attitude toward language calls for discussion. Bruno Snell has made us aware of the intellectual possibilities that were latent in the Greek definite article.[52] Its neuter gender in particular facilitated

[51] For "specious" words used to cover up selfish or brutal political manoeuvres see esp. 82.8, where we note μετὰ ὀνόματος εὐπρεποῦς at the beginning and εὐπρεπείᾳ δὲ λόγου near the end. However much hostility men had provoked by their actions, their reputation improved, provided they chose the right slogans.

[52] See his *Die Entdeckung des Geistes* (Hamburg, 3rd ed., 1955) 299ff. By beginning my cursory study of this development with Soph-

"abstract" thinking. When Homer uses the article, whether in the plural (τά τ' ἐόντα τά τ' ἐσσόμενα πρό τ' ἐόντα) or in the singular for a thought such as *Il.* 9.320: κάτθαν' ὁμῶς ὅ τ' ἄεργος ἀνὴρ ὅ τε πολλὰ ἐοργώς, he does not have individual men or objects in mind. His sentence has a more general meaning, yet there is nothing abstract in these words. Where later generations resort to the "abstract" τὸ ἀγαθόν or τὸ δίκαιον, their ancestors would have spoken of ἀρετή or of δίκη. Such are and remain concrete realities. They are felt, admired, revered, some of them even turned into deities.[53]

In the tragedies of Sophocles and Euripides, the neuter of the adjective has become established usage. In Sophocles' *Ajax*, a play of the 440s, we read Tecmessa's bitter reflections about those who did not appreciate τὸ ἀγαθὸν χεροῖν (964f.) in Ajax while he was alive but may now feel its loss acutely; we also find Teucer proudly defying Menelaus: ξὺν τῷ δικαίῳ γὰρ μέγ' ἔξεστιν φρονεῖν (1124). In the one instance ἀρετή, in the other δίκη could have served. From *Antigone* we may quote a well-known passage: σοφόν τι τὸ μηχανόεν τέχνας (ὑπὲρ ἐλπίδ' ἔχων, 365f.), which occurs in the praise of man's achievements. A

---

ocles, I do not suggest complete absence of these neuters in Aeschylus; but may τὸ δεινόν as used *Eum.* 517 and v. 698 honestly be called "abstract"? Perhaps *Pr.* 186f. (Zeus) παρ' ἑαυτῷ τὸ δίκαιον ἔχων is more to the point. Τὸ θεῖον (probably used as early as Anaximander) is a class of its own, and so, of course are the "powers" or "quality things" of the physicists, τὸ ψυχρόν etc. See further Snell, *Der Aufbau der Sprache* (Hamburg, 1952) 167 and H. Patzer, *Das Problem der Thukydideischen Geschichtsschreibung und die Thukydideische Frage* (Berlin, 1937), 91f., who rightly put collectives like τὸ Ἑλληνικόν (I 1.1) in a class by themselves (I 6.3 and τὸ ἑταιρικόν III 82.3 are comparable). For τὸ Ἑλληνικόν see also Hdt. I 4., VII 139.5 *al.*

53 Δίκη, Φόβος, Αἰδώς (cf. Hes. *Op.* 200) are perhaps the most obvious illustrations; on Ἔλεος see *LSJ* s.v. For personification in Greek language and religion cf. Wilamowitz, *Der Glaube d. Hell.* I (Berlin, 1932) 343 and *passim*; L. Deubner, "Personification" in Roscher's *Ausführliches Lexikon der Griech. u. Röm. Mythologie* (Leipzig, 1884-1937) III, 2069ff., esp. 2089ff., 2094ff; M. P. Nilsson, *Geschichte d. griech. Rel.*, I (Munich, 1941) 486f. and *passim*.

few lines later, there is a negated neuter ἄπολις ὅτῳ τὸ μὴ καλὸν ξύνεστι (370). The same expression τὸ μὴ καλόν recurs in the *Electra* (1087).[54] In the *Philoctetes* Neoptolemus is hopeful that τὸ δίκαιον is on his side (1251); in fact we may watch this definite or "abstract" neuter emerge from his altercation with Odysseus: a few lines earlier Neoptolemus uses plurals (ἀλλ' εἰ δίκαια, τῶν σοφῶν κρείσσω τάδε) and Odysseus replies in the singular, yet without the article (καὶ πῶς δίκαιον . . . , 1246f.). Noteworthy too in this play is the coincidence of norms to which we shall find a parallel in Thucydides: τῶν γὰρ ἐν τέλει κλύειν τό τ' ἔνδικόν με καὶ τὸ συμφέρον ποιεῖ (925f.).[55]

Do such neuters carry a claim to absolute validity? Not necessarily; even a passage such as Soph. *El.* 466f., τὸ γὰρ δίκαιον οὐκ ἔχει λόγον δυοῖν ἐρίζειν, ἀλλ' ἐπισπεύδειν τὸ δρᾶν, establishes no presumption. For the same Chrysothemis who thus reacts to Electra later refuses to cooperate in her outrageous project and sticks to what Electra derisively calls a personal, i.e. subjective δίκαιον: τῷ σῷ δικαίῳ (1037).[56]

In Euripides it is repeatedly stated how unsettled the true

[54] See *ibid.* v. 1469 (Aegisthus ready to honor τὸ συγγενές also in his enemy, Orestes). A quotation from a lost play includes ἥβης εἰς τὸ σῶφρον (frg. 718). On Deianeira's description of Iole as μεταιτία τοῦ μηδὲν αἰσχροῦ (*Tr.* 447ff.) cf. Jebb *ad loc.*

[55] In the *OC*, τὸ γενναῖον is conspicuous in Oedipus himself, and he in turn admires it in Theseus (vv. 8, 569, 1042). His gratitude for Athens is acknowledged in vv. 1125-7: τὸ γ' εὐσεβὲς μόνοις παρ' ὑμῖν ηὗρον καὶ τοὐπιεικὲς καὶ τὸ μὴ ψευδοστομεῖν. Cf. A. A. Long, *Language and Thought in Sophocles* (London, 1968) 49 n. 71, who notes a particularly wide range of abstract expressions in the *OC*. Although Long has of set purpose excluded Sophocles' use of such neuters from his purview (see p. 14), his book provides a most valuable treatment of many parallel developments toward a more abstract form of expression.

[56] "What is right according to you" Jebb *ad loc.* (for vv. 466f., too, Jebb's explanation seems most satisfactory). See also vv. 1041f. In Eur. *Hipp.* 1007, τοὐμὸν σῶφρον suggests an inherent quality, not like the τῷ σῷ in S. *El.* 1037, a personal and allegedly subjective point of view. Cf. Eur. *IA* 810f. and see n. 52 above for A. *Pr.* 186f.

meaning of τὸ δίκαιον and other normative concepts is.[57] Still, since we have found abundant evidence for the "abstract" neuter in Sophocles, we *a potiori* count on its presence in the younger and more "intellectual" Euripides. A minimal number of samples will confirm this expectation.

Someone brought up well, Hecabe assures us, οἶδεν τό γ' αἰσχρόν, κανόνι τοῦ καλοῦ μαθών (*Hec.* 600–602). Demophon, the king of Athens, explains to Jolaus that he has reasons for helping the harassed family of Heracles: τὸ συγγενές τε καὶ τὸ προὐφείλειν καλῶς πράσσειν . . . τούσδε τό τ' αἰσχρόν, οὗπερ δεῖ μάλιστα φροντίσαι (*Heracl.* 240–242).[58] In the *Helen* Menelaus has doubts whether it is the true καλόν for him to go down on his knees before Theonoe, upon whose assistance his own and Helen's fate depends (vv. 952f.); yet hard as he tries to preserve his dignity, he falters δακρύοις εἰς τὸ θῆλυ τρεπόμενος (v. 991). Most revealing—or puzzling—of all passages is perhaps τὸ σοφὸν δ' οὐ σοφία τό τε μὴ θνητὰ φρονεῖν sung by the Bacchants (*Ba.* 395f.), a "paradox" rightly described by Dodds as "the characteristic product of an age when traditional valuations are rapidly shifting."[59] Somehow this neuter, to whatever status it may aspire with the help of the definite article, does not measure up to the venerable noun σοφία. τί τὸ σοφόν; the chorus asks later (vv. 877–897), but what is the

[57] The most radical assertion is probably *Ph.* 499ff., See also *Or.* 492–95.

[58] For τὸ συγγενές, see also *ibid.* v. 6. Demophon's coordination of adjectives in the neuter with an infinitive likewise preceded by τό is one of very numerous passages that suggest a similar or identical function for both.

[59] *Euripides: Bacchae* (Oxford, 1944) *ad loc.*, where he (*inter alia*) refers to Thuc. III 82f. as providing a historical background. See also R. P. Winnington Ingram, *Euripides and Dionysus* (Cambridge, 1948) 11f., 167ff. and *passim*, and *BICS* 13 (1966) 34ff. H. Diller, *Abh. Mainz. Akad., Geistesw. Kl.* (1955), 463ff.; C. W. Willink, *CQ N.S.* 16 (1966) 229, 230 n. 1; D. J. Conacher, *Euripidean Drama* (Toronto, 1967).

answer? There are reasons to think that the hostile attitude to "abstract" wisdom persists throughout the play, and especially on the part of the chorus.[60]

As far as we can tell, the first prose authors deliberately to exploit these neuters for stylistic effects are again Thrasymachus and Gorgias. A passage in Gorgias' *Helen* is comparatively tame. Fear, he here argues, ἐποίησεν ἀμελῆσαι καὶ τοῦ καλοῦ τοῦ διὰ τὸν νόμον κρινομένου καὶ τοῦ ἀγαθοῦ τοῦ διὰ τὴν νίκην γινομένου (16). More striking instances may be quoted from the relatively small section that has reached us of his *Epitaph* for the Athenians. Here, between antitheses produced by other means, we find the warriors celebrated as πολλὰ μὲν τὸ πρᾶον ἐπιεικὲς τοῦ αὐθάδους δικαίου προκρίνοντες; later in the same piece they are described as αὐθάδεις πρὸς τὸ συμφέρον, εὐόργητοι πρὸς τὸ πρέπον, τῷ φρονίμῳ τῆς γνώμης παύοντες τὸ ἄφρον ⟨τῆς ῥώμης⟩.[61] Clearly the rhetorical desire for antithesis and *variatio* has discovered these neuters as good objects for experimentation.

The time for being wary of excess or mannerism having not yet come, Thucydides welcomed this discovery. As we have taken our last quotations from Gorgias' *Epitaphios*, we may fittingly begin our parade of Thucydidean ones by looking at the "Epitaph" of Pericles, ostensibly designed as a celebration of the Athenians killed in the first year of the war but more truly as a monument for Pericles and Periclean Athens.

Pericles bids the Athenians to take the men just buried as models for their own outlook: τὸ εὔδαιμον τὸ ἐλεύθερον, τὸ δ' ἐλεύθερον τὸ εὔψυχον κρίναντες μὴ περιορᾶσθε τοὺς πολεμικοὺς κινδύνους (II 43.4). The relationship of the three neuters brought together in this sentence should not be considered solely

[60] I cannot accept the arguments in favor of τὸ σοφόν in Marylin Arthur's otherwise admirable study, *YCS* 22 (1972) 176ff.

[61] If the preserved section is the conclusion of the *Epitaph* (as is generally and rightly assumed), we cannot know how lavishly Gorgias used these figures elsewhere in it. The two words at the end were added by Sauppe.

from the stylistic point of view. For τὸ ἐλεύθερον has a similar function as αἰδώς-αἰσχύνη in Archidamus' speech about the Spartan character (I 84.3). It is the "middle term" between τὸ εὔδαιμον, which is everybody's desire, and τὸ εὔψυχον, the quality so gloriously exemplified by the fallen warriors. Here again we are close to a syllogism in the first figure. However τὸ ἐλεύθερον has the full weight of its meaning; its connection with each of the two other "terms" is as important as their connection with one another, which it provides. Pericles surely wishes the Athenians to ponder the close interdependence of "happiness" and political liberty and again of liberty and a courageous facing of the dangers of war. To present this interdependence as identity is a solemn and forceful "simplification" appropriate to the stylistic level of this oration. Comparing our sentence once more with I 84.3, we notice as a further difference that Thucydides this time does not use nouns denoting the ἀρεταί, but makes his point by means of adjectives employed in the neuter. We may as well call them concepts, although it would not be easy to explain why a conceptual quality is more conspicuous in them than in the nouns of the other passage.

In another passage of the Funeral Speech: τὸ γὰρ φιλότιμον ἀγήρων μόνον (II 44.4), there is again a relationship between neuters of adjectives or, if we like, between concepts, but it is this time not a relation of identity. Rather, as μόνον indicates, one concept claims a monopoly on the other. In fact it is a claim made by a human quality on something normally associated with the immortal gods. No doubt we have entered the realm of logic; yet fascinated as Thucydides must have been with such formal aspects and possibilities,[62] his primary interest lies in the content. True values must be set apart from false.

62 Ed. Norden, *Antike Kunstprosa* (Berlin-Leipzig, 1898) I 98 n. 2 compares τὸ φρόνιμον τῆς γνώμης in Gorgias with τὸ θυμούμενον τῆς γνώμης in "Antiphon" (*Tetral.* I 3) and τὸ ὕποπτον τῆς γνώμης in Thuc. (I 90.2).

Having made this *caveat,* we may resume our formal analysis. The passages discussed suggest rather ambitious intentions, but we do not yet know how far Thucydides carried them. By using neuters of adjectives—as well as infinitives—with the article, Thucydides has risen above the level of facts and entered a realm where new perspectives beckon. Conceptual relations should make it possible to illuminate much that had so far been unknown because, generalizations apart, there had been no methods for advancing above or beyond the facts.

Still, not every passage that includes such a neuter lights up a previously dark and inaccessible corner of reality. Some merely indicate how natural it was for Thucydides to think in such ways. The "Melian Dialogue" abounds in neuters, and we should find it instructive to consider different uses of them with an open mind.

Do the Athenians not realize that by forcing Melos into subjection they might drive neutral cities into the enemy camp? Faced with this question, they reply that their most dangerous enemies are not ὅσοι . . . τῷ ἐλευθέρῳ πολλὴν τὴν διαμέλλησιν τῆς πρὸς ἡμᾶς φυλακῆς ποιήσονται but some other categories including τοὺς ἤδη τῆς ἀρχῆς τῷ ἀναγκαίῳ παροξυνομένους. οὗτοι γὰρ πλεῖστ' ἂν τῷ ἀλογίστῳ ἐπιτρέψαντες σφᾶς τε αὑτοὺς καὶ ἡμᾶς ἐς προὗπτον κίνδυνον καταστήσειαν (V 99). In these two sentences no less than three adjectives in the neuter are used to specify the true objects and causes of Athenian fear. If we ask how far the same thoughts could have been expressed in a more "traditional" form, the answer is not easy. By preferring τὸ ἐλεύθερον instead of ἡ ἐλευθερία in the former clause and τὸ ἀναγκαῖον instead of ἀνάγκη in the latter a nuance is gained; for it is not the condition as such but an attitude or habit engendered by it that determines the readiness of cities to risk their safety. For the last neuter, a less "abstract" equivalent does not suggest itself so readily. Granted that the irrational motive might have been specified as θυμός or, alternatively, that a participle such as οὐ λογισάμενοι might have been used (and the clause correspondingly reorganized), thanks to τῷ ἀλογίστῳ we find ourselves on a different, more intellectual plane of discourse, and look at men's doings from a distance.

Somewhat later the Athenians think it necessary to expose their partners' naïveté. If looking to the Lacedaemonians διὰ τὸ αἰσχρὸν δὴ βοηθήσειν ὑμῖν πιστεύετε αὐτούς, μακαρίσαντες ὑμῶν τὸ ἀπειρόκακον οὐ ζηλοῦμεν τὸ ἄφρον (105.3). Again the neuters determine the character of the thought as well as of the diction. Here it is easy to define the relation between the three neuters. To consider τὸ αἰσχρόν as an effective impulse suggests the presence of τὸ ἄφρον as well as of τὸ ἀπειρόκακον in those clinging to such illusions.[63] This is stated with reference to the Melians and, as it is worded, applies only to the situation at hand. The error of the Melians lies not in expecting an "abstract" neuter to have such influence but in making the wrong choice. We shall soon realize how great power some of these neuters may have.

Rebuffed, the Melians shift from τὸ αἰσχρόν to τὸ ξυμφέρον—(106) but to no avail. For although this is truly powerful and on many occasions proves the decisive motivation, under the present circumstances it will not, and the Athenians know why: οὔκουν οἴεσθε τὸ ξυμφέρον μὲν μετ' ἀσφαλείας εἶναι, τὸ δὲ δίκαιον καὶ καλὸν μετὰ κινδύνου δρᾶσθαι (which is not the Lacedaemonian way, 107). Unlike the passage analyzed previously, this appears to formulate something in the nature of a general truth. For its bearing extends far beyond the specific circumstances. Throughout Thucydides' work, τὸ ξυμφέρον is one of

[63] τὸ αἰσχρόν refers back to what the Melians themselves had called αἰσχύνη (104). The place of τὸ ἄφρον could probably have been taken by ἀφροσύνη, but τὸ ἀπειρόκακον could (as far as we know) only be replaced by a noun coined for the occasion to sum up a facet of the Melians' historical experience. ἄφρον and ἀπειρόκακον prompt very different reactions, and the verbs describing these give the impression of something desirable found in combinations with something very undesirable—until we realize the irony of μακαρίσαντες.

the most important and at the same time one of the most controversial concepts. Again and again we find his speakers engaged in clarifying its nature and influence on human action.

Toward this purpose, the "Melian Dialogue" makes a far from negligible contribution. To appreciate it fully, we should bear in mind Thucydides' tendency to use ξυμφέρον and χρήσιμον as synonyms, and we should not be too surprised if ὠφέλιμον also occasionally appears in this function. Early in the dialogue the Athenians have made clear that they consider τὸ δίκαιον as irrelevant (89) to the issue. The discussion must therefore concentrate on τὸ ξυμφέρον. The Melians, having no choice but to accept this dictum, may yet present their own version of τὸ ξυμφέρον. In their opinion, it resolves itself into τὸ κοινὸν ἀγαθόν (90), and the Athenians ought to realize how much damage a brutal use of force would do to their own interest and in particular to the prospects of their ἀρχή. On this subject, however, the Athenians recognize no authority but their own; rejecting the argument of the Melians, they explain how the ὠφέλιμον or χρήσιμον (91) of both parties may indeed, also from their point of view, coincide, but would for the Melians spell voluntary subjection, an unpleasant prospect, to be sure, but preferable to "the most dreadful" (τὰ δεινότατα) that they would suffer if they were conquered by force (93). Once more the Melians try their own approach to τὸ ξυμφέρον, for they still hope that the Athenians will reconsider the issue and find it possible to accept the Melian χρήσιμον as identical with their own. Evidently the correct understanding of this "abstract" entity has become a matter of life and death for the Melians, while for the Athenians it is, if not nearly so critical, still of no small importance for the best orientation of their policies.

Although some other neuters in the "Dialogue," such as τὸ εἰκός (96), τὸ ἀσφαλές (97), τὸ θεῖον (105.1, 2) might be discussed with profit, we may as well move on to samples in other sections.

The Melians are not the only people whose fate seems to depend on a correct understanding (not to say the true definition) of *τὸ ξυμφέρον*. The clarification that they attempt before the siege has a parallel in the argument of the Plataeans after a long siege when they find themselves at the mercy of the Lacedaemonians. In the course of their plea they try to enlighten their conquerors about a truly advantageous policy: *καὶ χρὴ . . . τὸ ξυμφέρον μὴ ἄλλο τι νομίσαι ἢ τῶν ξυμμάχων τοῖς ἀγαθοῖς ὅταν αἰεὶ βέβαιον τὴν χάριν τῆς ἀρετῆς ἔχωσι καὶ τὸ παραυτίκα που ὑμῖν ὠφέλιμον καθιστῆται* (III 56.7). Although there are difficulties of interpretation,[64] we understand that a long-range view is played off against *τὸ παραυτίκα που ὠφέλιμον*. In a similar spirit, a slightly earlier passage suggests a "balancing" (*ἀντιθεῖναι*, 56.5) of "larger" against "smaller" merits. To do so would prove advantageous to the Plataeans, whose record in the war against Persia should count for more than their present alliance with Athens. Such "balancing" would in the first place be an act of justice (*δίκαιον*, 56.5), yet expediency is here too in the offing.[65] Moreover, what made their record in the Persian War so praiseworthy was their readiness to do *τὰ βέλτιστα* rather than *τὰ ξύμφορα* (56.3). As we know from the "Melian Dialogue," *τὰ ξύμφορα* would have been associated with "security" (*ἀσφάλεια* 56.5); what

[64] The sentence structure is tangled to the point of obscurity, and I doubt whether conjectures should make it smoother; nor do I know of any that have succeeded. For the dative *τῶν ξυμμάχων τοῖς ἀγαθοῖς*, there is probably no grammatical justification; stylistically its "justification" is that it corresponds to *ὑμῖν*. The definition of the *ξυμφέρον* in III 56.7 might, like some others in Thucydides (e.g. of *φιλόπολι* by Alcibiades VI 92.4), be described as a "persuasive definition" in the sense in which A.W.H. Adkins (*CQ* 16, 1966, 206) tries to use the term for Eur. *Hec.* 844f., 901ff.

[65] See the train of thought 56.2–7.

the Plataeans preferred was "to dare the noblest with its dangers" (τολμᾶν μετὰ κινδύνων τὰ βέλτιστα).

Very often the ξυμφέρον finds itself competing in more or less open conflict with the δίκαιον. From the moral point of view, this conflict is crucial for Thucydides' conception of the war; he returns to it whenever a contest of speakers provides an opportunity. We have in our treatment of these contests (Chapter I) mentioned this issue, and some aspects of it will engage us when we deal with psychological theories (Chapter V); yet to trace the dialectic between these concepts in its formal manifestations only is unsatisfactory. None of the formal experiments leads us to the substance. In its substantial aspects the opposition of these concepts is a central problem of Athenian imperialism. Fortunately this large subject has been greatly advanced by some penetrating investigations of the last three decades.[66]

We select a few of the highlights: Even in the first ἀγὼν λόγων, the debate between the Corcyreans and Corinthians, both concepts are prominent. We have dealt with the reasons why the Corcyreans stress the ξυμφέρον, the Corinthians the δίκαιον.[67] From our present point of view, the most noteworthy passage of the Corinthian speech is I 42.1, where they warn the Athenian Assembly not to believe δίκαια μὲν τάδε (*scil.* their own arguments) λέγεσθαι, ξύμφορα δ' εἰ πολεμήσει, ἄλλα εἶναι. The coincidence of the two concepts is of course the most desirable condition. There is a prospect of its materializing—just once, and even then it evaporates on closer consideration. In the deliberation about the punishment of

[66] See, besides J. de Romilly's *Imperialism*, G.E.M. de Ste. Croix, *Historia* 3 (1954) 1ff., esp. 30ff.; H. Strasburger, *Saeculum* 5 (1954) 416ff. and *passim*; *Hermes* 86 (1958) 28ff. (esp. 29, n. 5); F. Wassermann, p. 27ff.; and others.

[67] See esp. 32.1; 35.5, 36.1 (yet also 34.1ff.); 37.2, esp. 4ff.; 39, 40.1ff.; cf. 42.1. In the Athenian decision the ξυμφέρον in effect prevails (see esp. 44.2), creating a precedent as it were for later issues. Note also on I 76.2 von Fritz, I 630, 634; also pp. 684ff., 720 and *passim*.

the Mytileneans, Cleon maintains that only the harshest treatment, the execution of the entire male population, would satisfy both principles (πειθόμενοι μὲν ἐμοὶ τά τε δίκαια ἐς τοὺς Μυτιληναίους καὶ τὰ ξύμφορα ἅμα ποιήσετε, III 40.4)—justice because no other punishment could match the gravity of their crime (39.2–4, 6), expediency because such a deterrent would safeguard the interests of Athenian domination (39.7f.). The two "concepts" are the same that we found in the *Philoctetes* converging toward a norm of conduct. There the convergence proved illusory, and in the present instance Cleon is shown to misjudge the situation. For as in so many instances of the *in utramque partem disputare* the second speaker, Diodotus, prevails; he takes his stand on τὸ ξυμφέρον to the exclusion of every other consideration and declares, after he has set forth his opinion, καὶ τὸ Κλέωνος τὸ αὐτὸ δίκαιον καὶ ξύμφορον τῆς τιμωρίας οὐχ εὑρίσκεται ἐν αὐτῷ[68] ἅμα δυνατὸν γίγνεσθαι. The "identity" here rejected would have been limited to the case under discussion. This makes it something utterly different from the basic conceptual identity of, say, ἀνδρεία, or any other ἀρετή, with ἐπιστήμη, theses familiar to us from the "Socratic" dialogues.

After this uncompromising repudiation of τὸ δίκαιον by the Athenians and the comparable, if slightly less dramatic, decision about Plataea (III 52–68) by the Lacedaemonians, pretences about justice are by and large discarded. As we have seen in the "Melian Dialogue" (V 89f.) the Athenians refuse

[68] If ἅμα seems redundant and ἐν αὐτῷ vague, we should nevertheless resist conjectures. To Thucydides himself the sentence may well have appeared both logically and stylistically satisfactory. We cannot know whether Diodotus' actual speech was prompted, wholly or in part, by humane motivations. If it was, Thucydides has preserved no trace of this (it has been pointed out to me that 43.2 may be thus understood; but does Thucydides use "hints to the reader"? I doubt it, and should think that 43.2 has a different function). The views set forth by Finley, 171, and von Fritz, I 687f., are admirable but do not allow for the dialectic between the two concepts.

to discuss τὸ δίκαιον at all.[69] Τὸ ξυμφέρον reigns unchallenged. A variation of it still worth listing is the line taken by Euphemus in his disingenuous speech to the citizens of Camerina. Certainly, he admits, Athenian policies are dictated by τὸ ξυμφέρον, but this principle correctly understood suggests one course of action in one area and a very different one elsewhere. As some "allies" serve the Athenian interest by contributing ships, others by financial support, so the Sicilian cities would help Athens most as strong and independent allies against Syracuse.[70]

From this pair of concepts we turn once more to other neuters. At IV 126.5, Brasidas prepares his soldiers for the strange fighting habits of the barbarians. It is important not to be affected by their wild looks, their noise and their gesticulations, for when it comes to action, they are not nearly so formidable since ἥ τε φυγὴ καὶ ἡ ἔφοδος αὐτῶν ἴσην ἔχουσα δόξαν τοῦ καλοῦ ἀνεξέλεγκτον καὶ τὸ ἀνδρεῖον ἔχει (IV 126.5 med.). Two central values of Greek conduct have an entirely different meaning for the barbarians: of τὸ καλόν these tribes have a very un-Hellenic conception; hence they lack a criterion also for τὸ ἀνδρεῖον. Some infinitives, turned with the help of the article into nouns, explain their outlook, and the next sentences clarify further: . . . πᾶν τὸ προυπάρχον δεινὸν ἀπ' αὐτῶν ὁρᾶτε ἔργῳ μὲν βραχὺ ὄν, ὄψει δὲ καὶ ἀκοῇ καταστπέρχον. ὃ ὑπομείναντες . . . ἔς τε τὸ ἀσφαλὲς θᾶσσον ἀφίξεσθε καὶ γνώσεσθε . . . ὅτι οἱ τοιοῦτοι ὄχλοι . . . (for those who hold their ground) ἀπειλαῖς τὸ ἀνδρεῖον μελλήσει ἐπικομποῦσιν (but for those who yield) κατὰ πόδας τὸ εὔψυχον ἐν τῷ ἀσφαλεῖ ὀξεῖς ἐνδείκνυνται (6). This description does

[69] Among later references to τὸ δίκαιον, VI 79.1 has hypothetical form. Brasidas (IV 85f., esp. 87.2) declares his expedition to the North to be ἐπ' ἀγαθῷ of the natives, but definite appeals to τὸ δίκαιον are hard to pin down in his speech. Nothing could be more *recherché* than the phrasing of 86.6, where ἰσχύος δικαίωσις contrasts with γνώμης ἀδίκου ἐπιβουλή.

[70] VI 84-86; note the principle enunciated in 85.1 and the emphasis on ξυμφέρον, *ibid.*

contain (partly in clauses here omitted) a fair amount of concrete and illustrative detail, but the "concepts" are integral to it. Do stylistic ambition and adventurousness suffice to explain this kind of phrasing? Such motives may account for the alternation between τὸ ἀνδρεῖον and τὸ εὔψυχον, but beyond such minor items I should not hold them responsible. Having undertaken to analyze a pattern of behavior familiar to himself from his Thracian environment but unknown to most Greeks, Thucydides chose to do so in the medium of concepts. The transition from concrete reality to "abstract" thought had become his habit, and he probably regarded it as conducive to a better understanding if he defined the nature of τὸ ἀνδρεῖον (τὸ εὔψυχον), τὸ δεινόν and τὸ ἀσφαλές in this type of fighting.[71] The last clauses of the description seem to introduce a humorous note; but I am by no means certain that Thucydides himself felt this element of humor.

Reference has been made earlier to Phormio's exhortation before the second battle in the Gulf. The Lacedaemonian fleet relies on its sizable numerical superiority, yet Phormio's arguments turn the enemy's advantage into an asset for his own men, a success of reasoning but essentially of the form in which the reasoning is cast. Whoever under such adverse conditions is ready to do battle must have μέγα τι τῆς διανοίας τὸ βέβαιον (II 89.6). The joining of another adjective, μέγα, to τὸ βέβαιον may show how far the new category of expressions has gone toward acquiring the status of a noun. Even more remarkable is what the next sentence offers: ἃ λογιζόμενοι οὗτοι (the Peloponnesians) τῷ οὐκ εἰκότι πλέον πεφόβηνται ἡμᾶς ἢ τῇ κατὰ λόγον παρασκευῇ. As Gomme observes, such language would hardly be effective with "simple men like the sailors."[72] Given the superior experience of the Athenians, the prob-

[71] τὸ ἀσφαλές occurs twice in this passage; the first time it refers to Brasidas' men, the second time to the enemy. For once there is no subtlety at work.

[72] Cf. pp. 100ff. with Gomme's comments on the sentences analyzed.

ability that this unexpected or indeed "unlikely" resistance will weaken the enemy's morale seems almost greater than that arguments thus worded should strengthen their own. However, such speculation is off the point; what matters is Thucydides' obvious enjoyment of a condition of things in which not τὸ εἰκός but its opposite could be introduced as effective. The frequent use of τὸ εἰκός facilitates, and at the same time adds point to, the unusual negative phrase. Commentators[73] have with some justification compared VI 34.8, where Hermocrates, advising his fellow citizens to meet the Athenian fleet on the high sea and at a good distance from Sicily, argues in support of his bold proposal: εἰ δὲ ἴδοιεν παρὰ γνώμην τολμήσαντας, τῷ ἀδοκήτῳ μᾶλλον ἂν καταπλαγεῖεν ἢ τῇ ἀπὸ τοῦ ἀληθοῦς δυνάμει. This time the meaning is less subtle, and anyone familiar with Thucydides' idiom will take this stylistic device—or intellectual experiment—in his stride.

The neuter τὸ μέλλον in the sense of "the future" had been current for some time, but to put this neuter at the mercy of another as in τὸ δὲ ἀστάθμητον τοῦ μέλλοντος ὡς ἐπὶ πλεῖστον κρατεῖ (IV 62.4) and to philosophize about the advantages of this condition as compared with its disadvantages was left for Thucydides' enterprising spirit. There is no limit to such explorations in the world of abstract entities,[74] and not the least of its attractions is that speculation on that high level is anything but futile. Viewing reality from a distance and from above reduces a multitude of impressions to their common denominator, a ἓν ἐπὶ πολλῶν, for whose successful handling new methods must be devised. Will the enterprise prove truly illuminating? Thucydides clearly thinks it worth-

[73] See Gomme *ad loc.*, where references and a critical discussion of earlier commentators will be found.

[74] For infinitives used in similar fashion see above, n. 55 (and 58). E. Schwyzer–A. Debrunner, *Griechische Grammatik* (Munich, 2nd ed., 1950) II 368, deal briefly with such constructions of the infinitive but are not very helpful for Thucydides, because their subject is syntax, not style.

while.[75] Philosophical and rhetorical theories were indeed to use "abstract" neuters, such as *τὸ ἀγαθόν, τὸ καλόν, τὸ πρέπον, τὸ καθῆκον, τὸ ἴδιον, τὸ σαφές*, to good effect, but with restraint. For scientific discoveries and generalizations, the more common resources of the Greek language—enriched by some new coinages—proved adequate.

[75] He was, it must be admitted, not invariably successful. A passage such as I 36.1, for instance, while entertaining as an experiment, is after all a grotesque aberration. For details, see my analysis *Hermes* 99 (1971) 407f.

V

EMPIRICAL PSYCHOLOGY AND REALISTIC GENERALIZATION

During the earlier centuries of Greek thought and literature, hardly any concept holds so dominating a position in moral issues as *hybris*.[1] How far literature reflects "life" in this aspect is difficult to know, but some corresponding, even if far less articulate, beliefs and superstitions must have formed the substratum of what we meet in the written documents. Were one to say nothing here of *hybris* prior to the fifth century and, in this century itself nothing about its central importance in Aeschylus and about its somewhat reduced place in Sophocles, Herodotus alone would suffice to prove its continuing vitality. For he almost invariably understands the story of a ruler's fate in terms of *hybris* followed by *nemesis* or divine punishment (jealousy of the gods maintains itself in innocent competition with the *hybris* pattern). Croesus, Cyrus, Cambyses, Darius, and Xerxes are not all of them throughout their rule guilty of *hybris*; but, at some point, a decision inspired by it starts them on the downward path.[2] The same is true of a number of minor figures. When

[1] For ὕβρις see besides C. Del Grande's monograph *Hybris* (Naples, 1947), Nilsson, *Gesch. d. griech. Relig.* (Munich, 1941) I 615, 694, and *passim*; E. R. Dodds, *The Greeks and the Irrational* (Berkeley and Los Angeles, 1951) 41ff.; Kurt Latte, *Kleine Schriften* (Munich, 1968) 13ff., 234ff. See also n. 2. In this chapter I have found it peculiarly difficult to specify what I owe to others. On questions related to φύσις, Patzer 90ff. has proved very helpful.

[2] In the account of Cyrus, for instance, ὕβρις is limited to the campaign against the Massagetae (I 201-216, esp. 212ff.). III 80.2f. may do duty for a fuller list of relevant passages. In general see Henry R. Immerwahr, *Form and Thought in Herod* (Cleveland, 1966) 310, and Helen North, *Sophrosyne* (Ithaca, N.Y., 1966) 28 and *passim*. Richmond Lattimore, *Story Patterns in Greek Tragedy* (Ann Arbor,

Herodotus changes over to the Greek side, different ideas begin to inform his account of exploits and achievements; in fact this new orientation should be recognized as a major aspect of his "development." Still, for his Oriental material, no other principle of organization compares in importance with *hybris* and its sequel.

As we turn from Herodotus to Thucydides, the contrast is striking. *Hybris* has ceased to hold sway; this last remainder of the divine powers who formerly directed the course of events has followed them into limbo. Thucydides prefers secular categories, and he has no difficulty in finding them; for the specific human impulses that were lurking behind the collective term *hybris* had long been known and would come to the fore as soon as the moral judgment and the religious perspective suggested by *hybris* were abandoned. To be sure, the word as such occurs at times, for instance in both of the conflicting explanations for the Mytilinean defection. Cleon's diagnosis takes us for a short spell back into the intellectual atmosphere of earlier generations: Unexpected prosperity of a community produces *hybris* in the cities (III 39.4).[3] Yet as we read on and learn about human nature and its lack of respect for mild rulers we know that we find ourselves in a changed, more sophisticated climate of thought. Also conceived in a new and more realistic spirit is Cleon's estimate of the psychological and political results to be expected if the brutal decision about Mytilene is rescinded. What will happen if the Assembly decides to limit the death sentence to the minority responsible for the secession? Allied cities witnessing a rebellion which, though crushed, is not

---

1964) 22ff. offers a warning, but his criteria are exclusively lexicographic. I admit that Croesus is no clear case. See also Lionel Pearson, *CPh* 52 (1957) 229f.

[3] Cf. Eur. frg. 437f. In Thucydides, see for ὕβρις also II 65.9. On I 38.4 and the very few other instances of noun and verb I can only agree with Huart, 473 n. 5 that they are "peu characteristique."

punished with the utmost severity, will be prone to defection, since they realize that the alternative prospects are success or a penalty which they can afford to pay (*ibid.* 7).

The opponent, Diodotus, completely disagrees with the psychological premises of this reasoning. It is, he argues (III 45), a matter of experience that no punishment however severe will deter a person bent on committing a crime.[4] For the motives that operate are powerful enough to disregard every threat of punishment. What are these motives? In specifying them (45.4–6), Diodotus begins with a distinction between poverty and its opposite, ἐξουσία which we may, however inadequately, render by "affluence."[5] Poverty "forces" men into daring deeds, while affluence produces a desire for more. The final result, we understand, is the same. In the closely parallel structure of the two thoughts, the "need" (ἀνάγκη) caused by desperate poverty is balanced by *hybris* and proud confidence (φρόνημα) both of which are engendered by wealth. Need and *hybris* are the immediate agents; both drive men into actions involving the greatest risk. If it is difficult for us to visualize "need" and *hybris* in analogous roles (for we think of the one as an external, of the other as a psychological condition), we may remember Thucydides' penchant for not truly symmetrical antitheses.[6] Next, Diodotus, looking beyond poverty and affluence, tries to cover other external constellations and events (ξυντυχίαι). Each of

[4] See esp. Stahl, p. 122. From the large bibliography on this contest I cite him because he makes an attempt (pp. 119ff.) analogous to my own to use Thucydides' "theoretical" statements for the understanding of the actual developments described by him.

[5] Gomme and others prefer "power"; J. de Romilly in the Budé translation "grandeur."

[6] See above Chapter IV. One may ask how far ἀνάγκη has become "internalized." Construction and meaning of a clause (ὡς ἑκάστη τις κατέχεται, 45.4) are disputed. J. de Romilly in her translation, Regenbogen (47), and Gomme *ad loc.* differ widely, and so do earlier commentators. My own interpretation is closest to Gomme (including the acceptance of ἑκάστῃ *scil.* ὀργῇ, for ἑκάστη).

them may carry men into hazardous courses; for each produces a "mood" (ὀργή) likely to have such effect.[7] The observations in III 82 about assimilation of tempers to external conditions—called τὰ παρόντα there, ξυντυχίαι here—coincide with Diodotus' point of view (this may encourage us to treat his opinions as in accord with Thucydides' own).[8]

Diodotus' argument includes some further points. In all such conditions man is led into danger ὑπ' ἀνηκέστου τινὸς κρείσσονος. Something "stronger" and overmastering is at work—stronger, evidently, than man who has no remedy against it. This is a remarkable admission of the suprahuman, quasi-demonic power that passions, moods, emotions, or whatever we may call these irrational forces exert.[9] If such is their hold, it is indeed futile—"very naïve" (45.7)—to look to laws or terror as restraints upon "human nature." When Medea's passion, her θυμός, governs her deliberations, she cannot help doing what she realizes will be the source of her own misery.

But we have not yet exhausted Diodotus' psychology. In each such undertaking, he goes on to say, hope and desire (ἔρως) play a fatal part, desire by giving the lead and conceiving the plot, hope by the wishful thinking that expects to find the path smooth and assumes that the incalculable τύχη will favor the undertaking. They, too, are irresistible: "Invisible as they are, they prove stronger than the dangers

[7] *Hdt.* III 80.3 is remotely comparable.

[8] The archaic thought: man's νόος (or θυμός) is like the day which Zeus brings about (*Od.* 18.136f.; Archil. 68 D. 131 W.) is not too different in conception; for the reference to Zeus has something conventional, and Archilochus' καὶ φρονεῦσι τοῖ' ὁκοίοις ἐγκυρέωσιν ἔργμασιν (132 W.) takes us still closer to Thucydides. Cf. Hermann Fränkel's familiar article: "Man's 'ephemeros' nature . . . ," *TAPhA* 77 (1946) 131ff., esp. 135. Finley, *Essays* 34, reminds us that in Sophocles φύσις remains unchanged even in catastrophe. On ὀργή in Thucydides see also Regenbogen, *Kleine Schriften* (Munich, 1961) 235.

[9] See Pericles' reference in II 64.1 to the νόσος, another ἀνήκεστον (47.4; note 50.1); cf. Adam Parry, *BICS* (1969) 106ff., esp. 115f.

that are in view." Decidedly, this "rationalism" is far from underrating the intangible (as we might say for "invisible"), irrational forces.[10] And if Diodotus, in the last sentence, has referred to τύχη, but only as included in the optimistic calculations of "hope," he immediately afterward (45.6) gives τύχη itself a place in his scheme of motivations. This is another completely irrational factor; for as Diodotus himself points out, τύχη presents itself, *scil.* as good fortune, when least counted upon and leads individuals and cities to overrate their resources in critical situations. Only after all this has been carefully set forth and we have become convinced of man's helplessness does Diodotus use the words "human nature" (45.7). It has been the subject of the entire argument.

In this scheme of causation, *hybris* has its place, but compared with the large territory that it formerly occupied it is a rather small place. An unprejudiced examination of what makes people rush to their doom reveals impulses at work that must be designated by words other and more specific than *hybris*. But these impulses operate not only in decisions of so critical or catastrophical a nature. The new psychology applies everywhere in man's life. It is a purely secular psychology[11] whose principal tenet is the distinction between reason and a variety of irrational inclinations. The latter may cooperate with reason and doubtless often do so; yet the instances of

[10] For Diodotus' psychology see F. Wassermann, pp. 36ff. W. Müri, *MH* 4 (1947) 252ff., 268ff., is important also for the place of φύσις and ὀργή. Huart, pp. 141ff., counts 76 instances of hope (ἐλπίς) in Thucydides against 14 in Herodotus. On the arguments of Diodotus cf. R. P. Winnington-Ingram, *BICS* 12 (1965) 70ff.

[11] J. de Romilly, *Imperialism*, 327 observes: "Hybris becomes something strictly human." Her chapter on the psychology of imperialism (pp. 322ff.) does include many passages that could illustrate *hybris*—if indeed this concept had the same place in Thucydides' thought as in Herodotus'. Del Grande (see n. 1) professedly argues on this assumption (in the "Melian Dialogue": "Tucidide da la mano al Erodoto," p. 248). I trust that I have made clear why I take a different view.

conflict between them and reason are of far greater interest. In the contest between Cleon and Diodotus this conflict is in the offing: On Cleon's view, reason ought to keep potential rebels conscious of the brutal punishment that awaits them. His arguments are, however, not formulated in terms of reason and emotions. Not reason, but fear and a policy of terror should keep at bay the irrational forces bent on a secession.[12]

Is a clear-cut theory of the opposition between reason and irrational forces more than we may expect in this age which extols reason and tends to look at matters in perspectives suggested by reason?[13] We may as well accept the testimony of the *Protagoras* (352b), where people in general are said to know about the conflict between knowledge (ἐπιστήμη) and a variety of impulses, each of them stronger so that it "drags knowledge about like a slave." Here the forces opposed to knowledge are pleasure and pain, desire, fear (ἡδονή, λύπη, ἔρως, φόβος), and the untranslatable θυμός. No generic concept is used to comprehend them. Not much later, however, we meet the word πάθος (352e6) and are meant to understand quite literally a "suffering"; whoever "suffers" fear or a strong desire, is unable to act in accordance with what he realizes to be best.[14]

The only concept common to the argument in Thucydides

[12] For much that follows cf. Huart's work, of which I learned only after the first draft of this chapter was completed. Moving along lines parallel to mine, he has caused me to make some corrections and to shorten where I had nothing to add to his observations.

[13] III 45.4. Fear, too, would normally be considered as something irrational. In the present context this is irrelevant; what matters is that while the δεινά resulting from a policy of frightfulness are "seen," the irrational impulses are "invisible," and yet stronger (45.5). For δέος and φόβος, Thucydides' words for "fear," cf. J. de Romilly, *Classica et Mediaevalia* 17 (1956) 119ff. (δέος slightly more intellectual). Cf. also Huart, pp. 124ff.

[14] Only reason is "active," and everything that interferes with it renders man "passive." Cf. *Prt.* 352c,e. In Latin *passio* seems to have acquired the analogous meaning only with Christian authors such as St. Augustine.

and the *Protagoras* is "love" (= strong desire). Nevertheless in a broader sense both are concerned with the same topic, the power of man's irrational drives and the impotence of reason when confronted by them.

If after Thucydides and Plato we still wish to hear Euripides, we should listen to Phaedra as she explains "how the life of mortals is ruined" (*Hipp.* 375-430). The more general and theoretical section of this discourse has again one item, pleasure, in common with the passage of the *Protagoras*, yet none with Diodotus' analysis. This need not surprise us, since Phaedra lists tendencies that stand in the way, and slow down, the right resolution, whereas the other two passages refer to strong impulses capable of competing with such resolutions by pursuing different goals. Nevertheless *eros*, present in the other two contexts, deserves a place also in Phaedra's disquisition; for it is the cause of her "illness" and in her own case the explanation for "why life is ruined." Very appropriately it makes its appearance as soon as she passes from the general argument to the specific form in which it applies to herself (vv. 391f.). Her "theory" places on the one side γνώμη and γιγνώσκειν (vv. 377, 380), εὖ φρονεῖν (v. 378), and also ἐπίσταστθαι (v. 380),[15] on the other sloth, pleasure (for which she offers two illustrations), and "bad shame," the last item designating inhibitions of the wrong kind that prevent us from acting as true knowledge bids us to (vv. 381-387). These opponents of true knowledge give the impression of being chosen at random; whether all of them are especially relevant for Phaedra, as the recent editor of the play suggests, need not detain us now.[16] On the whole

[15] See vv. 377ff. and for the obstacles vv. 381-387. Here too ὕβρις is absent. Although in Euripides the word appears more often than in Thucydides, by comparison with earlier writers its place seems peripheral. This development requires further study. *Hipp.* 474 and *Ba.* 375, 555 (576, but note also v. 247) recall the traditional pattern—but in a problematic fashion.

[16] Cf. my critical comments (*AJPh* 88, 1967, 87f.) on Barrett's

there is certainly the largest interaction between the new psychological convictions and the study and analysis of human actions. Experiments and discoveries take place in the realm of theory as well as in the observation of practice.

Phaedra is not content with theorizing. Having discovered why the right knowledge does not normally issue in corresponding action, she is determined to be an exception and to this end has devised a strategy that includes complete silence about her "illness" and, if nothing else will avail, suicide by starvation (vv. 401ff.). But despite her clear realization of the issue and despite her refusal to make concessions, she yields, if only an inch, and finds herself trapped.[17] Eros has proved stronger. Euripides, who very probably in his "first" *Hippolytus* had allowed Phaedra readily to surrender to her passion,[18] this time makes us witness Eros slowly but surely triumphing over a most stubborn effort to resist him. Phaedra's gradual yielding is the subject of a minute and almost clinically precise study. Astonishingly enough, the gain in scientific accuracy is at the same time a gain in poetic quality.

In the *Medea*, another passion, a fanatic desire for revenge and for punishment of her treacherous husband, proves irresistible. She herself admits that her θυμός has taken control of her plans,[19] and there is not as in Phaedra a struggle between reason and passion, but Medea feels one passion, her ferocious hatred of Jason, fight with another, the love for her

commentary. For the inhibiting effect of "bad shame" see my article, *Hermes* 101 (1973), 420ff.

[17] Cf. *Hipp.* 310-352 and the developments beginning at vv. 490ff. which culminate in the decisions of vv. 724-731.

[18] The inevitable uncertainty of the reconstruction is known. Still even Barrett, pp. 30f., though particularly cautious admits a "shameless Phaedra" for the earlier play. See below, n. 70.

[19] See the concluding lines of her monologue (*Med.* 1079f.) as interpreted by Hans Diller, *Hermes* 94 (1966) 267ff. William W. Fortenbaugh, *GRBS* 11 (1970) 233ff., has done well to treat *Hipp.* 373ff. and *Med.* 1079f. in relation to Aristotle's bipartite psychology.

children. Reason, though telling her what misery she will inflict upon herself (v. 1088), has no power of its own. Its resources serve her desire for revenge. At the height of the conflict, when we have watched her waver back and forth between one strong impulse and the other, she persuades herself that the brutal plan must run its course, and in words of deep compassion bids her children farewell.[20]

Unable to conquer her passionate desire for revenge, Medea is, despite all differences, comparable to Phaedra, who, desperately as she fights the power of *eros*, in the end succumbs. It may be this overwhelming force of love that made it the prototype of any emotion so powerful that, when it takes possession of individuals or of groups, it leaves them without remedy or defense. Diodotus' "incurable" (ἀνήκεστον) is uniquely appropriate.[21] He uses both *eros* and "incurable" in speaking of the state of mind in which communities, disregarding all counsels of prudence, all dangers, and warning examples, rush into an adventure whose chances of success are highly dubious (III 45.4f.). For Thucydides himself, the

[20] Love for her children also rebels against her resolution before the final monologue; see e.g. vv. 790ff., 923ff.; still, it is clearly in the fluctuations of the monologue (vv. 1021-1080) that the conflict reaches its crisis. Like Phaedra's struggle, it represents a great enrichment of psychological insight. For an analysis of the monologue cf. Schadewaldt, *Monolog und Selbstgespräch* (Berlin, 1926) 194-198. Contradictions in the monologue brought into focus by recent studies (see G. A. Seeck, *GRBS* 9, 1968, 291ff., with references to Regenbogen, *Eranos* 48, 1950, 21ff., and others) must be admitted but in my opinion also accepted and have little or no bearing on Medea's psychology. In the text I still consider the excision of vv. 1062f. as the best solution, despite Seeck's vigorous arguments to the contrary. M. D. Reeve (*CQ* 22, 1972, 51ff.) carries merciless logic to extremes. His rationalism is alien to Euripides' own, and his paper actually shows what kind of inconsistencies are possible in Euripides.

[21] Gomme in his paraphrase *ad loc.* does justice to the place of ἀνηκέστον in the syntax and thought of the sentence. I should say the same of H. P. Stahl, p. 122, but have misgivings about the rendering in the Budé edition and cannot extract much meaning from O. Regenbogen, p. 167.

Sicilian expedition is inspired by ill-founded hopes and a far too sanguine opinion about the ease with which the enterprise could be accomplished. Being determined on it, the Athenians are unwilling to heed Nicias' prudent warnings. An *eros*, we read, is taking possession of young and old alike (VI 24.3) and, as Diodotus described it, this *eros* is accompanied by an optimistic hope (εὐέλπιδες ὄντες), in this instance for safe return. If the excessive eagerness (ἄγαν ἐπιθυμία, 24.4) discourages any thought of arresting it, it certainly may be said to defy cure.[22]

Early in this chapter we mentioned Herodotus' application of the *hybris*-punishment scheme to the Oriental monarchs and his occasional use of it elsewhere. In each instance we may assume that the information at his disposal justified such organization of his narrative. Still, we may doubt whether the *hybris* pattern was as appropriate to the conduct of any Persian king as it would have been to the Athenians when voting and setting out for the Sicilian War. And yet there is no hint of *hybris* in Thucydides' account. Ἔρως and the other impulses that we have mentioned, most noticeably hope (ἐλπίς), take its place. Nor is divine wrath or jealousy aroused; instead the catastrophe is due to a sequence of mistakes, each of them aggravating the results of the preceding, and one of the worst being caused by a piety that Thucydides, normally so reserved in such judgments, sees fit to stigmatize as excessive.[23]

The secular psychology recognizes "compulsion"; yet no matter how strong it may be, neither Thucydides nor, as a

[22] Note also the comments in III 65.4 on another instance of unrealistic ἐλπίς engendered by a παρὰ λόγον εὐπραγία. Here it is the cause (αἰτία) for serious miscalculations. For an ἔρως στρατείας see also Eur. *IA* 808f., where it is however οὐκ ἄνευ θεῶν (cf. v. 1264). Most recently ἐλπίς in Thucydides has been studied by Harry C. Avery, *Hermes* 101 (1973) 1ff.

[23] See VII 50.4 on the eclipse of the moon, Nicias' reaction, and Thucydides' comment on it.

rule, Euripides ascribes it to the operation of a suprahuman power. Daemons who formerly used to work upon man from without or within have lost their standing. What exerts such force must be a part of man's own make-up. ἦθος ἀνθρώπῳ δαίμων, Heraclitus' saying (22B119 D.-K.),[24] applies to many a character in Euripides (for Medea θυμός would fill the place of ἦθος). Still, under very specific conditions the "incurable" affliction may in Euripides take the shape of a god who asserts his power over willing and unwilling, rational and irrational alike.[25] In the *Bacchae*, where Dionysus appears in person, the city is seized with a new strange frenzy; most individuals are drawn into the whirl, the most rational and reluctant falls victim to a ruse. Nevertheless, the play is not simply a victory of passion or "collective" madness over reason. Its significance extends farther; it shows us the Greek mind overpowered by the emotionalism of an Oriental religion.[26] The barbarians (vv. 13ff., 55ff., 482ff., 604, etc.) conquer the Greek *polis*—not by the numerical superiority of a huge army but by something far stronger, their fanatic devotion to a miracle-working savior god who releases man from the miseries of life. Euripides strikes us as centuries ahead of his time. Even if the play was conceived and worked out in

[24] I do not know whether Eur. frg. 1018, where our νοῦς is the god for each of us, is comparable. See E. R. Dodds, *CR* 43 (1929), 99.

[25] The victory of Aphrodite over Phaedra's determination remains the most familiar example; see esp. vv. 359ff. I know how controversial it is and appreciate Lesky's observations in *Euripide, Entretiens sur l'antiq. class.* VI (Vandoeuvres-Genève, 1960) 136. Still the statement made in my text may, I trust, stand. See also Pasiphaë's defense in the *Cretans* (frg. 82.21 Austin); and note the quick transition from δαίμων to σύνεσις, *Or.* 394-396 (cf. νόσος in v. 395, λύπη in v. 397, the reference being essentially to one and the same condition). In *Tr.* 929ff. (esp. 940ff., 983ff.) the issue between Helen and Hecuba is in part whether Helen herself or Aphrodite is responsible. We should not look for Euripides' own answer in the debate.

[26] Cf. Dodds, in the "Introduction" to *Euripides: Bacchae* (Oxford, 1944) xx ff., and *HThR* 33 (1940) 171ff., on the invasion of Athens by foreign cults of a comparable type at the time.

Macedonia, it reflects the psychological exhaustion of Athens at the end of a long and terrible war. As in this, so in other late plays of Euripides the confidence in reason is on the wane. Σοφίζομαι δὲ καὶ . . . τέχνας πορίζω πανταχῇ νικώμενος says Agamemnon (*IA* 744f.), admitting the defeat of his rational devices.

We return to earlier plays, having so far dealt only with Medea and Phaedra. In *Andromache* we witness a violent outburst of jealousy on the part of Hermione, who is seconded by her father Menelaus.[27] In the *Hecuba*, the aged queen, thrown from her high position into misery and captivity, deprived of her last two children one after the other, ultimately collects what is left of her strength to take the most fiendish vengeance on Polymestor, the treacherous murderer of her youngest son. Indignation at his foul deed combines with the final stroke of grief to transform a warm-hearted mother into a savage plotter of cruelty.[28] Alcmene's hatred of Eurystheus prompts her to kill him, although his life has been spared by Athens. It is a strong hatred; built up in the course of many years, it has hardened into a firm, yet cold determination, which does not reach the same pitch of intensity as Hecuba's passion.[29] In fact there are in the preserved plays no other characters so completely in the grip of a passion as Medea, Phaedra, and Hecuba—unless it be Eteocles in the *Phoenissae*, one of the latest plays (whereas the other three are "early"). His ambition, centered upon the

[27] *Andr.* 147ff.; cf. vv. 309ff. I do not question the fundamental differences between the conception of this play and e.g. *Medea* (see Kitto, pp. 231f.).

[28] See esp. *Hec.* 736ff., 787ff., the developments beginning vv. 953ff., and the account (mixed with accusation) of Hecuba's plot (vv. 1145-1183). Cf. Pohlenz, *Die Griech. Tragödie* (Göttingen, 2nd ed., 1954) I 280. D. J. Conacher, *AJPh* 82 (1961) 1ff., and *Euripidean Drama* 155ff., despite polemic against Pohlenz, gives essentially a refinement of the same opinion. See also frg. 1038.

[29] See *Heracl.* 941ff., cf. vv. 1022ff., 1045ff. On Alcmene cf. G. Zuntz, *The Political Plays of Euripides* (Manchester, 1955) 36f.

tyranny of Thebes, vents itself in the notorious hyperbolic declaration: εἴπερ γὰρ ἀδικεῖν χρή, τυραννίδος πέρι κάλλιστον ἀδικεῖν, τἄλλα δ' εὐσεβεῖν χρεών (vv. 523f.). To the same trilogy belonged the *Chrysippus*, where Laius, seized by homosexual desire, yields, although he knows it to be wrong and unwise (frgs. 840f.).[30]

Lycus, the tyrant of Thebes, claims to act not from enmity but merely in the interest of his safety when, during the absence of Heracles in Hades, he exterminates Heracles' family; he is ready to argue about matters as remote from the issue as the value of bow and arrow, and he certainly knows nothing of the daemonic power that drives Medea and tortures Phaedra.[31] Finally Creusa in the *Ion* steels her heart and tries to be as indifferent to right and wrong as anyone else who plots murder in Euripides; her gentle soul is driven on by despair when the violence that she once suffered has suddenly and most poignantly been brought home to her consciousness.[32]

Euripides is too great a poet to confine himself to the standard passions and their usual manifestations. He knows more about the human heart. He knows, and with his eye free to watch, his mind free to study the darker, often concealed phases of experience, he ventures ahead to new explorations. He knows how adulteresses tremble in the darkness of their

[30] See *Ph.* 499ff., esp. 503ff. (note Iocaste's description vv. 531ff., 549ff.), 588-642 (624 etc.). For the date of the *Chrysippus* see *Schol. Eurip.* I 244 Schw.; for the content *TGF* 839ff. Cf. Snell, pp. 63f. It is understandable that some scholars (Schadewaldt, *Monolog*, 251 n. 3, Webster, *The Tragedies of Euripides*, London, 1967, 111, *al.*) would prefer for this play a date before the *Phoenissae*. Cf. again Lesky, pp. 138f. In the *Aeolus* incest was an ingredient of a plot that we can no more reconstruct than that of the *Cretans*. *Aeolus* must have been produced before the *Clouds* (see *TGF* s.vv.).

[31] *HF* 140ff.; Lesky, too (pp. 138f.), holds that "Wissen um die gefährlichen λόγος-feindlichen Urmächte" was most productive in the period including *Med.*, *Hipp.*, *Hec.*

[32] See *Ion passim*, esp. vv. 747ff., 934ff., 970ff., 985ff.

bedchambers and fear that the walls may disclose their secret to the husband. Interpreting the Erinyes of Clytaemestra as pangs of conscience, he visualizes Orestes as physically and mentally destroyed by the consciousness of his deed.[33] More conclusively than any other Greek author does he prove that not only conscience but also repentance antedates Christianity.[34] His Electra is so bitter about what she regards an unbearable degradation that, although trying to appreciate her husband and his forbearance, she is unable for any length of time to keep up an urbane tone of conversation. Euripides knows the phases and symptoms of a despair that sometimes turns with accusations against the gods and at other times seeks its satisfaction in abusing a fellow human being.[35] For the special grief of a new widower returning home from the funeral of his wife he has as intimate an understanding as for the feelings of an exile permitted a few hours visit of his home town.[36] He also knows what experiences make a woman's heart change from love to hatred and realizes (unlike some of his critics) that even a character so savagely

[33] *Hipp.* 415ff.; *Or.* 253-279, 396, 407ff. (see also *El.* 1177ff., 1190ff., etc.). Orestes' psychological (and physical) suffering in *Or.* has, as far as I am aware, not yet received the close study for which it calls. For some good points see Lesky, pp. 137ff.; for some others, Wesley D. Smith, *Hermes* 95 (1967) 29ff., though he overstates his case. On "conscience" see F. Zucker, *Semantica, Rhetorica, Ethica* (Berlin, 1963) 96ff. A. Cancrini's recent monograph *Syneidesis* (Rome, 1970) includes too much under this heading.

[34] For repentance see *Alc.* 935ff.; *Hipp.* 1408ff. (1458ff.); *El.* 1177ff. On Admetus Lesky, p. 145, is closer to the truth than A. M. Dale in the "Introduction" to her edition, xxv ff.; valuable, too, are his observations about a "Labilität" of Euripides' characters.

[35] See e.g. *HF* 207ff., 217ff., 339; *El.* 198ff., 404, 408; *Ion* 859ff. (881ff.). Note also a passage such as *IT* 344-353. Iphigeneia considers herself ἠγριωμένη as result of her dreams. Fortunately this is not borne out.

[36] Cf. Walter Jens' perceptive observations, *Eurip. Sämtliche Tragödien* (Stuttgart, 1955) "Einleitung" xi ff. For "loneliness" he refers to Admetus after the burial and to Clytaemestra in *IA* (1173ff.); for the exile to Polynices, *Ph.* 366ff.

determined as Medea will shed tears when she has to go through with the murder of her children. Aeschylus knew the agony Agamemnon suffered when his beloved daughter had to be sacrificed; indeed he probably created the excruciating choice between two evils (Ag. 205ff.). Euripides takes up the subject in his *Iphigeneia in Aulis* and throughout large parts of his play develops with far more sympathy and delicacy the desperate struggles in the soul of the king. He has observed manifestations of madness and of neurosis and is said to be almost scientifically accurate about the gradual process of awakening from a trance.[37]

No more than Euripides does Thucydides consider himself restricted to a limited number of standard irrational motives. Of the new manifestations of human brutality and shameless egotism that the war brought into the open we have already spoken. The atrocities in Corcyra showed Thucydides how low human beings could sink. New too and "like nothing" (VII 71.2) within the realm of normal experiences was the intense excitement—most of all the "fear"—of those who watched the last battle in the harbor of Syracuse. Most probably this account of various and changing emotions is, like much else in his work, a mosaic of information received from different quarters, each of his informants supplying some of the details. Thucydides with his superb power of synthesis, which will engage us later (in Chapter VI), fashions them into a compact whole (VII 71). The reader is forced into continuous psychological participation with the sufferings of the crowd, which, unable to help, watches from the shore how the battle develops. With extreme vividness (ἐνάργεια) Thucydides conveys the fluctuations between hope and fear, the alternating gain and loss of courage. It was a physical, not merely a psychological experience for the onlookers, whose bodies responded to every new impression:

[37] Cf. Dodds, *CR* 43 (1929) 99f.

καὶ τοῖς σώμασιν αὐτοῖς ἴσα τῇ δόξῃ περιδεῶς ξυναπονεύοντες ἐν τοῖς χαλεπώτατα διῇγον (71.3).[38] In the end, one single shout of dismay and despair was the response of all to the defeat (71.6). Such minute description of psychological responses, at once objective and sympathetic, opens a new field for Greek narrative art. Thucydides, who discovered it, immediately produced a masterpiece that probably remained unmatched, despite all efforts of later writers to make history as dramatic and pathetic as possible.[39]

Thucydides and Euripides are students of *ἀνθρωπίνη φύσις*, human nature as it actually is, something markedly different from Sophocles' *ἀγαθή* or *εὐγενὴς φύσις*. In a small way, the orator Antiphon, too, makes his contribution to this subject, e.g. when he sets forth the motives that impel human beings to commit a grave crime such as murder (5.57ff.). Yet the concept of "human nature" and the words for it are familiar from Thucydides, where many arguments, discussions, and individual pronouncements relate to the subject. Of chapters that include the actual phrase, probably the best known is his comprehensive description of changes in moral outlook (III 82f.). These changes, first revealed in the Corcyrean atrocities, manifest themselves in actions, in valuations, and most directly in the connotations of the words applied to human conduct. Curiously the same sentences in III 82 embody Thucydides' belief in the basic constancy of human

38 Cf. Huart, p. 140.

39 Less dramatic but no less perceptive is the re-creation of the atmosphere of paralyzing fear that in 411 helped the Four Hundred to seize power. Here Thucydides (VIII 66) does not work up to a climax; instead he sets forth symptom after symptom of people's reaction to the intimidation, relying on the cumulative effect of this procedure. The result is mutual distrust throughout the *demos*; nobody dares to speak out. The tone of the chapter is detached, and it may be in point to remember Thucydides' critical view of democratic mentality and institutions. The reader, nevertheless, sympathizes with people helpless in this condition of terror.

nature and his conviction that its manifestations are bound to vary with the changing circumstances. The two ideas are complementary, for human nature changes in a regular, more or less predictable manner. In peace and prosperous conditions, individuals and communities are in a friendlier mood, whereas war, that brutal teacher, through its "unwelcome necessities" renders men's tempers correspondingly ruthless. For the proposition that man's moods (*ὀργαί*) depend on external circumstances, Thucydides in III 45 provides wealth and poverty as concrete illustrations; in III 82, peace and war serve the same purpose. Insights of the kind were nothing entirely new. Homer and other early poets had formulated them in simpler ways.[40] Still, it was only in the course of a war, and of a war creating quite unusual living conditions, that the extent to which civilized human beings could alter their habits and become barbarized came to light.

Thucydides' description of the plague also includes, side by side with the physical sufferings, observations about unusual human behavior that came into the open because there were no longer reasons for concealing less reputable desires. Probing for norms recognized (*scil.* by implication) in such new behavior, Thucydides sees pleasure and profit in control: *ὅτι δὲ ἤδη τε ἡδὺ πανταχόθεν τε ἐς αὐτὸ* (text uncertain) *κερδαλέον, τοῦτο καὶ καλὸν καὶ χρήσιμον κατέστη* (II 53.3).[41] Among psychological motives, Thucydides gives prominence to the impression caused by sudden changes, especially of an economic kind. After the unexpected death of wealthy people, men formerly poor would suddenly find themselves affluent and would wish to enjoy as quickly as possible what for a

[40] See again Fränkel, *TAPhA* 77 (1946) 135, esp. his reference to *Od.* 18.130-140. For the different *ἦθος* of war and peace cf. also Thuc. I 120.3f.

[41] For the phrasing cf. V 105.4 and for *κατέστη* used in a "subjective" sense (*scil.* in the outlook of the Athenians then and there) cf. p. 109 and n. 49. For the text of II 53.3 as quoted above I follow Gomme after pondering his comments *ad loc.*

time was theirs, yet might no less quickly pass on to others. The realization that pious worshippers of the gods suffered the same fate as others deprived divine punishment of its former deterrent effect, nor would the thought of worldly tribunals frighten men who did not know whether they would live to face them.

Thucydides thus became acquainted with modes of human conduct for which he had not been prepared. He observes and records but at the same time uses his penetrating mind to "explain" his observations. His explanations are experiments, a fact we easily forget because the apodictic tenor of his presentation keeps us spellbound and prevents us from wondering about alternative or additional causes.

Although Thucydides treats his subject, the Peloponnesian War, by and large as a sequence of political and military events, no rigid principle excludes moral developments; in fact we have found him giving attention even to changes of usage (Chapter IV). During the plague, Thucydides had been in Athens and had witnessed the changes in people's conduct. What happened in Corcyra had probably been reported by eye-witnesses, and as the war continued he realized its significance. For, unlike the human instincts and passions released by the plague, the brutalities of Corcyra were the first example of something destined to become increasingly frequent.[42]

Numerous passages in Thucydides throw light on human nature but relatively few frankly declare that they bear on this topic. Cleon, while criticizing the preferential treatment accorded to the Mytileneans within the League, supports his strictures by the generalization: *πέφυκε γὰρ καὶ ἄλλως ἄνθρωπος τὸ μὲν θεραπεῦον ὑπερφρονεῖν, τὸ δὲ μὴ ὑπεῖκον θαυμάζειν* (II 39.5). Though spoken by Cleon, the words are germane to Thucydides' own realistic appraisal of man. In this instance,

[42] See III 82.1 (the dubious version in 84.1 says the same in plainer language).

the desire to look upon the world in a disillusioned spirit has been carried to cynical conclusions. Slightly less provocative but not truly different in outlook is a statement of Hermocrates: "I do not blame the Athenians, if they avail themselves of the opportunities offered them by the mutual hostilities between Sicilian cities": πέφυκε γὰρ τὸ ἀνθρωπεῖον διὰ παντὸς ἄρχειν μὲν τοῦ εἴκοντος, φυλάσσεσθαι δὲ τὸ ἐπιόν (IV 61.5). Obviously certain tendencies of human nature exist διὰ παντός. They are merely revealed or intensified by war.

Other generalizations if less extreme in tone and content are nonetheless inspired by the same uncompromising realism. We did nothing that is not human, declare the Athenian delegates at the pre-war convention in Sparta, when we yielded to the three most powerful motivations—honor, fear, and self-interest; they caused us to accept the hegemony when it was offered and not to let it go afterward. At all times the weaker has to suffer encroachment from the stronger (I 76.2), and to rule over others is simply a part of human nature (I 76.3). Here we also learn that nobody resorts to arguing about justice as long as he has the power to acquire something by force.

Since human nature is worth knowing also in its less rough aspects, we may choose a few of them at random. Man will at times respond most favorably to actions that hardly deserve to carry great weight: ἡ γὰρ τελευταία χάρις καιρὸν ἔχουσα, κἂν ἐλάσσων ᾖ, δύναται μεῖζον ἔγκλημα λῦσαι (I 42.2). Similarly, help extended in a particularly critical situation will be remembered and will influence the feelings of the recipient in a decisive manner. Whoever has acted thus will, even if previously an enemy, thereafter be considered a friend; conversely he who in a crisis is on the opposite side passes from the number of friends to that of enemies (I 41.3).

Pericles knows that the adverse effect of the plague upon Athenian morale corresponds to a habitual reaction to the unexpected: δουλοῖ γὰρ φρόνημα τὸ αἰφνίδιον καὶ ἀπροσδόκητον καὶ *τὸ πλείστῳ παραλόγῳ ξυμβαῖνον* (II 61.3). When Nicias seeks to prevent the large expedition to Sicily, he argues that the Athenians will inspire more fear as long as they remain distant; next in his order of preference would be a brief display of power without serious involvement. Such a display would prove effective because *τὰ διὰ πλείστου πάντες ἴσμεν θαυμαζόμενα καὶ τὰ πεῖραν ἥκιστα τῆς δόξης δόντα* (VI 11.4). His appeal to a general rule governing human responses is the more noteworthy if, as has lately been suggested,[43] earlier experiences in Sicily bear out his argument. Yet it is not by reference to them that Nicias—in truth, Thucydides—supports his contentions.

Alcibiades' principal explanation of why the Lacedaemonians should occupy Decelea is that the Athenians fear nothing more than this contingency. No greater hurt can be inflicted upon the enemies than by learning what they fear most and presenting them with just this as a *fait accompli* (VI 91.6).

This generalization is not likely to be taken from the common stock of strategic or political principles; it is formulated *ad hoc* to support the proposal that it fits so perfectly. Of other generalizations probably formulated for the first time I should instance *τὸ ἀντίπαλον δέος μόνον πιστὸν ἐς ξυμμαχίαν* (III 11.2), used by the Mytileneans to justify their secession. The Athenians will soon no longer treat them as allies because power—and fear—are no longer evenly balanced. This piece of realistic political wisdom would apply to more than one situation. While others too must have known it by instinct, they may have lacked the acumen and the almost cynical frankness to put it in words, and since the next sentence

[43] Cf. von Fritz, I 735, 738. If Thucydides kept so close to Nicias' actual speech—something exceptional but not on that account impossible—either of them would have transposed "historical" experience into generalization. It is, however, well to remember that the "limited intervention" of 427-24 ended rather ingloriously (IV 58-65).

contains an argument in support of the generalization, Thucydides' originality is probable. It would be a fair specimen of his outlook—cool, disillusioned, resolutely opposed to conventional pretenses. Broadly speaking, the propensity to generalize is so strong at the time (at least in literature; how far it reflects an actual habit of life we cannot know)[44] that it operates on the slightest excuse, or even without excuse, and not only for the larger issues of life or politics but also for minor problems.

Not simply the realistic but the pointedly and self-consciously realistic quality of these generalizations is the novel element. In the debate about Mytilene, Cleon urges the Athenians to envisage how the Mytileneans would have treated them if the roles were reversed. What he says is no everyday thought. In fact it is shrewd; yet the contingencies envisaged are so contrived that the intention of parading cleverness is palpably an end itself: *μάλιστα οἱ μὴ ξὺν προφάσει τινὰ κακῶς ποιοῦντες ἐπεξέρχονται καὶ διολλύναι* (J. M. Stahl: *διόλλυνται* MSS). This generalization may be traced back to a rule of still wider application, and the speaker—again, of course, the author—does not miss this opportunity: *ὁ γὰρ μὴ ξὺν ἀνάγκῃ τι παθὼν χαλεπώτερος διαφυγὼν τοῦ ἀπὸ τῆς ἴσης ἐχθροῦ* (III 40.6).

Whoever has recourse to such thoughts professes to handle a situation with a certain authority; for the implication is that he has seen comparable ones and knows how people usually act.[45] The pleasure of theorizing and discovering at every turn

[44] Finley, if I understand him correctly, takes a more positive view; see his *Essays* x f., 32f., 109f.; and *Thucydides* 65ff., where "capacity for abstraction" is "the very hallmark of the period" (pp. 66f.), though Thucydides' personal bent in that direction is not minimized.

[45] One more passage may be briefly considered. The Athenian envoys in Sparta, explaining why their city, despite its remarkable fairness toward the "allies," is exposed to criticism on their part, come forward with the generalization: *ἀδικούμενοι* (*scil.* in their own opinion) *οἱ ἄνθρωποι μᾶλλον ὀργίζονται ἢ βιαζόμενοι* (I 77.4). Surely a paradoxical

a truth not previously brought to light would prove attractive to bright minds in this age when traditional opinions were discredited and the individual intellect felt emancipated. No attempt is ever made to integrate a large number of these newly uncovered verities; that man's impulses are selfish is an insight that underlies a good number of these propositions, but such thought is never used as a kind of first principle from which to deduce other generalizations.

Turning once more from Thucydides to Euripides, we may begin by quoting Hecuba's reply to Agamemnon's qualified promise of help (*Hec.* 864-867): οὐκ ἔστι θνητῶν ὅστις ἔστ' ἐλεύθερος· ἢ χρημάτων γὰρ δοῦλός ἐστιν ἢ τύχης, ἢ πλῆθος αὐτὸν πόλεος ἢ νόμων γραφαὶ εἴργουσι χρῆσθαι μὴ κατὰ γνώμην τρόποις. As so often, Euripides is going out of his way. None of the obstacles mentioned actually applies to Agamemnon (although πλῆθος πόλεος comes close to στρατός).[46] It cannot help Hecuba's case to theorize about the fact that nobody is "free." Is it so great a surprise to her? Or is the theorizing an emotional relief? Given her extreme misery, neither the one nor the other hypothesis is truly satisfactory. Not to Hecuba, but to Euripides has this realization come, and he sees fit at this juncture to announce it. The validity of the thought rests on expanding the range of the word "freedom" (ἐλεύθερος) beyond the political sphere. Euripides does not compete with Thucydides in the elaborate phrasing of generalized statements (samples

---

conduct, yet Thucydides is able to account for it: τὸ μὲν γὰρ ἀπὸ τοῦ ἴσου δοκεῖ πλεονεκτεῖσθαι, τὸ δὲ ἀπὸ τοῦ κρείττονος καταναγκάζεσθαι. The latter condition was in fact endured, and without protest, by the same men who are now so vocal whenever they think that they have not been fairly treated (cf. 77.3, 5). Thus, the initial generalization is both empirically confirmed and psychologically explained.

46 Cf. H. F. Johansen, *General Reflection in Tragic Rhesis* (Copenhagen, 1959) 158, who in regard to his subject finds a peculiar technique in this play. He treats with special care the formal varieties occurring in generalizations, something of minor interest for my present purpose. On concepts of "freedom" in *Hec.* see St. G. Daitz, *Hermes* 99 (1971) 217ff. 221.

of which we have examined in Chapter IV); nor is he by and large as ambitious to come forward with new insights. *Hel.* 417ff.: ὅταν ἀνὴρ πράξῃ κακῶς ὑψηλός, εἰς ἀηθίαν πίπτει κακίω τοῦ πάλαι δυσδαίμονος can hardly have struck the audience with the force of a startling revelation, and ἀνάγκης οὐδὲν ἰσχύει πλέον slightly later (v. 514) in the same play is explicitly introduced as being no new wisdom but σοφῶν ἔπος (we hardly need such recommendation to accept it). There are many other instances, e.g., *IA* 333 γλῶσσ' ἐπίφθονον σοφή, where originality is dubious and can hardly have been Euripides' primary concern. Even the fascinating psychological theories of *Hipp.* 375ff. which it has taken Phaedra many a night's profound reflection to discover may have cost Euripides himself considerably less effort and need neither express his firm conviction nor be as original as we are prone to regard them. For interest in the effect of knowledge on conduct was not confined to Socrates and Euripides, and the originality of *Hipp.* 377ff. may lie in a slight variation of an opinion favored at the time by many.

Nevertheless, since Euripides' name is associated with a new realism, and this realism determines his treatment of entire plots, of characters, and of many matters of detail, it would be astonishing if the realism were not apparent also in his γνῶμαι and his experiments with generalization. We did after all recognize some originality in Hecuba's reaction to Agamemnon, although the novelty needed a word of comment. And we are free to read Medea's entire argument about the position of women (*Med.* 230-247) as a sequence of generalizations[47]—or alternatively as one basic proposition supported by other general statements sufficiently modern to shock the conventionally minded. Original thoughts may be extracted from Ion's broodings about the drawbacks of tyranny (*Ion* 621-632); some of what he says has been cast in the form of a general insight. A verse quoted from the *Scyrioi*

[47] See Johansen, *op. cit.*, 128.

(frg. 683): σοφοὶ δὲ συγκρύπτουσιν οἰκείας βλάβας would, if necessary, receive light from the prudential talk of the worldly wise nurse in the *Hippolytus*: ἐν σοφοῖσι γὰρ τόδ' ἐστὶ θνητῶν, λανθάνειν τὰ μὴ καλά (see vv. 465f.). New too and more realistic than tragedy used to be are the derogatory remarks about the "race" of heralds (e.g. *Or.* 89ff.) and, more important, the laments about the sad fate of exiles. The former may reproduce a contemporary prejudice, the latter certainly reflects an increasingly familiar experience; if Jocaste for αἱ δ' ἐλπίδες βόσκουσι φυγάδας, ὡς λόγος (*Ph.* 396) admits a debt to conventional opinion, Polynices' answer stresses the bitter realities obscured by this opinion: καλοῖς βλέπουσαί γ' ὄμμασιν, μέλλουσι δέ (v. 397). A fragment (904): ἄκρας εὐηθίας ἅπτοιτ' ἂν ὅστις τὴν φύσιν νικᾶν θέλει may fittingly conclude this selection from Euripides since it sums up much that we have said about his characters.[48]

More than once we have found or suspected traditional wisdom in Euripides' general statements. Yet tradition in this case is not only a broad but a vague concept. We must allow for the most variegated legacy. From the beginning, i.e. from the days of Homer and Hesiod, there had not only been normative *gnomai* designed to influence people's conduct but others of a rather empirical and, we need not hesitate to say, prudential cast. Παθὼν δέ τε νήπιος ἔγνω (Hes. *Op.* 218) would be confirmed by experience, and even a more daring assertion such as ἀλλ' ὅταν σπεύδῃ τις αὐτός, χὡ θεὸς συνάπτεται (A. *Pers.* 742)[49] would often be borne out and therefore continue to give confidence to men in trouble. Yet

[48] Johansen repeatedly observes that a remark may be gnomic in meaning or effect without being so in form. On p. 156 he instances *Or.* 804ff.: κτᾶσθ' ἑταίρους, μὴ τὸ συγγενὲς μόνον a general advice prompted by Pylades' unflinching loyalty. Cf. Thuc. III 82.6, where increasing confidence in friends at the expense of kinsmen is said to be a "trend."

[49] I believe, although without possibility of proof, the sentence to be a kind of proverb. The "cooperation" is not normally toward disaster.

this saying clearly includes an element of *a priori* belief and may in this respect be classed with the numerous affirmations in early poets that divine Justice comes without exception (e.g., Sol. 13.31 W.). A large number of maxims and generalized thoughts were bound to be handed on from generation to generation and would be quoted even after the conviction behind them had faded. In Euripides we have to reckon with several alluvial strata of *gnomai*, some of them normative, others empirical. If we treated the statement about envy aroused by a "wise tongue" as empirical and unlikely to be a new discovery, we may yet, despite the similarity of thought, look on Medea's pronouncement (v. 294) χρὴ δ' οὔποθ' ὅστις ἀρτίφρων πέφυκ' ἀνήρ, παῖδας περισσῶς ἐκδιδάσκεσθαι σοφούς as normative. Not a few Athenians would agree with it, yet the σοφία by which Euripides supports it, describing the reaction of different groups to children thus brought up, may have been something unusual. In Thucydides, the speakers are by and large above repeating outworn commonplaces; they reflect the author's disillusioned outlook to the extent that they would rather shock than please the bourgeois. In a desire for originality *à tout prix* they sometimes come forward with a piece of wisdom whose surface profundity dissolves on examination: τὸ γὰρ ἄπραγμον οὐ σῴζεται μὴ μετὰ τοῦ δραστηρίου τεταγμένον (II 63.3) is, soberly considered, a pretentious phrasing of what could better and with less puzzling effect be expressed by the first five words alone.

The distinction between normative and empirical generalizations, if somewhat artificial for the earlier periods, does prove useful for the authors of the late fifth century, especially again for Thucydides. It is a high degree of folly, declares Pericles in his last speech, to go to war if it is unnecessary and the prevailing conditions are satisfactory; but if the choice is between losing your independence and risking war with a good prospect of victory, to shun the risk is "more blameworthy" than to accept it (II 61.1). The judgments here pronounced put the opinion in the class of normative *gnomai*. Although dealing with an issue vital for Athens, Pericles (not to say, once more, Thucydides) thinks it wise to begin his defense by stating a fundamental truth about good and bad policy. From this he passes abruptly to the concrete situation.[50]

Generalized, too, yet allowing for different circumstances, is a normative statement by the Corinthian delegates at the first convention of the Peloponnesian League. As long as Sparta remains passive, the Athenians will move from success to success: καὶ ἡσυχαζούσῃ μὲν πόλει τὰ ἀκίνητα νόμιμα ἄριστα, πρὸς πολλὰ δὲ ἀναγκαζομένοις ἰέναι πολλῆς καὶ τῆς ἐπιτεχνήσεως δεῖ (I 71.3). No little experience would seem to lie behind this; still, since the sentence includes a statement as to what is best and ends by implying a necessary reform, it is more than a summary of experience. Rationality carried to a length previously unknown inspires normative as well as empirical generalizations.[51]

Gnomai of both types have a wide range. They may summarize or recommend an entire way of life. Archidamus first defends the Lacedaemonian traditions against misunderstandings, then comes forward with his "value judgment": πολύ τε διαφέρειν οὐ δεῖ νομίζειν ἄνθρωπον ἀνθρώπου, κράτιστον δὲ εἶναι ὅστις ἐν τοῖς ἀναγκαιοτάτοις παιδεύεται (I 84.4). The clause embodying his ideal is brief; but throughout this chapter, although he seemed merely to explain, to describe, and to justify, he has spoken in glowing language of the peculiar Lacedaemonian virtues. In substance, even if not in form, his account has set up a *paradeigma* of life.[52]

50 Cf. Hermocrates' general reflections about war and peace, their motives and καιροί in IV 59.2f. at the beginning of his speech; here too the application follows immediately (59.4).

51 Flexibility versus reluctance to change is also an issue in the contest between Cleon and Diodotus (III 37-48). The arguments have been analyzed in Chapter I, pp. 38ff.

52 Note e.g. μάλιστα and μόνον in 84.2 but also in 84.1 the insistence

This glorification of Sparta is challenged from a distance by Pericles' Funeral Oration, at once a description, an explanation, and a eulogy of the Athenian life. Values and virtues of this life are extolled, the superiority, in fact supremacy, among all forms of personal and community life is established.[53] There are touches of realism, to be sure, in the Oration, but taken as a whole it is an idealization. Athens as it had been and as the historian fondly remembers it becomes imperceptibly the ideal city.[54]

Surely if there is a *paradeigma*, an integrated ideal of life embodying human values of the highest order, it must contrast sharply with the brutal realities set forth throughout the *History* without mercy or illusion. The discrepancy, though in principle of the same kind, is far greater than the difference between normative and empirical *gnomai*. Are there other survivals of a nobler outlook on life? About the place of "Justice" (τὸ δίκαιον) we have formed impressions in Chapters I and IV, and may conclude that, though sometimes treated with respect, it never enjoys real power. Courage fares better; whether going under the name of εὐψυχία or another, it remains something essential.[55] An even more venerable legacy from the past was τὸ καλόν, the noble, honorable, glorious.

on freedom and a most glorious reputation. For "l'idéal et les vertus" including also the "valeurs," subjects to be discussed on the following pages, cf. again Huart's treatment, pp. 441ff.

[53] See e.g. II 37.1 (παράδειγμα), 39.1ff.; 40.2, 5; 41.3. Μόνοι recurs in 40.2, 5; 41.3, κράτιστοι *ibid*. 3.

[54] Cf. Jaeger, *Paideia* I 408f.; K. Reinhardt, *Von Werken und Formen* (Godesberg, 1948) 259ff., *al*. Idealization is traditional in the Athenian epitaphs, though Thucydides handles it very much in his own way; cf. Strasburger, pp. 20ff. (contested by Diller, *Gymnasium* 69, 1962, 199f. = *WdF* 98, 55ff.). Even power is idealized (e.g. 41.3), as I should argue against Hellmut Flashar "Der Epitaphios des Perikles," (*SHAW*, 1969, 1ff.), some of whose observations (pp. 22ff.) I welcome. For the other views of scholars see above, pp. 32f. and n. 35. Here I merely add that Archidamus' corresponding account in I 84 could hardly be called "realistic."

[55] Cf. above pp. 100ff., 107, 110.

Unlike τὸ ἀγαθόν, which may stand for the virtuous but also for the useful, τὸ καλόν promises no material advantage. In Thucydides, it makes rare but perhaps, on that account, all the more noteworthy appearances. In the very first contest of speeches, the Corinthians argue that for a colony such as Corcyra, even if it has legitimate grievances about the mother-town, it would be καλόν to bear them with patience (I 38.5). Oddly enough, the Funeral Oration includes, with the exception of the well-known φιλοκαλοῦμεν (II 40.1), no reference to τὸ καλόν (still it is present, though not explicitly present). The one event of the War where speeches as well as narrative give prominence to καλά and τὸ καλόν is the last battle in the harbor of Syracuse. After the Syracusan commanders have reminded their men ὅτι μὲν καλὰ τὰ προειργασμένα καὶ ὑπὲρ καλῶν ὁ ἀγὼν ἔσται (VII 66.1), the men think it καλόν (70.7) when the fight goes well and in the hope of cutting off the enemy's escape exert themselves περὶ τοῦ πλείονος ἤδη καλοῦ (71.1).

Considered as a whole,[56] the harvest for τὸ καλόν is far from large. In the "Melian Dialogue" the Lacedaemonians are accused of misusing time-honored value concepts such as καλόν and δίκαιον (V 105.4). Knowing from III 82 that the application of specious words to disreputable actions became widespread during the war, we would not credit the Lacedaemonians with a monopoly in this practice. Thucydides in his own language does not participate in the misuse of words. The slight role of τὸ καλόν in his work is easily understood, yet at times we may wonder whether its antonym, τὸ αἰσχρόν, did not retain a stronger hold on men's minds. People indifferent to τὸ καλόν and perhaps even to preserving the reputation of it may yet have recoiled from the prospect of seeing themselves "disgraced." However, the evidence does not suffice to hold this view with confidence.[57]

[56] II 53.3 is one of the few passages not yet mentioned.

[57] Once again the "Melian Dialogue" is particularly important (see V 104, 105.3, 111.3, yet also III 58.1, IV 38.3); cf. Huart 457ff., esp. 459.

There is much in Thucydides to suggest a cleavage between the dominating spirit of realism and the "ideal" that is limited to episodic appearances. Euripides leaves us with the same impression. More important than the normative *gnomai* preserving traditional morality are entire plays conceived in a "patriotic" spirit. Defense of supplicants, protection given to fugitives were part of Athens' mythical and idealized past. These noble deeds became a stock topic of the public epitaphs, and the best known stories of the kind form the "myth" of the *Suppliants* and the *Heraclidae*.[58] Here we find an exaltation of democracy; νόμος rules, φύσις is given no chance of questioning it. Civic virtues and military valor are properly celebrated.[59] In the *Heraclidae* Iolaus carries his heroism to the most improbable length; as a reward, so to speak, a miracle takes place and secures for his irrational daring an equally irrational success.[60] In these plays the realities and values of *Medea* and *Hecuba*, even of the *Trojan Women* and of *Heracles* have no place. For a student of Euripides it is almost disquieting to find himself in a world where unwritten laws are honored, where the wicked are defeated and punished, the innocent given protection.[61]

Having met a sporadic recognition of τὸ καλόν in Thucydides, we are bound to wonder what became of it in Euripides. Once more we must not look at the characters whom we

[58] Cf. Strasburger, pp. 2ff. esp. 23, who also compares Plato's *Menexenus*. Fundamental for the appreciation of these tragedies is G. Zuntz's book; he too has frequent references to the *Epitaphioi* (e.g., pp. 13ff.). No other preserved play is in the same category; of those known to us (optimistically speaking) in outlines, *Erechtheus* has the strongest claims (cf. Webster, see n. 30, 127ff., and the new papyrus published by Colin Austin, 33ff.).

[59] For democracy see esp. *Supp*. 429ff.; for νόμος *ibid*., 558ff.

[60] *Heracl*. 680ff., 843ff.

[61] Despite Zuntz's successful efforts to understand an apparently so different Euripides, serious problems remain, and it is not astonishing that Diller (*Gnomon* 32, 1960, 230f.) and Conacher (pp. 95ff.) are not everywhere in agreement with him.

would consider representative of Euripides' new approach to life. In striking contrast to these, others represent an idealistic outlook. The hallmark of such an outlook is a readiness to sacrifice one's life for a group, a city, or a worthy cause. If the *Alcestis* was composed before the realistic spirit had reached the high-water mark, we had better turn to the *Heraclidae* for our first illustrations. Here Iolaus as well as Macaria offer their lives to save the members of Heracles' family.[62] As matters stand, only the death of Macaria can serve the purpose. The other examples—if we keep to the preserved plays —are found in two of the last tragedies. In the *Phoenissae*, it is Menoeceus and in *Iphigeneia at Aulis* Iphigeneia herself, both of them very young persons, who decide to accept this fate when they learn how much depends on their death for a large community.[63] To cling to life, φιλοψυχεῖν (*Heracl.* 518, *IA* 1385), would under the circumstances be a disgrace, an αἰσχρόν (*Ph.* 999 etc.); to offer it is a noble action, a καλόν bound to secure glory.[64] Iphigeneia, as is well known, differs from the others in that she first joins her mother in laments and protests (vv. 1211-1252, 1279-1335); yet, when the situation in Aulis becomes so critical that a fight between Greeks and Greeks seems imminent, she suddenly changes her mind.

62 Vv. 453ff., 474ff., 500ff. The play, even if as early as Zuntz (pp. 81ff.) and others are inclined to put it, would yet be later than *Medea*. For the subject of self-sacrifice cf. Johanna Schmitt, *Freiwilliger Opfertod bei Eurip.*, Religionsgesch. Versuche u. Vorarbeiten 17.2 (Giessen, 1921); Hans Strohm, *Euripides. Untersuchungen zur dram. Form*, *Zetemata* 15 (Munich, 1957) 51ff. See also Karl Reinhardt's brilliant essay, "Die Sinneskrise bei Euripides," in *Tradition und Geist* (Göttingen, 1960) 238; Kitto, pp. 252ff.; R. Lattimore, *Story Patterns*, 47ff.

63 *Ph.* 985ff., esp. 991ff.; *IA* 1368-1401, 1416-1420, 1435ff. *passim*.

64 For important observations on καλόν and αἰσχρόν see A. W. H. Adkins, *Merit and Responsibility* (Oxford, 1960) *passim*; esp. 186ff. on its problematic position in the city of the fifth century. Some passages in Euripides are discussed by him in CQ 16 (1966) 194ff. (I do not invariably agree, e.g. should hesitate to accept Odysseus' arguments *Hec.* 303ff. so readily at face value as Adkins, pp. 197ff.)

She herself tells why. Far more than her personal fate is at stake, and even for herself death does not just mean horror but would secure a unique merit and a glorious memory.[65] In the lost tragedies, self-sacrifice, or more precisely the readiness for it, has been postulated for the plot of the so-called *Phrixos B*;[66] unfortunately, however, next to nothing is known about the particular circumstances and the antecedent events.

In all instances the heroic decision is made with enthusiasm; yet this enthusiasm does not exclude careful arguments on the part of those ready to die. What is at stake and what would happen to the others—and to themselves[67]—if they clung to their lives? Surely these enthusiasts and idealists look different from Sophoclean characters. Ajax, Antigone, Electra, and others may also reason, but their reasoning explains the only course that their noble nature has allowed them.[68] In truth they have no choice, even if they use arguments to justify before the bar of reason what they will do because it is a vital necessity for them.

Εὐγένεια and considerations of τὸ καλόν inspire Polyxene in the *Hecuba*, when she accepts and indeed welcomes the

[65] See esp. vv. 1368-1401; she understands the issue in terms reminiscent of her father's explanation vv. 1255-1275. The criticism in Arist. *Poet.* 15, 1454a31ff. is familiar. Of modern misjudgments H. Funke, *Hermes* 92 (1964) 284ff., records a staggering number. As Schmitt, *op. cit.* 137, points out, in *IT* 24ff., 359ff. Euripides still has the same version of Iphigeneia's sacrifice as Aeschylus in the Ag. This underlines the novelty of *IA*.

[66] See esp. Webster, pp. 132f. Cf. also Schadewaldt, *Hermes* 63 (1928) 1ff., 12f. In the *Erechtheus* it is, according to all we know, not the victim but the parents who show patriotic readiness for the sacrifice of their child (see esp. *TGF* 360, 362).

[67] See esp. *Heracl.* 507ff.; cf. Polyxene in *Hec.* 349ff. (see below) and Joh. Schmitt, *op. cit.* Cf. H. Strohm, *Euripides* (see n. 62) 50ff., also p. 62. Something different from self-sacrifice for a community yet no less high-minded in outlook is Pylades' eagerness to die with his friend Orestes. See *IT* 674ff.; *Or.* 1070ff. (1085ff.). Note that in both instances αἰσχύνη and the reputation motif contribute to his determination.

[68] See e.g. *Aj.* 457ff., 470ff.

Greek decision to sacrifice her on the tomb of Achilles. She too supports her willingness by visualizing the alternative fate that would await her. Why should she prefer a life of slavery with its humiliations?[69] It may appear unfair to deny her a place by the side of Sophocles' noble natures who, as we just said, also reason. Do we feel that for her the arguments are really decisive, not as in Sophocles secondary, and is her conduct when she gets ready for the sword perfect, indeed, but almost too perfect or too consciously perfect? No doubt she knows as well as Antigone and Sophocles' Electra what is noble and what is ignoble or disgraceful, nor need we suppose that she knows it only by reason, not by nature (φύσει). But the compelling influence of "nature" is simply not so convincing, not so obvious and unmistakable. Moreover, in Euripides "nature" does not mean the same as in Sophocles.

Yet there is also the "reformed" Phaedra of the second *Hippolytus*.[70] Here if anywhere we should feel close to reality while we listen to her principles and resolutions. This play has nothing of the high-flown, overemphatic idealism we have encountered in some other plays. Phaedra's desperate effort to follow the right course is as convincing as the struggle between her determination and the stronger power of sexual passion or as her argument with the down-to-earth common sense of the nurse. Her concern about τὸ καλόν, about τὸ εὐγενές, and about her εὔκλεια is genuine, and it would not be right to judge her in the light of vv. 403f.: ἐμοὶ γὰρ εἴη μήτε

69 Cf. above n. 65; see e.g. vv. 347f., 372ff. (382f.) and Talthybius on her death, esp. vv. 546ff., 557ff., 579f. Cf. D. J. Conacher, *AJPh* 82 (1961) 6 and n. 11.

70 For Phaedra in the first *Hippolytus* and the difference between her character there and in the second *Hippolytus* a reference to Bruno Snell, *Scenes from Greek Drama* (Berkeley, Cal., 1964) Chs. II, III, IV, should now suffice. The opinions advocated by W. S. Barrett, pp. 30ff., and others are critically discussed by Snell, with whom I agree on the changes made by Euripides in Phaedra's character and action. I should however keep Socrates out of the reconstructions (see n. 82). See also Kitto on the "virtuous" Phaedra of our play, pp. 203f.

λανθάνειν καλὰ μήτ' αἰσχρὰ δρώσῃ μάρτυρας πολλοὺς ἔχειν. Surely her reputation worries and influences her,[71] yet she also mentions earlier and later in this speech more substantial reasons for conducting her life well.[72] Something else may give us pause. It has taken her long nights of thought to settle her views about life (vv. 375ff.). Could we imagine Aias, Antigone, or Electra going through such intellectual efforts to find their bearings? If we approach this play with Sophocles in mind, we may be willing to grant Phaedra some nobility of "nature." But, once more, in Euripides "nature" has different connotations—it is the nurse rather than Phaedra who takes her stand on it (vv. 437-475).

Somehow, wherever we look at two great authors moving ahead with their time, the impression is the same. The time-honored values have not completely passed out of existence; they may even, as in the Funeral Oration, be recast in a more sophisticated and by this token more up-to-date form. But vitality has gone elsewhere, and whoever accepts the great tradition in the new versions would not qualify as a conservative but as an idealist. And what evidence is there that the new version reflects a creed and is more than a literary tribute to the past?

Earlier in this chapter, while dealing with the emergence of a secular psychology, we discussed the supremacy of reason, λόγος, and referred to irrational forces disputing this supremacy. Fear, grief, "shame," and the desire for pleasure are, like reason itself, part of human nature. So is θυμός.[73] When their objectives do not meet with reason's approval, they may attain

[71] Cf. vv. 489, 687. The extent to which τὸ αἰσχρόν in *Hipp.* (and elsewhere) depends on reputation still needs investigation. See e.g. Ar. *Av.* 755ff.

[72] See vv. 375-390, 409-412, 413f. (vv. 409ff. might on a pedantic interpretation even suggest that standards of reputation are liable to change; yet Phaedra would be none the happier if what is now αἰσχρόν were to become καλόν.)

[73] See above pp. 129, 133f.

them nevertheless and thereby prove stronger than reason. Different from these enemies in each individual human being are the suspicions and hostilities that reason is apt to arouse in the population at large. Whenever reason increases its power, the opposition to it (nowadays known as anti-intellectualism) is likely to grow at the same pace, if not faster. It need not reach the dimensions of a movement, still less of an organized movement; nor need it produce its own ideology. Its strong weapon is slogans. Men believing in reason and progress are suspected of not sharing the conventional opinions. From the *Clouds* and from the lawsuits against Socrates and other "atheists," we know how fatal could be the accusation of not believing in the gods of the city or of introducing new deities.[74] In Thucydides, the Spartan king Archidamus and the Athenian Cleon, different as they are in all other respects, are at one in praising ἀμαθία μετὰ σωφροσύνης. To be, or act as, "more intelligent than the traditions" (τῶν νόμων σοφώτερος) may have been one of the formulas in which the suspicion against those given to arguing and discussing crystallized.[75] Archidamus feels proud and safe because in Sparta young people are not taught the dangerous habit of independent thinking.

Thucydides knew why he presented Cleon in such an anti-intellectual attitude. If it is well for the individual to be guided by reason, it is well also for the community. As long as Pericles governed the destinies of Athens, they were, as Thucydides judged in retrospect, guided by λόγος. Pericles himself when setting forth his qualifications for political leadership begins with his capacity of γνῶναι τὰ δέοντα (II 60.5).[76] This is followed by his ability to communicate his

[74] Cf. Ar. *Nub.* 1452ff., 1506ff.; cf. K. J. Dover's "Introduction" xxxv ff.; Dodds, *The Greeks and the Irrational,* 188ff., who synthesizes the evidence for "the reaction against the Enlightenment."

[75] I 84.3, III 37.3f.

[76] Cf. Huart, pp. 309ff., on the importance of γνώμη in Thucydides' speech (on Pericles also, 439; ἀμαθία 279). Note Thuc. II 65 on the

political judgments effectively, while two other character traits guarantee that his intellectual powers are immune to corruption. There is no word here about his record in directing or carrying out military and other enterprises (nor is anything of the kind included in the brief appreciation of Themistocles I 138.3).[77] It has from time to time been pointed out that Greek words like *γνώμη* and *φρόνησις* cover more than an intellectual act. They combine, it is held, knowledge and the readiness to act in accordance with it. *γνώμη* in particular suggests an effort to live up to an outlook or a decision.[78]

In the Funeral Oration, Pericles—countering Archidamus' praise of Spartan *ἀμαθία*—credits the Athenians in general with confidence in reason and with the capacity to use it to advantage. Athenians think before they act, undertake what reason bids them do, and the vigor of their activities is not impaired by antecedent reflection.[79] This is their peculiar character and their peculiar strength: in fact *κράτιστοι . . . οἱ τά τε δεινὰ καὶ ἡδέα σαφέστατα γιγνώσκοντες καὶ διὰ ταῦτα μὴ ἀποτρεπόμενοι ἐκ τῶν κινδύνων* (40.3). We recall Archidamus' very

---

correctness of Pericles' judgment, including his prognosis of victory (*ibid.* 5, 10ff.). The superior power of his intellect controlled the emotions of the populace (*ibid.* 8f.). See also H. D. Westlake, pp. 32, 36, 39. Adam Parry, *YCS* 22 (1972) 57ff., should be compared also for the next paragraphs, although he carries good ideas and some correct observations to unwarranted conclusions.

77 See also the judgment about Antiphon VIII 68.1, which in some respects is reminiscent of Pericles' statement about himself, although Antiphon's political activity had to be very limited.

78 See e.g. F. Zucker, *Semantica*, 48ff. Epic phrases like *ὀλοφώια εἰδώς, ἀθεμίστια εἰδώς* foreshadow this attitude. Cf. Dodds, pp. 16f., and Harold Patzer's very careful disquisition, pp. 44ff.

79 II 40.2f. The same people think and act. As for Pericles *μὴ προδιδαχθῆναι λόγῳ* is a *βλάβη*, so in Diodotus the *λόγοι* are *διδάσκαλοι τῶν πραγμάτων* (III 42.2). Archidamus and Cleon would be of the contrary opinion. For thought as directing action in Thucydides see Hans Herter, *RhM* 93 (1950) 133 and *Studi in onore di G. Funaioli* (Rome, 1955) 133ff.

different definition of the κράτιστος in I.84 (see above p. [151]).

Doubtless Pericles as well as Thucydides knew what Phaedra knows in the second *Hippolytus* and what in the Platonic *Protagoras* Socrates and Protagoras admit to be known and believed by οἱ πολλοί:[80] knowledge is dragged about by the human passions and emotions, which treat it as their slave rather than as their master. If Pericles no more than Protagoras and Socrates (or Plato) agrees with the crowd, this does not mean that either Pericles or Thucydides is blind to the "realities of life." Rather, like Socrates and Plato, so Thucydides and for once also his Pericles are engaged in building up another and better reality. About ordinary reality Thucydides, Pericles, and Socrates certainly, and Plato, probably even at that early stage of his life, had no illusion; and if Plato ever had any, he lost them at the time when Socrates was condemned and put to death.[81] Ordinary reality would at best occasionally approximate the postulated better order of things. The Funeral Oration is unique, and we have tried to define its unique character. If reason is in it said to lead and to lead unhampered and with the best results, we need not on that account look for a "Socratic influence"—unless thoughts about the relation between reason and emotion were at the time a monopoly of the Socratic circle.

In the passage quoted above, the Athenians readily face

[80] Plato, *Prt.* 352b ff.

[81] Socrates would hardly have enjoyed the confidence of parents or indeed of the youths themselves to the degree suggested in early Platonic dialogues (e.g. *La.* 180b ff.) if he had been a mere theorist without an understanding for human beings as they are. As for identifying the Socrates of the *Protagoras* with the historical Socrates, I should be thoroughly sceptical of such attempts. He certainly is not the entire Socrates. See n. 82. Plato himself, I admit, cannot at so early a phase be credited with the mature (and disillusioned) wisdom about mankind known from later works, e.g. *R.* IV 431b-c, VI 488a ff., 496a ff., and most of all from the *Laws*; but we need not on this account think of him as blind to the "facts."

the dangers, even if they have a clearer idea of them than others. The subject here in the offing is the relationship between knowledge and one particular excellence, courage. It is familiar to us from early Platonic dialogues such as *Laches* and *Protagoras*, yet references to it occur also elsewhere in Thucydides' speeches.[82] Of all Greek excellences courage (ἀνδρεία) seems most reluctant to accept either an identification with or a guidance by knowledge. In the Funeral Oration knowledge is an advantage for action, including obviously military action, not a cause for hesitation (ὄκνος, 40.3). This, we repeat, is true of the ideal Athenians; yet, later in Book II, the admirals of the Peloponnesian fleet seem to envisage a different kind of Athenians. While admitting the presence of knowledge in the Athenian sailors—albeit a more technical kind of knowledge—courage may or may not follow in the wake of this knowledge; for when fear arises it causes fighters to forget their knowledge, which thus becomes useless (II 87.4). Phormio, when "answering" on behalf of the Athenians, disagrees, yet even he remains at some distance from the position of the Funeral Oration. He does see a causal relation between "experience" (ἐμπειρία) and

[82] *Prt.* 353c ff.; 358a ff.; *La.* 194e ff. (cf. above, pp. 100ff.). Reluctant as I am to discuss the "Socratic problem," I can in this context hardly shirk the question how Socrates' trust in knowledge differs from that of some—perhaps of many?—contemporaries. Simply to say that he "identified" excellence (ἀρετή) and knowledge would be no answer. With his confidence in knowledge, he surely is not so isolated that Eur. *Hipp.* 377ff., as far as it is polemic, must be polemic against him. In my opinion, no discussion of the Platonic Socrates should omit Nietzsche's playful definition of him as πρόσθε Πλάτων, ὄπιθεν δὲ Πλάτων, μέσση δὲ Χίμαιρα, though some progress has been made since Nietzsche, lately in particular through the brilliant essay of Gregory Vlastos (in the collection of papers edited by him, *The Philosophy of Socrates*, Garden City, N.Y., 1971, pp. 1ff.). I do not go far with him in accepting Plato as "authentic" witness (and understand the *Apology* differently), but on a crucial point I emphatically agree: knowledge itself, so vitally necessary, is not known but ought to be known and must continually be sought.

daring (θαρσεῖν 89.2). Pericles appreciated something different: the clear realization of the dangers which does not interfere with the readiness to face them.[83]

To consider how "thought" directs action, we may again look at the Funeral Oration. The Athenians are urged to emulate the courage and spirit of the men who have just been given public burial: τὸ εὔδαιμον τὸ ἐλεύθερον, τὸ δ' ἐλεύθερον τὸ εὔψυχον κρίναντες μὴ περιορᾶσθε τούς πολεμικοὺς κινδύνους.[84] The "judgment" contained in the words that precede and depend on κρίναντες determines the attitude (μὴ περιορᾶσθαι) to the perils of war; in fact the way from correct judgment to the right attitude seems straight and clear.

At the convention in Gela, Hermocrates (IV 58-65) causes the delegates to think new thoughts about the policies pursued by their cities. Again and again he bids his hearers realize the true nature of the issue and perceive what intentions the Athenians pursue while intervening in Sicily and how readily the cities of Sicily play into their hands.[85] Not content with pressing home these insights, Hermocrates adds others of a more general kind, theorizing about human nature and the large gap between man's wish and achievement.[86] His counsel prevails; the questions dividing the Sicilian cities begin to look minor; they are settled (65.1), and Athenian intervention is, for the time being, brought to an end. We readily believe that Hermocrates on this occasion made a statesmanlike speech and produced a strong impression. But did the speech really suffice to produce, without much further arguing, bickering, and diplomatic manoeuvring, a settlement

[83] Brief allusions to the problem in Book VII (61.3; 63.4; 66.3; 67.1) seem likewise based on the equation of ἐπιστήμη with ἐμπειρία.

[84] II 43.4. For the phrasing see Chapter IV (pp. 114f.).

[85] IV 60.1; 61.2 (if not rather 1f.); 63.2. The relevant part of 63.1 is unfortunately obscure; probably right insights as well as the course of action resulting from them are specified, as is the case also in 61.2.

[86] See esp. 61.6 with its reference to the thought preceding it in 61.5; 62.3; 64.1.

of all troublesome conflicts between the cities?[87] And—to ask a rather impudent, unorthodox question—are the political reflections of the speech not in good part at least, intended for us, the readers of the *History*? Be that as it may, in Thucydides the whole turn of events is a triumph of true insight—forms of γιγνώσκειν occur throughout the speech (60.1, 61.2, 62.3, 63.2, cf. 61.6).

Pondering the key role of "thought" in political and military events, we cannot help being amazed at the precise information Thucydides professes to have about the projects and thoughts of leading personalities. Did he really know these plans or did he rely on inference and reconstruction? In one particular case, imaginative reconstruction has been proved. Readers who enjoy the dramatic episode (IV 27) in which Cleon is forced to take over the command at Pylus would yet like to know how Thucydides could be so positive about what Cleon at each stage thought, expected, believed, or realized. The fact is that Thucydides writes with unwarranted confidence. He has reconstructed these mental processes,[88] a hazardous venture, since his mind, wherever Cleon was concerned, was not free of *ira et studium*—hence the numerous errors in the psychological explanations. Thucydides completely ignores the information which Cleon had of Demosthenes' plans for an attack,[89] and which Thucydides himself mentions in the following chapter (IV 29). We shall come back to his procedure in Chapter VI, while dealing with his reconstruction of historical events.

[87] Cf. Gomme's admirable comments on this speech (III, 520ff.). The envoys came to bargain and to negotiate, not to receive instruction about the principles of politics.

[88] See the cogent arguments of A. G. Woodhead, *Mnemosyne* 4th Ser. 13 (1960) 312f. Cf. also Westlake, pp. 69ff. Von Fritz, I 696, seems to take a different view.

[89] Cf. again Woodhead, *Mnemosyne*, 314f. Thucydides, I take it, misinforms his readers because he has persuaded himself to hold the erroneous view.

Unlike this experiment involving a man he disliked, the reasons Thucydides gives for Demosthenes' change of mind and readiness to attack Sphacteria have a good chance of being authentic.[90] Yet even with this assumption Thucydides himself must have contributed a great deal. For it is improbable that Demosthenes, when in the mood to reminisce about his strategic thoughts and decisions, would produce something as admirably organized as the account of IV 29 and 30. How much importance did he, or did others whom Thucydides questioned, attach to the forest fire on Sphacteria? We cannot know. In Thucydides its role is pivotal. He begins in IV 29.3 by explaining why before the fire Demosthenes was averse to the idea of attack. This explanation, preceded by a few words on the topographical conditions, burgeons out into a most carefully constructed system of reasons and causes, partly coordinated, partly subordinated to one another (29.3f.). In the end, for good measure, a place is also found for the psychological effect of a previous defeat suffered by Demosthenes in comparable circumstances (30.1). While reading this, we already know something about the fire that made him change his mind (29.2). In the following two paragraphs (30.2f.) details are given about this fire, its causes, origin, and extent, and then finally about the new strategic considerations to which the increased visibility produced by the fire gave rise. No individual, however gifted as narrator, could in conversation present complex matters in such perfect arrangement, nor is Thucydides likely to have accepted an "authoritative" account and incorporated it in the *History* with only a minimum of formal, especially stylistic adjustments.

The strategic plan governing the attack finally resolved upon is set forth in IV 32. Again much of it probably goes

[90] See Gomme's list of the scholars who consider Demosthenes himself one of Thucydides' chief sources (III, 485; cf. his *Essays*, ch. 7).

back to Demosthenes himself. But Thucydides has recast it in such manner that every item of the plan appears in its clearly defined function. Moreover, he may easily have used a further "source." In the actual development of the fighting, so much corresponds to the "plan" that we cannot help suspecting this plan to be reconstructed from what happened when the battle was joined. Thucydides may, in part at least, have abstracted the γνώμη from the ἔργον (cf. 33.1), and if Demosthenes himself "remembered" how one success and another materialized according to plan, his "recollections" of the plan, perhaps also in part *ex eventu*, would serve Thucydides as welcome, if barely necessary, confirmation. The account of the fighting, convincing as it is down to the smallest detail (chs. 33f.) gives the impression of a clever strategic project being carried into effect step by step. Are we to such a degree the victims of Thucydides' suggestive power, or did strategic planning for once celebrate a complete triumph? The answer must be conjectural and subjective. While not questioning the success of the strategic γνώμη, I would allow Thucydides by a few touches here and there to contribute to this proof of its controlling power over events.[91]

At present, however, we are not studying Thucydides' methods of reconstruction but his conception and appraisal of human reason. What may we say about this subject? It operates, naturally enough, along causal lines, and the chapters just analyzed throw some light on this causality. For there is no break in the tenor of the narrative when, in the battle of Sphacteria, we move from a rational scheme planned by a human mind to causal sequences in the physical world, such as the origin of the forest fire, its spreading due

[91] Cf. J. de Romilly, *Histoire*, 123ff., esp. 129f. The light-armed (ψιλοί) may have come to play a larger part in the action than had been envisaged. Cf. von Fritz, I 696. This is possible; but 32.4, unfortunately disfigured by a corruption, contained more than is now apparent.

to the wind, and finally the destruction of a large wooded area (30.2).

On the other hand, even if reason basically operates alike in human beings, there are differences between one man's thinking and another's.[92] Anyone who knows about the typical ways of human φύσις uses reason more expertly than a person content to surmise what will happen, yet unable to understand it as a manifestation of this ever-constant entity. Pericles (as we have seen) has a broader outlook and a larger perspective than his fellow citizens; in addition he shows, especially in the Funeral Oration, an exceptional sense of value. Yet the latter finds no place in Thucydides' final appreciation of him.

Thucydides and others doubtless knew some men to be more intelligent than the average. In the *History* Themistocles and Archidamus are praised for ξύνεσις, Pericles and again Archidamus for πρόνοια.[93] Yet it does not often happen that an individual is in straightforward language called "stupid" or that a mistaken decision is without further ado traced to lack of intelligence.[94] More frequently a man in public life is by a particular emotion, by ambition, or by a

[92] With Euripides in mind, we might also ask whether the reason of men and of women operates in identical ways. For a clear-cut answer, we should have to meet them in comparable situations. In Chapter I our study of the *in utramque partem disputare* has found persons of both sexes equally resourceful and conforming to the same patterns. The superior aptitude of women for τέχναι (schemes, intrigues) is conspicuous in Euripides and at times actually stated, e.g. Eur. *IT* 1032; *Hipp.* 480f.; cf. *Philologus* 87 (1932) 7 and n. 21 (= *Kleine Schriften* I 147).

[93] See Thuc. I 138.3, 79.2; II 65.5ff. (Brasidas' ξύνεσις IV 81.2 seems a matter of political expediency.)

[94] It is rather the institution of democracy as such (VI 89.6) that is called an ἄνοια; see, however, for an occasional use of ἄφρον, V 105.3, of εὐήθεια, III 45.7 (Diodotus about Cleon's proposal). In Euripides cf. μωρία *Med.* 371. However, words like μωρία, ἀφροσύνη, etc., have moral as well as intellectual connotations (see e.g. S. *Ant.* 470; *OT* 433, 540) and the latter need not by any means prevail.

personal interest prevented from making the best use of his intelligence.[95] This is reported of as honest a man as Nicias, whereas little or nothing interferes with Demosthenes' use of his mind, so that we may regard his thoughts in Pylus and in Sicily as illustrating the normal process of reason. Another example of reason functioning in a straight and normal way is furnished by Brasidas. In IV 105.1, Brasidas has to make up his mind how to secure the possession of Amphipolis, whose inhabitants are divided in their political sympathies. He evidently knows of the call for help that the pro-Athenian faction has sent to Thucydides, knows that Thucydides happens to be in Thasos, at half a day's distance from Amphipolis, and knows something about the ships at his disposal. We might as well say that he knows what was known in Amphipolis, and, since the pro-Lacedaemonian party[96] there was in contact with him, this is natural. What then went on in his mind? The question makes it necessary to decide how high an opinion he had of Thucydides. Having learned about Thucydides as owner of gold mines in the region, he feared his reputation and influence—what he thought of his strategic and other abilities should matter too, but for reasons easy to understand nothing is said about this. It suffices that Brasidas could visualize the hopes and expectations that Thucydides, if allowed to arrive in Amphipolis, would arouse in a large body of the citizenry. Further help on land and sea would be expected to follow. Realizing how essential it is to use the very short time before the arrival, Brasidas offers extraordinarily mild and attractive conditions, whereby he immediately achieves his purpose (105.2–106.2).

We may have made too much of Brasidas' knowledge and reasoning. Actually, thought is not the obvious common denominator for the variety of motivations mentioned by

[95] Cf., as the most comprehensive statement to this effect, II 65.10.

[96] See IV 104.4–105.1, 106.1f. For what follows cf. O. Luschnat, *RE* s.v. "Thukydides" 1099.

Thucydides. Fear, worry, eagerness operate as well, all of them activated by the specific information about Thucydides.[97] How reliably Thucydides could learn what Brasidas knew, feared, hoped, and thought and how close to the historical reality his account of the motivations takes us is another question. Brasidas himself, a man, we may presume, of action (cf. 81.1) rather than of reflection, might not have found it easy to analyze the part played by each of these heterogeneous motives. All of them are true to type, realistic, and likely enough consciously or subconsciously to influence a keen and energetic commander. This, of course, may be as easily an argument against as for their accuracy.[98]

We have ventured to show Demosthenes and Brasidas as reasoning in a normal or typical fashion. For just as ἐσθλοὶ μὲν γὰρ ἁπλῶς, παντοδαπῶς δὲ κακοί, so, we believe, the manifestation of reason is uniform in contrast to the larger and almost infinite variety of emotional conditions. Nevertheless men fundamentally rational have yet their individuality. It is as an example of such a man, i.e. a man reasonable, yet nevertheless individual in outlook and even influenced by personal interests, that we here give brief attention to Nicias.[99]

In the winter of 422/1 various special causes and an atmosphere of general discouragement have created a mood for peace on both sides. Nicias, who does not wish to imperil his record of successful campaigning,[100] and, who is by tempera-

[97] δεδιὼς . . . πυνθανόμενος . . . ἠπείγετο . . . μή would be the skeleton of the sentence (IV 105.1), which includes no word meaning "decision."

[98] An extreme and under the circumstances somewhat ironic suggestion would be that what we here read is a description of how Thucydides himself would have reacted, had he been in the position of Brasidas.

[99] See for him also III 51; IV 27.5ff.

[100] V 16.1. Problems found by Gomme (*ad loc.*) in the thought and, after others, also in the text of the sentence appear less formidable after J. de Romilly (in the "Notice," pp. xxvii f., and the notes to her Budé text) has treated them in the light of Thucydides' habits. She notes

ment averse to toils and perils, considers his personal interests better served by ending the war. The ἀκίνδυνον of the city coincides with his own. We recognize the same Nicias afterward, when he wisely opposes adventurous enterprises; and from such situations it is not a far cry to others where he wavers and is reluctant to act, although the circumstances require a determined step taken without delay.[101] His superstitious habits (VII 50.4) may be an additional trait, although we easily visualize them blending with his other characteristics.

It goes without saying that Alcibiades and other individuals cast in a major role are likewise consistent in the essential quality and ultimate orientation of their thought, no matter how often they change their policy.[102] We content ourselves with this impression; for it would not be easy to pursue this line of inquiry much farther. To isolate "thought" from a complex pattern of motivations has been precarious even in some of the passages analyzed on the preceding pages. For whenever personal preferences play a part, it becomes hazardous to decide whether we should speak of "thought" influenced (or modified) by less rational motives or whether it is better to recognize emotions, desires, personal ambitions, etc., as "having a firm hold on the deliberations" (κρείσσων τῶν βουλευμάτων, *Med.* 1079) and prescribing the way that thought is to take.[103] Moreover, much of the thought in

(ad 16.1) the "sévérité" of his judgments. See also Westlake, pp. 93, 95, and especially the excellent comments by Karl Reinhardt on Nicias in Thucydides (*Von Werken und Formen* 276).

[101] From a good number of noteworthy passages I choose VII 48.2ff., where Thucydides professes to know that his actual (τῷ ἔργῳ, 3) intentions differed from what he announced as his settled opinion and where he is again, as in V 16, greatly concerned about his personal safety and rather shrewd in judging the chances.

[102] For Alcibiades, see an extensive account in Westlake, pp. 212ff.; cf. also P. A. Brunt, *REG* 65 (1952) 59ff.

[103] See e.g. VIII 89.3.

question consists of political plans and intentions, as in one instance where Thucydides feels sufficiently confident to specify the political preferences of an entire group by stating their first, second, and third choices, while in another he wonders which of three alleged intentions behind Tissaphernes' course of action is likely to be the truth.[104] On all such occasions a sure grasp of realistic, utterly unsentimental political calculations is evident; yet such political thoughts and plans do not illustrate the kind of λόγος that we have in mind when we look upon the opposition between reason and the irrational emotions as the core of the new psychology. We gladly believe that this was a psychology appropriate to the men and women of the late fifth century, and if we had any doubt about this, the firm command and the confidence with which the great authors of the period employ it would reassure us. So perfect indeed is this confidence and so thoroughly are we convinced that we forget the experimental nature of this approach. Euripides and Thucydides are pioneers as well as masters in the new knowledge of man.

[104] VIII 91.3; 87.

VI

RATIONAL RECONSTRUCTION

Events of the Peloponnesian War

In Chapter V we became acquainted with a new approach to the problems of human motivation. In the generation of Thucydides, realistic analysis took possession of a subject in which formerly divine operation had been allotted a large share. Antiphon the Orator uses the realistic psychology in the interest of his clients. Euripides and perhaps other tragedians of the time show men and women "as they (really) are" in their acting and suffering; and Thucydides thinks in terms of the new psychology to explain the conduct of individuals or communities directing the course of historical events. The events themselves are treated in the same spirit of rational and realistic probability. In the famous chapter on "methods," Thucydides emphasizes the pains he has taken to ascertain the facts.[1] He has not seen fit to write them down as he learned them "from the first person who happened to come along"; nor has he allowed his own opinion free play; but he has trusted himself only in the (relatively few) instances when he had actually witnessed the events, while for everything else he has used the reports of others after examining them with the greatest "accuracy."[2] This was the

[1] See I 22.2f. Fortunately it is not necessary here to review the very extensive discussion of these sentences. ἔργα τῶν πραχθέντων are the words of special interest to us. What do they cover? Thucydides seems to ignore not only (as von Fritz points out, I 620) his own selection of the facts to be included but also what he contributes to their interconnection. The reason is simply that he had not carried the theoretical analysis of his procedure so far.

[2] ἀκρίβεια is the word used here (and also with reference to the speeches in 22.1), σαφές in 22.4. Professor Martin Ostwald suggests to me that the "examining" applies also to events which Thucydides had

more necessary since in many instances the reports conflicted with one another. He had to decide on the relative trustworthiness of each in the light of the reporter's sympathies and powers of memory. These criteria cannot always have been known to him beforehand; often enough he must have formed his judgment about them in the actual process of listening and inquiring, and hardly less often when he had an opportunity for comparing one version with another.

In the collection of his material, Thucydides was indefatigable, for the amount of fact included in his work is stupendous. To us, however, as we ponder his achievement, the connection established between events seems an intellectual feat of—at least—the same order as the ascertaining of them. Regardless of how much or how little a particular informant would tell him, the decision about the interrelation of events, their integration into a convincing narrative remained Thucydides' own responsibility, and he was more than ready to accept it. If he incorporated a version with little or no change,[3] the reason would be that he considered it reliable. Yet we should certainly not underestimate the amount of information dismissed by him as biased, intrinsically improbable, or irrelevant.[4]

If Thucydides in spite of his efforts could not obtain as good or as complete reports of major developments as he desired, he himself had to coordinate the results of his inquiries.

---

witnessed. I am aware of two opinions on this point and admit that syntax and general considerations favor Ostwald. Perhaps the sentence in my text should be modified. Whether Thucydides really did not trust himself sufficiently is another question.

[3] Incorporation with no change is almost impossible, since adjustment to his own style and to the tenor of his presentation was necessary throughout. For the process of collecting information cf. Edouard Delebecque, *Thucydide et Alcibiade* (Aix-en-Provence, 1965) 11ff., esp. 35.

[4] For a case where material of considerable interest was dismissed or ignored see below on Corcyra pp. 208ff.

In fact larger sequences must always have been organized by his own mind, and it is difficult to imagine that even in shorter sections he simply repeated what he learned without asserting his own rational interpretation to give the account its line and logic. Besides ascertaining the temporal sequence, he had to establish convincing causal relationships. We know the standard to which he tried to conform. It is *to eikos*, a concept of probability based on the ways in which men or things normally work.[5] Thus defined, the *eikos* seems to leave little scope for individual differences. Indeed, although Thucydides had a keen eye for individuals with their capacities and weaknesses (he shows to what extent Alcibiades' character was responsible for the Sicilian adventure, Pericles' wisdom for the strategy of the Archidamian war, or Nicias' hesitations and superstitions for fatal delays in Sicily), by and large it is a generic rather than an individualized kind of probability that prevails in his work. Human nature is and will remain the same; so presumably is and will the nature of things. This is why the pattern of historiography created by Thucydides involves a certain uniformity. The same rationality shapes and organizes everything,[6] including the reconstruction of irrational behavior.

This uniformity may give us a measure for the degree of freedom that Thucydides took not only in filling out gaps in his material but also, and no less, in synthesizing such

[5] See on τὸ εἰκός above pp. 13ff., 166ff. This concept, it may well be argued, guides Thucydides also in VIII 64.5, a very remarkable passage. The Athenians, who have set up an oligarchical government in Samos, try to effect the same change in some allied cities. In Thasos they succeed, but, as soon as they have left, Thasos breaks away from the Athenian League. After reporting this, Thucydides expresses his belief that this development was paralleled in other cities. He has no positive knowledge to this effect, yet postulates such secessions as a matter of historical probability.

[6] Cf. J. de Romilly, *Histoire*, 51, on the "tendance à l'unité" as related to "vraisemblance" (εἰκός), "rigueur," and an "enchaînement" of psychological causalities in particular.

material as was available. No ancient historian has the same confidence that by using his reason to the fullest extent he recovers the "truth." Others do not have the same devotion to truth or lack the power of his mind (often, to be sure, both of them are absent). Thucydides lived and is conceivable only at the historical juncture when the intellect had gained its freedom and had not yet learned to use it with moderation. To synthesize historical material so boldly was certainly an experiment. The Ionian rationalism of Hecataeus has something premature; it is arbitrary—at times frankly subjective. Herodotus felt obliged to keep closer to his informants.

Since Thucydides does not let us know his raw material, analysis of his narrative is our only way of finding out how he proceeded. To this we shall now turn, and, like others before us, shall see that Thucydides' transforming activity went very far indeed.

We may first examine a relatively short section embodying operations in a peripheral area of the war. The expedition of a large pro-Lacedaemonian coalition against the Acarnanians (II 80-82) and the sea battle between the Athenian admiral Phormio and the Corinthians (83f.) are, roughly speaking, simultaneous. Beyond this temporal relation there is a more significant interdependence. The Ambracians and the Lacedaemonian commander of the expedition count on the Corinthians for assistance, yet in the end proceed without waiting for their fleet;[7] on the other side the Acarnanians (81.1), being allies of Athens, ask Phormio for aid, and he, although unable to comply with their specific request, helps them effectively by watching the movements of the Corinthian fleet and intercepting its attempt to reach the coalition. Thucydides' over-all organization of his material is simple: he first reports the large-scale expedition against the Acarnanians and its failure (81.4ff.), then, turning to the

[7] See II 80.3f. (where the Corinthians are ready to assist Ambracia) and 8.

Corinthians ostensibly to explain why their fleet could not provide the expected help, describes the sea battle that developed between them and Phormio, when they tried to move past him in Naupactus (83, esp. 4f., 84). Thus we have two, so to speak, parallel accounts. Each works up to a climax and then concludes in a lower key.[8]

In reconstructing the expedition against Acarnania, Thucydides, it seems reasonable to suppose, depended on information supplied by Lacedaemonians for their own preparations, for their agreement with the Ambracians, probably also for disposition of the forces in the army, and most of all for the remarkably full catalogue of tribes that participated in the expedition and of their leaders.[9] From the same source he may have learned about the movements following the defeat and about the inglorious disbanding of the army. The decisive battle itself is however described from the side of the victorious Acarnanians; and we read not only of their strategic manoeuvres but also of the expectations and calculations that prompted them. Although when we come to psychological motives[10] we must make allowance for Thucydides' own contributions, we can hardly dispense with an "Acarnanian" source besides the Lacedaemonian. As usual, there is no gap between reports from different sides; and in this instance it is particularly easy to identify the point of their juncture. The Chaonians, evidently the least disciplined contingent in the motley Lacedaemonian-Ambracian alliance,

[8] For references from one account to the other and for the function of these references in the composition of these sections see below p. 179.

[9] 80.1f., 5-8. Throughout this chapter the enemies of Athens are the subject; so they are again in 81.2-4, 7f., 82.

[10] Especially in 81.5, perhaps also in 81.4, Thucydides' informants, when telling him about the Chaonians and describing their impetuous conduct, may of course have mentioned their over-confidence and explained it by their reputation. We are free to think of Thucydides as eliciting by his questions one or the other additional item or receiving confirmation for his tentative synthesis.

cannot like the others move forward in orderly fashion, but rush ahead, proud of their reputation as the most warlike tribe and confident of capturing the town of Stratos single-handed (so far Thucydides probably drew on what he learned from their allies, who contrasted the impetuous conduct of the Chaonians, 81.4, with their own orderly movements). Realizing their chance, the Acarnanians launch simultaneous attacks from front and sides, crush the Chaonians thoroughly, and thereby create terror in the other "barbarian" contingents of the army.[11] Here Thucydides is likely to draw on reports of the victors; yet when the barbarian troops fall back on the main body of the army, which after such inauspicious beginnings gives up the expedition, he owes his information again to a Lacedaemonian source. Still no matter where we draw the lines between his sources, they are visible only to a critic scrutinizing the account with analytical intentions. The story of this expedition reads as a perfectly integrated account that, owing to its intrinsic logic, the reader accepts without hesitation.

For the complementary story of Phormio's fight with the Corinthians (83f.) reasons for assuming information from both sides are less compelling. Nevertheless I incline to this view, because this battle is followed by another that includes items of Lacedaemonian provenience (85.1ff., 86.6). For the first battle, the Athenians could report enough about the equipment of the Corinthian fleet and its conduct during and to some extent also before the engagement.[12] Intentions behind the Corinthian manoeuvres were not hard to guess, and if Thucydides had an opportunity—and why should he

[11] 81.5 (where the participles γνόντες and ἡγησάμενοι mark the change to the other side) –7. In 81.8 the explanation why the inhabitants of Stratos do not attack may be Thucydides'.

[12] In 83.4 Thucydides mentions the names of the Corinthian commanders, adding that each of the allied cities had its own commander. If he did not know the names of the latter, he would hardly see the need for making efforts.

not?—to question Phormio, he would receive an expert's diagnosis of Corinthian tactics and the most authoritative explanation of the plan by which the Athenian sailors themselves operated so successfully.[13] The Athenians could watch the Corinthians react to their movements. For a time these movements were designed to avoid actual clashes; their aim was to create uncertainty and confusion. Thus they prepared the best conditions for the moment when the breeze would begin to cooperate with them. As soon as this happened (84.3), the *peripeteia* to which Thucydides has so carefully worked up materialized. The description of the battle itself (84.3) has much in common with others, especially that of the final struggle on Sphacteria.[14] Several difficulties, dangers, and causes of confusion harass the Corinthians at one and the same time. Thucydides has found it possible to pack the development of the entire fighting into one sentence (84.3), yet in spite of its length, the sentence does not lack clarity and is so breath-taking that the reader safely finds himself carried to its conclusion. For Thucydides' mastery of concentrating a large amount of material within a short compass we shall soon meet other instances. This time a long subordinate clause shows us the Corinthians struggling in vain against the adversities created by the breeze, and as this clause unfolds we see more and more complications result from their efforts; in the midst of this abundant detail (and a corresponding variety of syntactical constructions), Thucydides still supplies explanations of a more basic type (ἄνθρωποι ἄπειροι . . .). Then, after we have watched the Corinthian plight become increasingly desperate, the main clause finally begins: Phormio gives the signal; the attack for which all antecedent harassment was a preparation takes

[13] For the relation between "intelligence" and the resulting action in Thucydides' battles see above, Chapter V. On confusion as part of the strategic γνώμη see J. de Romilly, *Histoire*, 168ff., 172 and n. 2.

[14] See below p. 204.

place, and brief indications of a few successive stages show the attack to result in complete victory.

We understand why the fleet of the Corinthians and their allies cannot provide effective help for the Ambrakians. Yet when we have come to the end of the sea battle we have lost sight of the operations in Acarnania. Moreover this sea battle is, as we have mentioned, followed by another. Although describing the second more fully (II 85–92), Thucydides himself does not suggest that it has any bearing on the events on land. Probably it had none. Despite some initial interrelation, the actions in the Gulf and those in Acarnania each take their own course. As far as we can judge, Thucydides had no alternative to presenting them in separate accounts with their own structure, and to explaining by a few interspersed remarks (80.8, 83.1, 84.5, cf. 80.2ff.) how the naval action affected the operations on land.

Book VIII, owing to its unfinished and presumably unrevised condition, lends itself more readily than the other books to an analysis from our point of view. Integration has here not reached the stage where all seams have been removed.[15] We shall, however, stay clear of the most controversial sections and begin with a relatively simple and as it were transparent unit. VIII 25–27 describe an Athenian attempt to recapture Miletus, which Alcibiades shortly after the Sicilian catastrophe had caused to break away from Athens and join the Peloponnesian League. The attempt to regain it begins with a battle before the city. Although the

[15] In this century Schwartz, 72ff., went farthest in discovering uncoordinated drafts. Many of his conclusions have not stood up well under later criticism (which was initiated by M. Pohlenz, G. G. N., 1919, 96ff.; 1920, 56ff.). The most recent treatment is by von Fritz, I, 757ff. Wilamowitz's analysis of Book VIII (*Hermes* 43, 1908, 578 ff.) remains important.

allies of Athens are beaten and only the Athenians themselves are victorious, this suffices for the investment of the large city. The narrative is straightforward and its entire content may go back to an eyewitness or participant, who, no matter to which side he belonged, was alert to significant details like the cavalier attitude of the Argives, who attacked καταφρονήσαντες ὡς ἐπ' Ἴωνας κτλ.[16]

The beginning of chapter 26 brings the reversal. The imminent arrival of fifty-five ships from the Peloponnesus and Sicily becomes known in the Athenian camp. At this point Thucydides has to go back in time and explain the sudden appearance of this naval force; in particular he must, however briefly, inform us that the Sicilians had decided to take part in "what remained to be liquidated of the Athenians" (26.1: τῆς ὑπολοίπου 'Αθηναίων καταλύσεως). In addition, the arrangements made in Sparta and the movements of the fleet prior to approaching Miletus had to be recounted. Here Thucydides incorporates material known to him from other sources. During a sojourn in the Peloponnesus he would easily acquire information about those subjects.

In chapter 27 he returns to the Athenians and the main line of action. Most of their leaders are willing to remain and fight the large fleet; only Phrynichus, realizing how much is at stake for Athens and how unwise it would be to expose its weakened forces to the danger of a major defeat, opposes his fellow commanders by making these points and in the end convinces them, although with difficulties and at the price of losing the Argives as active allies.

Thucydides cannot easily resist the opportunity of sum-

[16] Alternatively it may have been supplied by Thucydides himself, who considered it "in character." The question is of a type with others concerning psychological motivations. At the end of the same chapter the Athenians turn to the investment of Miletus, expecting through its conquest to recover the loyalty of other cities, surely an obvious expectation for which Thucydides did not need an "authority." But where are we to draw the line between obvious and less obvious motivations?

marizing intelligent arguments, especially if, like those used by Phrynichus, they illuminate conditions and prospects in a general fashion. Moreover, being in Book VIII more ready than elsewhere to express his own opinions, he gives Phrynichus special praise for his prudence as shown on this and other occasions.[17] Since Phrynichus was dead before Thucydides returned to Athens, Thucydides probably learned the specific arguments he used from one of the other Athenian commanders or, if this was not possible, from somebody who knew them second-hand.[18] The action against Miletus having thus been broken up, there is nothing further to report about Athenian enterprises in this season.

Phrynichus' determined reaction in 27.1 to the sudden arrival of the fifty-five ships may be read as the immediate sequel to the first sentence of chapter 26, where the news of their arrival reaches the Athenians. The background information on these ships forms a separate strand in a primarily Athenian narrative. To speak of "integration" would be pretentious; it should be enough to say that there is no disturbing interruption of a coherent narrative. Even in a final version of Book VIII this would be the right place to insert the background information about the boats—unless, of course, Thucydides had more to communicate, having learned about important differences of opinion in Sparta or between Sparta and its allies, Sparta and Syracuse, etc.

So far we have said nothing about 26.3, where Alcibiades appears on horseback and urges the Peloponnesian commanders by all means to prevent the investment of Miletus. Did Thucydides learn about him again from another source? Perhaps from Alcibiades himself?[19] As chapter 26 now reads,

[17] On Phrynichus cf. Wilamowitz, *Hermes* 43 (1908) 603.

[18] Wilamowitz believes that even Thucydides' judgment about Phrynichus reflects that of his informants. Given Thucydides' intellectual independence, this is not easy to believe.

[19] See the impressive reasons offered by P. A. Brunt, *REG* 65 (1952) 59ff., for whom Alcibiades is the informant on whatever is read about his

without his persuasive appeal the Peloponnesians might not have decided to oppose the Athenians before Miletus. From this point of view his role seems crucial; the reference to it organic. Far less organic is the statement in the same context that Alcibiades—and Tissaphernes!—had participated in the battle fought outside Miletus. This looks like a footnote—or a later addition. Still we should beware of rash conclusions. As we know, Alcibiades had played an essential part in winning Miletus for the Peloponnesian cause. In the events concerning Miletus, Alcibiades had his place, and so, we may assume, did he in Thucydides' information about them. Thus we could understand that, although knowing from the beginning of Alcibiades' presence in the battle, Thucydides reserved mention of it for a point where Alcibiades' intervention had a decisive effect.

VIII 31–43.1, a larger section set off from its surroundings, is a unit, yet a complex unit. At the beginning we find ourselves on Chios, which after the Sicilian catastrophe has broken away from the Athenian League but which the Athenians are particularly anxious to reconquer. We again distinguish several strands in Thucydides' account,[20] and it is quite probable that they correspond to different sources of information. He reports what happens in Chios, yet the actions of the Spartan admiral Astyochus must be followed up even after he has left Chios; in addition other Spartan

activities, influence, etc. See also E. Delebecque, *Thucydide, passim.* Westlake's skepticism (pp. 231f.) is ill-founded. If Book VIII is an "unrevised draft . . . probably written soon after the events," this does not exclude additions (Westlake makes concessions, e.g. pp. 243, 245, 248).

20 Von Fritz, I 773f. speaks well of "Ereignisstränge" worked out independently and sometimes more, sometimes less integrated. I should include our section among the "more"—even though not yet completely—integrated. On chs. 57ff. as sequel to 29-44 and about the relation of 45-56 to 29-44 see Wilamowitz, 588ff., L. Bodin, *REA* 14 (1912) 26ff., Delebecque, 77ff.

naval operations, even if at first not directly related to Astyochus', interact with them later; and finally Athenian strategy too requires attention. In chapter 31 we accompany Astyochus in his enterprises on the coast of Asia Minor until he hears of a new chance of winning Lesbos through cooperation with its anti-Athenian faction. He himself is ready to take this opportunity, but the allies refuse to participate. Frustrated, he returns to Chios, where within a short period (ch. 32) his situation and resources improve considerably, so that when, once more, hopeful messages and calls for help arrive from Lesbos he insists more strongly on moving to the support of the rebels. Again, however, he meets with opposition, this time primarily on the part of the Chians. The result is a serious break between him and the Chians; he leaves Chios in a fit of temper, warning the people not to count on his help if they should find themselves in danger (33.1ff.). As we shall see, these ill feelings will have their influence when, five chapters later (38), Thucydides resumes the narrative at this very point.

On leaving Chios, Astyochus heads for Miletus, but some information—actually, as it turns out, misinformation—causes him to move first to Erythrae, and it is only due to this change of plan that he does not encounter a detachment of the Athenian fleet on its way to Chios, where it debarks on the side opposite to that left by Astyochus. A new crisis seems in the offing. We can appreciate what care has gone into reconstructing the temporal sequences as well as coincidences; yet we also understand why Thucydides, having stayed so long with Astyochus, decides to concentrate on events elsewhere for a while.

In chapter 34 we read of clashes between Athenian and Chian ships, and in chapter 35 of operations undertaken by a Lacedaemonian fleet to secure Cnidos and of Athenian countermeasures. When in chapter 36 Astyochus appears again, he has reached Miletus, where the Peloponnesians decide to draw up a new treaty with Tissaphernes (37)—whether Astyochus himself had a hand in it is not clear, and there are other problems regarding the treaty. Still, rightly or wrongly, this is the place where Thucydides decided to insert it.[21]

Meanwhile, the situation in Chios has greatly deteriorated. Chapter 38 shows the Athenians having progressed dangerously close to the city of Chios itself. Since Astyochus left, the Chians have suffered many hard blows. Thucydides sums up their experiences with extreme brevity; they have been defeated in "many battles," have suffered much from internal discord, in the course of which some leading men have been put to death for treason and the government has "from necessity" turned into an oligarchy (38.3). A closer look at these condensed statements suggests that Thucydides probably could have told us more. He might—this must always be admitted—have done so, had he been able to revise the Book; yet we may as well suppose that he had a reason for being so brief and that the reason was either his sense of proportion or the wish to return without much delay to Astyochus' relations with Chios. In any case, at 38.4, the possibility envisaged by Astyochus when he left Chios has materialized; the Chians ask him for help, and he turns a deaf ear (οὐκ ἐσήκουεν). We know the cause of this unwillingness, but the unwillingness in turn functions as a cause of other events. Astyochus is denounced in Sparta by Pedaritus, the Lacedaemonian commander in Chios (38.4), and another Peloponnesian fleet is sent to Miletus for various reasons and purposes,[22] one of

[21] Wilamowitz, 589, argued that the treaty of ch. 37 was ignored and presumably unknown in ch. 45. Some of his arguments have been invalidated (cf. von Fritz, I 760). Still, even if Thucydides found the correct chronological place for the treaty, the reason why it was needed is not adequately stated (ὁμῶς 36.2 betrays a certain embarrassment).

[22] The main purpose is to cooperate with Pharnabazus, whereas the fleet in Miletus has its treaties with Tissaphernes. Ever since the early chapters of Book VIII we know about the rivalry between these two

which is to keep a watchful eye on Astyochus and, if it seems indicated, to depose him from his command (39.1ff.). Again we have reached a point where the narrative leaves Astyochus. For some time we have to concentrate on this newly dispatched fleet.

This fleet runs into unexpected difficulties. On the way it encounters ten Athenian ships and, although it beats them, there is ground for apprehension that the fleet's movement will be reported to Athenian headquarters in Samos and that Athenian forces will try to intercept it before it can join the main body of the Lacedaemonian navy in Miletus. Giving way to this apprehension, the commanders change their course, sail first to Crete, and from there to Caunus on the southern coast of Asia Minor. From Caunus they send a message to Astyochus, asking him to escort their fleet to Miletus (39.4).

Astyochus, to whom we thus return in chapter 40, finds himself at this point beset by urgent requests from two sides, Chios and Caunus. We know the causal sequences that lead up to both of them. In Chios the crisis has continued to worsen. This time Thucydides allows himself a fuller and more relaxed description. He informs us not only of the military progress made by the Athenians, the mass desertion of slaves, and the damage they inflict on Chios (40.2), but also of the specific pleas used by the Chian envoys when they meet with Astyochus (40.3). Although reluctant to go back on his threats, Astyochus is on the point of relenting when the new request for help comes from Caunus. Deciding to give it priority, he moves with his boats to Caunus. The Chians are left in their desperate plight. As the account of Book VIII continues, Thucydides has to deal with so many new developments—especially again with negotiations be-

---

satraps for an alliance with Sparta and joint naval actions (39.1 harks back to 8.1 and beyond it to 5.4ff.; 6).

tween the Peloponnesians and Tissaphernes and later with the complex machinations of Alcibiades—that he can only now and then afford a brief glance at the fate of the hard-pressed Chians (55.2–56.1, 60.2, 61.1ff.). In the end, they have the good fortune that the Athenian forces employed against them are needed for an emergency arising elsewhere (chs. 62f.).

Actually, since Astyochus moves with his fleet first to the aid of those in Caunus, Thucydides has an excuse for giving this operation priority in his narrative. We are prepared for Astyochus' experiences on the way, for we know that the fleet recently sent from Sparta unexpectedly encountered Athenian boats, some of which escaped and reported to their headquarters in Samos about this Spartan force. This was why the Lacedaemonian commanders had changed their course. What they feared has happened; and when Astyochus' fleet is sailing from Miletus to Caunus, the Athenians even know the Peloponnesian fleet to be in Caunus, and have sent a task force to watch it (42.3f.).[23] Astyochus encounters this force under weather conditions unfavorable to both sides, yet, as it turns out, worse for the Athenians, who, while fighting a part of his fleet, believe it to be the whole. When the truth dawns on them, they turn to flight, and Astyochus is able to join his fleet to that waiting in Caunus.[24]

Looking back at the section analyzed (31–43.1), we may wonder whether Thucydides could just as well have reported this sequence of events from the Athenian point of view and indeed kept up—more or less continuously—an Athenian "line" in his narrative. He actually begins with the Athenian

[23] We pass over some stops on the way and the happy pillaging in Cos (41.2).

[24] Although the fleet in Caunus does not immediately sail to Miletus, its original destination, we may assume that it arrives there at some later time (cf. 63.2). Still there is no longer mention either of this or of other original instructions, such as watching Astyochus.

decision (ch. 30) to use a part of their recently increased forces for operations against Chios. Yet being in exile at the time, he probably received more material from the Peloponnesian side and, as a result, organized his narrative around Astyochus, the Chians, Peloponnesian fleets, etc. However, he does know a good deal about Athenian deliberations and operations, and while some of this knowledge may (theoretically speaking) go back to sources in the other camp, not all of it can have originated there. For not only does Thucydides show himself well informed about constitutional changes in Athens, but the same is true about other developments there and in Samos, in fact even about specific matters such as Phrynichus' protest.[25] As Samos was the headquarters, whoever reported to him, e.g. about the political upheavals there, would also know details about the military expeditions.

In principle, we may as well assume, Thucydides could have organized his narrative from the Athenian point of view; yet actually it would have been a reorganization, and we understand that, if he ever gave thought to it at all, he regarded other phases of his work as more urgent. We cannot know whether the concentration on Sparta—and after Sparta on Chios—has excluded some strategic deliberations in Samos and various other items of considerable interest. Conversely, had he presented the entire story from the Athenian side, he might have had to sacrifice material of no less interest, such as the temperamental reactions of Astyochus (important for his later refusal), the reasons why he could not intervene on Lesbos, and—greatest loss of all—the two requests for help reaching him simultaneously. I prefer not to speculate

[25] First reactions in Athens to the Sicilian catastrophe (VIII 1.1ff.) are (I admit) general rather than particular. Wilamowitz, 585, rejects the idea of Athenian sources. What we read in 33.2–34 is the sequel to ch. 30; both deal with Athenian operations, and I find it difficult to believe that Thucydides learned about them from Peloponnesian informants. I should not call it impossible.

whether (and how) Thucydides could have retained the denunciation of Astyochus to the authorities in Sparta, the instructions given in Sparta to the eleven men sent with the new fleet, and the difficulties experienced by his fleet. The second treaty of the Lacedaemonians with Tissaphernes (ch. 37) does not even in the present account have an "organic" place; what might have become of it if the chapters surrounding it had been rewritten from an Athenian perspective?

Regardless of how he organized his presentation, Thucydides had to practice the art of selecting, omitting, and condensing. At first reading, this may not be apparent; his narrative seems so straightforward that we forget the "reconstruction" that has produced it. To be sure, reconstruction is not here at its boldest, most experimental; no profound insight, no speculation has determined the arrangement of facts, but cool reflection has decided what to include and in what sequence. About the conditions found by Astyochus in Miletus, about the other Spartan fleet, and especially about the sufferings of the Chians,[26] Thucydides obviously does not tell all he had learned; but for whatever he does relate, he has seen to it that the reader knows antecedents and causes. At times interruptions in the coherent narrative are necessary to take care of events happening elsewhere at the same time, yet Thucydides has here—as we shall notice again and again—made a virtue of necessity; for while he deals with these subjects, his readers have the impression that time is passing, and this is the right frame of mind in which to read the sequel of the "main" story.[27]

[26] About continuous Athenian success in Chios and about the task force sent against Caunus and its setback, Book VIII even as it stands contains whatever seems essential. Perhaps there are other phases of Athenian strategy of which we remain ignorant.

[27] For comparable instances see pp. 200f. On chs. 45ff. where Alcibiades becomes important and should be considered as a source for

The sections of VIII dealing with the change in Athens from democracy to the government of the Four Hundred and then again to that of the Five Thousand are not an ideal subject for our kind of analysis because we do not know how satisfied Thucydides himself was with this account. Did he consider some phases sketchy and provisional, hoping to improve them some day when he had come to know more of the inside story or when he had finished other parts of his work? Speculative questions of this type are in principle justified, and there are instances where the impulse to answer in the affirmative is almost irresistible.[28]

The actual deliberations and decisions which established the government of the Five Thousand—the best constitution that Thucydides has known (97.2)—are reported in a very few sentences; we must content ourselves with a statement about πυκναὶ ἐκκλησίαι passing resolutions on "law-givers and other questions pertaining to the (new) constitution" (*ibid.*). The brevity[29] is particularly striking if compared with the rather detailed account of preliminary developments. For on these Thucydides presents a careful and indeed remarkably graphic description, setting forth how the navy in Samos remained opposed to the immediately preceding government of the Four Hundred and how it preserved the spirit of "freedom" (chs. 73–77). We also read (ch. 89) in some detail why and how hostility to the Four Hundred developed in Athens after everybody had at first been cowed into submission. Similarly the countermeasures of the oligarchs are set forth, with special emphasis on the ominous "fort" they

Thucydides and on their later insertion see Delebecque's attractive suggestions (77ff.; he refers to Wilamowitz and Bodin for similar views).

[28] See e.g. below pp. 192f.

[29] A concomitant event, the loss of Oenoe through the treachery of one of the oligarchs, is set forth in ch. 98 at what we may consider normal length.

built in Eetoneia (90.1ff.). Why Theramenes and Aristocrates, although belonging to the Four Hundred, turn against them, how cleverly the former, especially, goes to work, what impression his versions about secret plans make on the masses and at what junctures they become most effective, all this and much else is well-known to Thucydides, and he passes it on.[30] The entire account is both dramatic and rich in concrete events. Throughout it we sense that conditions are becoming increasingly explosive, and Thucydides certainly intended to convey this feeling. Finally, at the height of the crisis, confused as the situation must have been, Thucydides has yet succeeded in finding out precisely what happened in the Peiraeus and what in the city. He leads us to the point where the tension is so acute that a fight would have taken place had it not been for the timely intervention of some senior men, one of whom reminds the excited people that the enemy is watching from close by (92.8).

Atmosphere rather than information is produced when Thucydides mentions the mysterious assassination of Phrynichus and the hardly less mysterious confessions of someone connected with the murderer, who under torture reports "meetings of many people" in the homes of the polemarch and others. "Nothing further," Thucydides continues, "happened as a result of it" (92.2 med.), yet it sufficed for Theramenes and his accomplices to move ahead more boldly, especially since at the same time a Peloponnesian fleet appeared between Aegina and Epidaurus, and Theramenes knew how to arouse suspicion that it had been called by the oligarchs with treacherous intent (92.3). Atmosphere has influenced the developments. We know (above pp. 141f.) Thucydides' uncanny power of recreating it. Here he has

[30] I take it that the motives of the two oligarchs for changing sides are stated in 89.2, even though I am at a loss how to understand the sentence, have seen no satisfactory explanation (or correction), and am not even sure that the scholiast understood it.

used this power of imagination in the service of his reason to isolate stage after stage of the developments. It is almost impossible to resist the spell of his reconstruction.

Generally speaking, we have no reason to doubt the large role played by Theramenes during this critical situation; nor need we guess how Thucydides became so familiar with his doings. Still it must have been difficult for him to decide by what stages opposition against the Four Hundred grew and consolidated. Much had happened in secrecy; some people active at the time were dead when Thucydides returned to Athens, and others had an interest in suppressing or distorting the facts. In view of all this, we must allow for some incompleteness in Thucydides' reconstruction and for the possibility that he allots some individuals or events more importance than they actually had.[31] Did the meetings reported by the man put to the torture actually take place? And if so, for what purpose? Thucydides does not tell us, presumably because he himself does not know. Regarding the "fort" in Eetoneia, he inclines to the view that the suspicions were not groundless (91.3) and in support of it states what condition of things would have been most to the liking of the Four Hundred, what would have been their second choice, and what their third. Here he may be correct—or at least approximately correct—if indeed the oligarchs were so unanimous in their intentions and so sure to what length they would go. But we may as well recognize another productive use of his own reason in the reconstruction of their preferences.

[31] He knows about and appreciates the success which Thucydides of Pharsalus had with his words of wisdom (92.7). This fact and, as prior conditions to it, the turmoil in city and Peiraeus are inserted while we think of Theramenes as being on the way to the rebellious hoplites in the Peiraeus. Here protest actions lead to the destruction of the fort in Eetoneia. For Thucydides this is the most important result of Theramenes' intervention. I am unable to construe *φοβούμενοι* in 92.11, and suspect a lacuna (conceivably left by Thucydides himself).

Some promises made by the Four Hundred (93.2) keep the excited masses quiet. They wait for an assembly on a specified day. At the time agreed upon, the people convene full of expectation, when suddenly the approach of a Lacedaemonian fleet is announced. Thucydides is not sure what caused this appearance of the fleet, yet feels obliged to tell what was believed at the time and what he himself considers possible. Comprehending the beliefs in one sentence and his own hypotheses in another, he next turns to something he knows far better, which forms the natural sequel in his narrative, namely the political and military effects of this unexpected fleet. Both are appalling. For the fleet, appearing suddenly, while Athens is in the throes of a political crisis, causes nothing less than the loss of Euboea. Thucydides reports the Athenian measures designed to counter the attack upon this island. Preparations for a battle to retain Euboea were frustrated owing to the disaffection of the Eretrians, who handicapped the Athenians and thus played into the hands of the enemy.[32]

In the meantime the excitement of the Athenian population has shifted from the internal crisis to Euboea, where its vital interests are threatened. Thucydides moves his narrative correspondingly from the one theater of events to the other. About the futile efforts in Euboea he had gathered just enough material to fashion a coherent account. Next he

[32] Although the Peloponnesians are successful throughout 95.1–6, their conquest of Euboea is not complete; what happened is treated in one brief sentence (95.7.2), and Thucydides seems to have much less information about it. Collusion of the Eretrians with the Peloponnesians is made clear enough in 95.4; so is its adverse effect on the outcome of the battle. As *καιρός* for inserting it Thucydides chose the point where the Athenian commanders call their men to the boats—and find them absent. We may wonder how in 95.4 the *ὅπως*-clause became separated from *οὐδὲν γὰρ ἐπωλεῖτο ἀπὸ προνοίας τῶν Ἐρετριῶν*; (*ἀλλ' ἐκ τῶν* . . . disrupts the thought, just as badly as the *ὥσπερ*-clause in 48.1 where *ἐς αὐτούς* besides *ἑαυτοῖς* adds to our uneasiness. Schwartz, pp. 358f., proceeds in a very radical manner. Cf. n. 34 below).

describes the profoundly discouraging effect of the great loss upon Athenian morale, setting forth in a few sentences how gravely it hurt the prospects just at that point. Nor can he deny himself the satisfaction of indulging in reflections of a more general type (96.4f.). The Lacedaemonians could have exploited their success with results catastrophical for Athens, and it was after all a great advantage to the Athenians to have the slow moving Lacedaemonians as their principal enemies. Only after indulging in this piece of reasoning does Thucydides complete his account of the constitutional changes, and we have already seen how disproportionately brief and condensed this account is by comparison with the antecedents.[33] Still, while this section of Book VIII (chs. 89-98) is in many ways uneven and we should regard it as provisional, Thucydides has made the most effective use of his material, communicating not only the cause-and-result sequence of some developments but much of their dramatic quality as well.

If we wish for a contrast we may consider the great care Thucydides has taken to describe the previous change from democracy to the oligarchy of the Four Hundred.[34] Here however the situation and, correspondingly, his task were different. For in that instance the new form of government was most unpopular, running counter to the cherished traditions. Thucydides realizes fully how great a psychological resistance had to be overcome. For a hundred years the *demos* of Athens had enjoyed freedom and power (68.4). At first

[33] For a summary statement about the new constitution see 97.1; 97.2 contains, besides the reference to "numerous additional assemblies," Thucydides' own judgment about its merits. On Thucydides' reflections (here and elsewhere in Book VIII) see Schwartz's brilliant remark, pp. 88f. See also J. de Romilly, 84.

[34] I do not, however, suggest that, in the account as we read it, the organization of the material has everywhere been completed. Absence of a final revision is the obvious diagnosis e.g. for the relation of 82.2 to 86.4. The similarity cannot be explained by supposing the danger at 86.4 to be more acute. See Schwartz, pp. 78f.

(53), while the idea of a constitutional reform is still closely connected with the recall of Alcibiades and with hopes for his influence in Persia, there is nevertheless passionate protest on the part of the citizens. To calm it, Peisander, who is most active at this point in the interest of the oligarchic faction, discusses the war with each leader of the protest actions individually, causing him to realize that there is no hope unless the new proposals are accepted.[35]

Later, when Alcibiades' promises have come to nothing, the unraveling of the events and the building up of rationally acceptable sequences becomes difficult. Developments in Athens as well as in Samos are important; they have not only to be reconstructed but as far as possible to be correlated with one another. We select a few characteristic features of this reconstruction.

Peisander, who operates as messenger and propagandist between Samos and Athens, serves also for Thucydides as a link between his description of developments in both places (chs. 49, 53f., 63.3–65.1, 67f.). But while dealing with the first phase of the revolution in Samos, Thucydides becomes engrossed in the tangled machinations of Phrynichus (48.4–51). Pleased as Thucydides may have been to know the whole "truth" about them, the private dealings of an individual monopolize our attention for an abnormally long stretch.[36]

[35] Delebecque, p. 145, has a rather artificial theory about the role given by Thucydides to Peisander. His analysis of chs. 53ff. and 73ff. is attractive, it should stimulate further efforts. The same is true of ch. 63 (pp. 146ff.), where he exaggerates the difficulties. E.g. Alcibiades' "unwillingness" (63.4) is no problem but amply substantiated by ch. 56. Delebecque and others correctly advocate the presence, side by side in Book VIII, of various blocks unamalgamated and reflecting earlier and later information; but there is also deliberate composition.

[36] Phrynichus' intrigues (48.4–51.3) produce no political results but turn into a question of life and death for himself. Marveling how Thucydides disentangled the complicated plot, we can only hope that he had enough information and applied his acumen felicitously. See von Fritz I 765 and below, n. 92.

Later, when Peisander returns (63.3ff.), the atmosphere in Samos has changed. The hopes originally connected with Alcibiades have vanished, yet there is all the more confidence among the oligarchic leaders in their own strength and resources, and the readiness for a new type of government has also grown stronger. It seems to be a better guarantee for effective warfare.

In Athens psychological conditions are more complex, yet all-important. Realizing this, Thucydides here, too, dwells on the atmosphere. Distrust and mutual suspicion are general. So much happens stealthily and is apt to intimidate people that they no longer know whom to trust. Rumors are spread, false impressions created, nobody is able or dares to find out the truth. Thucydides, although he was not present to experience this state of mind, must have heard about it—partly perhaps from other exiles, partly after his return, yet without using the resources of his own imagination he could not have conveyed the psychological effects of terror. Another device to explain the success of the "conspiracy" is his no less masterly characterization of the men primarily responsible for it. Peisander, Antiphon, Phrynichus,[37] and Theramenes had the exceptional qualities of intellect that were necessary for this enterprise. In a chapter altogether unique in his work (68), Thucydides makes it a point to acquaint us with each of them and his peculiar capacities. Because engineered by such men, τὸ ἔργον οὐκ ἀπεικότως—i.e. in accordance with τὸ εἰκός—καίπερ μέγα ὂν προυχώρησεν (68.4). How smoothly "the great enterprise," *scil.* the overthrow of the democratic institutions, proceeded, we learn in chapters 69 f. A few steps taken with determination after favorable conditions for them have been created suffice to cow the *demos*. However, before we read much farther, new contacts taken up with Samos

[37] That Thucydides realizing to what extent the success of the daring plot depended on the leading personalities gives so full a portrait of them is a signal proof for the flexibility of his method.

(71.4, 72) furnish Thucydides with an unobtrusive transition to the new developments that are afoot (ἐνεωτερίζετο). These are hostile to Athens and the Four Hundred in power.[38] In Samos it suffices for Thucydides to identify the most active personalities, Thrasybulus and Thrasyllus (73.4), but closer characterization of them is not necessary. All the more does he dwell on the psychological conditions, the high morale and the spirit of opposition, if not downright hostility to Athens.[39]

Throughout these sections Thucydides shows an almost uncanny gift for penetrating to the decisive causes, no matter whether they are unusual individuals, clever machinations, a state of morale, or an emotional atmosphere. About the ἔργα τῶν πραχθέντων his information seems at times to be defective, but for what he knows he has found a place where it has its function in the historical sequence, and we must hope that from the chronological viewpoint these places are correctly chosen.

When we move on to larger units, we have even more reason to admire the intellectual powers brought to bear on their reconstruction, yet we also see reconstruction pass into

[38] In ch. 72 the Four Hundred send ten envoys to Samos, fearing that there may be hostility. The fear is more than justified, and the hostility has actually grown to such dimensions that the envoys think it better to bide their time in Delos (77). Later, when arriving in Samos (86), they find Alcibiades practically in control, are given a very emotional reception, and sent back with a message entirely at variance with their mission (86.6).

[39] See chs. 73, 77. Note the sanguine opinions reported 76.3–7 at remarkable length. I pass over some episodes of the revolution, e.g. the negotiations with Agis and his reactions (70.2; 71). It is always of special interest to see at what point Thucydides decided to insert subjects of the kind and whether he inserted them as a unit or each phase as chronology demanded. In this instance he has preferred the former course.

"composition," and composition becomes meaningful where it suggests a judgment about particular situations and their significance. Weight and length accorded to events may depend on the relative importance which Thucydides gives them.

The episode of Pylos and Sphacteria will serve as the first illustration. Some of Thucydides' sources can be identified with reasonable certainty.[40] They include his own recollections of Athenian assemblies, extensive descriptions given by Demosthenes (as likely as not to Thucydides himself), probably also an official memorandum by the commanders of the Athenian fleet, the text of a short-range treaty concluded for the period of negotiations, and finally—although not everybody would agree on this—supplementary knowledge derived from inquiries made by Thucydides when he spent some time in the Peloponnesus. Despite so many sources, there are gaps in his information about strategic movements, especially of the Spartan fleet, while vagueness, incompleteness, or inaccuracy in matters of topography betray lack of personal familiarity with the territory.[41] Varied as his material was, it had to be supplemented by Thucydides' own reconstruction of motives and intentions. In this and in the synthesis of facts learned from different quarters he proceeds with his characteristic sovereign confidence.

To be more specific, the official Athenian commanders are likely in their report home to have disclaimed all responsi-

[40] See E. Schwartz, pp. 290ff. and his excellent conclusions p. 294; Wilamowitz, *SBBerl Ak.*, 1921, 308ff.; Gomme III 485 (with further references) and *Essays* 125ff. I follow each of them in some points, parting with them on others.

[41] Wilamowitz, *SBBerl Ak.*, 307. The topographical studies of G. B. Grundy, *JHS* 16 (1896) 1ff., and R. M. Burrows, *ibid.* 55ff., suggest that Thucydides had not visited the region. Burrows thinks he consulted the commanders of the Athenian fleet. See also Grundy's much later discussion in his *Thucydides and the History of His Age* (Oxford, 2nd ed., 1948) 122ff.

bility for the adventure in Pylos, pointing out that in accordance with their instructions they had proceeded onward in the direction of Corcyra.[42] Several details in the first chapters give the impression of going back to this official document. On the other hand Demosthenes could supply Thucydides with a full version not only of what happened when the fleet was marooned for a few days in Pylos and what he and his men did afterward but also of his personal judgments, and of his plan for the invasion of Sphacteria and the tactics to be employed on this occasion.[43] Lacedaemonian sources suggest themselves for the countermovements (including the reason why at first they were so slow, IV 5) as well as for later apprehensions and discouragement on that side.

In a few instances, it is fairly clear that Thucydides synthesized Athenian and Lacedaemonian information. In chapter 13 he knows from the Lacedaemonians what they did before and after the Athenian boats returned to Pylos from Zacynthus, from the Athenians what impressions they had of the situation and how difficult it was to orient themselves about the strategic conditions and arrive at a decision. Similarly in chapter 26, he first describes the deteriorating morale of the Athenians in Pylos, while on the island the Lacedaemonians show no sign of yielding; next, making the Lacedaemonians his subject (26.5), he explains the reason for their endurance. Some of the ingenious devices by which they were able to provision themselves were detected by the Athenians, who then tried to cut them off (7f.); but what became known thus could hardly suffice for an account as full and convincingly organized as that in chapter 26.[44]

[42] Wilamowitz, *SBBerl Ak.*, 309 f., thus explains the improbabilities in chs. 2-5.

[43] See below pp. 202f.

[44] See Schwartz, pp. 293f. for the synthesizing of reports from both sides.

About the final battle on Sphacteria, where fusion of Athenian with Spartan information is again almost certain, more will be said later.

Although the Lacedaemonian fleet was closing in on the men in Pylos, Demosthenes succeeded in dispatching two boats to the naval commanders in Zacynthus asking them to return and help. This action, decisive for the later success, is inserted (8.3) in the description of the Lacedaemonian operations, which is thus for a moment interrupted. To us this may seem the obvious place for mentioning the step, but we should not underrate the careful thought with which it has been chosen. No less obvious may appear the point for introducing Demosthenes' long-time connections with the Messenian natives;[45] they are used as an argument by him when he urges his fellow commanders to fortify Pylos in what "was once Messenian land" (3.2), and there was no equally good reason for referring to them earlier.[46]

Far more precarious were decisions concerning the location of other topics. In 29.2 Cleon, having been charged by the assembly to liquidate the resistance on Sphacteria, chooses Demosthenes as his "chief of staff" because he knew that "he had plans for an invasion of Sphacteria." Demosthenes may even have asked the Athenians to send him additional troops (30f.) and have specified the kind of soldiers he needed.[47] His project developed in the atmosphere of discouragement spreading in Pylos when the Lacedaemonians showed no sign

[45] IV 3.3; cf. III 94.3 and esp. 95.1.

[46] *Scil.* as far as we can tell; yet there is something tantalizingly mysterious about ch. 2. Being sent out as a private citizen, Demosthenes is given far-reaching permission about the ships. Had Demosthenes in Athens given indications of what he had in mind, and had Thucydides never heard of this?

[47] In 30.3 no such request for reinforcements from Athens is mentioned; yet the grammatical subject of (στρατιὰν ἦν) ᾐτήσατο is, we tend to assume, Demosthenes. Cleon certainly knows what kind of troops will prove useful (28.4).

of weakening. We have read of this atmosphere in an earlier chapter (26.1–7) and may wonder why Demosthenes' project is not recorded in that context. Since it was known to Cleon, the latter's behavior in the Assembly, his attack on Nicias and emphatic insistence on a more active strategy, are not the empty boasts and demagogic manoeuvres Thucydides makes them appear to be, nor would the reader see them in this light if he had previously learned of Demosthenes' intention. Thucydides, by the arrangement and sequence that he has chosen, tries to force on us his own judgment of Cleon. After indulging in a dramatic presentation of Cleon as the victim of his arrogance and lack of judgment, he furnishes the information apt to suggest a different understanding of Cleon's conduct.[48] Yet what reader would go back and revise his impressions?

In the preceding chapter we scrutinized the considerations of Demosthenes and the responses of Cleon. Both illustrate, even if not to the same degree, the psychological devices that Thucydides had at his command. Yet in the case of Cleon, prejudice has influenced this psychology.[49]

The story of Pylos and Sphacteria is twice interrupted by chapters dealing with other areas of the war. The first instance of the kind (ch. 7) is brief, and the matter may as well have been inserted for no more profound reason than that it took place at the same time (7.1). But chapters 24 and 25, dealing with events in Sicily and southern Italy, have a function in the main narrative. Although the events are again simultaneous, chronology merely provides an excuse; the true purpose is to create a feeling for the long time passing and the increasing hardships endured by the Athenians in Pylos. When we

[48] Cf. 29.2 and the very full report about Demosthenes' strategic considerations extending through this and the next chapter. His intentions are not mentioned in ch. 27 either. Cf. above, p. 164, for comments on the presentation of Cleon.

[49] See again above, p. 164.

return to them (ch. 26), nothing at all has changed. We understand how demoralizing the effect must have been. The discomforts of life in their improvised camp are felt so strongly because no end is in sight and winter is approaching.

Thucydides is astonishingly brief (23.1) about the shady pretexts under which the Athenians retain the Lacedaemonian fleet, although they were pledged to return it after the truce had run out; nor does he say more of the Lacedaemonian response than that they protested and called the action an injustice. He seems to have known some details but refers to them as *οὐκ ἀξιόλογα* (23.1). At the end of the Pylos episode, he is equally brief about continued Lacedaemonian peace feelers in Athens (41.3f.). We should imagine them to have been important. Here he may actually not have known more, for these moves took place after he had been exiled.[50] In the former instances the brevity and cavalier treatment are less easy to explain.

Besides the decisive battle on the island, one long and essential part of the account has not yet been discussed. It is the speech of the Lacedaemonian envoys who are negotiating in Athens about the men cut off on Sphacteria and about the feasibility of concluding a treaty (chs. 17–20). This speech serves Thucydides as a vehicle for conveying the deeper significance of the Pylos-Sphacteria episode. Elsewhere he is engrossed in the events, their mutual relationships, causes, and consequences; much, he shows, is due to mere chance, yet not a little is the result of deliberate planning. Here he rises above the factual aspects to view the "episode" in the perspective of the whole war. It has a very definite meaning. A great success has been played into the hands of the Athenians, who had no right to expect it.[51] This

[50] Wilamowitz, *SSBerl Ak.*, 312; Gomme *ad loc.*

[51] *Scil.* and even less right to expect such success to continue; see esp. 17.4f.; 18.4. Cf. H. Erbse, *RhM* 96 (1953) 55. For the thought content and the significance of this speech see Eduard Meyer, *For-*

was their chance to conclude the war on very advantageous terms. To do so would have been in accord with the spirit of Pericles, with his foresight and his awareness of the unpredictable turns a war is liable to take.[52] The Lacedaemonian experience, very effectively summarized by the envoys from this point of view (see esp. 18.2), was undeserved and improbable; for this very reason it should be a warning to Athens and a reminder of the irrational vicissitudes of war. Has Athens itself not experienced the unpredictable (or "unforeseeable," ἀπροόρατον) in dimensions startling even to Pericles? The envoys' speech brings home to us what a unique opportunity of quitting the war with honor and success Athens let slip. The events of Pylos and Sphacteria were a part of the war, and the narrative treats them as such. This speech by contrast defines the very special function of the "episode" in the great drama. A present-day historian need not accept this interpretation; he may even consider it an attempt to find more "reason," λόγος, in history than it actually has. Still, that a "meaning" is here sought and found will hardly be contested.

The chapters dealing with the final battle (32–35) still call for analysis. If Thucydides received a first-hand report from Demosthenes, this would include his plan for the invasion and the fight on Sphacteria. Although we know that Thucydides' confidence in reason may show itself in reconstructing plans from events, and have (in Chapter V) studied instances of the kind, Sphacteria seemed to be an exception and the realization of the γνώμη in some measure true to the facts.[53]

schungen zur Alten Geschichte (Halle, 1899) II 351f. and *Gesch. des Alt.* (Stuttgart, 1901) IV 17ff. After others, Erbse carries Meyer's views farther.

52 Some of the details are not of the kind to be foreseen. We shall come back (pp. 214ff., 221f.) to the reconstruction of plans and thoughts.

53 For γνώμη and its realization cf. J. de Romilly, *Histoire,* 123ff. (Sphacteria, 129ff.). See also the suggestions below, pp. 204ff.

For the battle as such, communications from both sides must be assumed. We may experiment with the idea that Thucydides had talked only to Athenian participants and owes the Lacedaemonian reactions to an imaginative use of the *eikos*, but even the richest imagination could hardly reconstruct the abundance of specific items in chapters 33–35.[54] The battle itself begins as planned; still in chapter 33.2, a few additional features are mentioned, no less than six being of a causal type: (1) the "light-armed" (ψιλοί) fighters could manoeuvre easily because they were mobile (κοῦφοι), and thus (2) could without effort outdistance their pursuers; in this they were helped (3) by the difficulty and (4) roughness of the ground. The latter of these qualities is in turn explained by (5) the lack of all previous inhabitation. Onto such territory the Lacedaemonians could not follow (6) since they wore heavy armour. After a while they had to slacken their pace in pursuing the "light-armed" (34.1). This in turn improves the morale and intensifies the activity of these; yet two other factors help at the same time; for the "light-armed" (a) realize their numerical superiority and (b) gain courage because, now that matters have come to a test, the Lacedaemonians do not prove as formidable as had been expected (this original apprehension again is suggested and at once explained by two participles, 34.1). Against such background we understand that these fighters renew their attack with increased vigor.

At this point (34.2) Thucydides changes again to the Lacedaemonians. They are in a state of consternation (ἔκπληξις). Of the shouts which help to cause it we read earlier (34.1), nor do the words "being unaccustomed to this manner of fighting" (34.2) introduce an entirely new notion to us. Still, Thucydides wishes to remind us of these causes as

[54] "Can anyone fail to see that much of the narrative is from accounts given by the Spartan soldiers themselves?" Gomme, *Essays*, 129; see also his remarks on the interrogation of captives, 125, 130.

operative before he adds one more, the clouds of dust rising from the newly burned forest.[55] The simultaneous effect of missiles, stones, and dust leads to new trouble; it was impossible for anyone to see what was in front of him. The description of all misfortunes that beset the Lacedaemonians culminates (34.3) in a sentence beginning with an understatement: *τὸ ἔργον ἐνταῦθα χαλεπὸν τοῖς Λακεδαιμονίοις καθίστατο.* Their plight has become worse, since (1) their cuirasses afford them no protection against the missiles, (2) their spear shafts are broken (as a result of being hit), (3) being unable to see what is ahead of them, they do not know how to move, (4) the shouts make it impossible for them to hear any commands. Two participle constructions, while not adding anything to the facts, sum up the psychological condition produced by this accumulation of misfortunes: danger surrounded them on every side and in despair they saw no way of defending and saving themselves (34.3). Thus they decided to withdraw to their last refuge, the almost impregnable position at the end of the island.[56] In the sentence recording this, two facets of the situation are mentioned for the first time: "many of them had been wounded" and they had "to move backward and forward always over the same ground" (35.1).

It is hardly necessary to comment on the singularly concentrated presentation of a large amount of material and the coordination effected by assigning to each element its best place. Stories that Thucydides received from participants of either side would in all probability be vivid and substantial (even if we bear in mind that everybody must have been absorbed in the fighting and suffered from limited visibility);

[55] We have read about the fire in 29.2–30.2.

[56] The final securing of access to this position—a repetition on a smaller scale of what happened at Thermopylae (36.3)—and the negotiations ending in the surrender of the Lacedaemonians (37) are less rewarding subjects for an analysis.

most could tell him of several developments that deserved to be incorporated; two, three, or even more men would concur in recalling identical conditions; yet at times one man might remember an item that the others had forgotten or never noticed. Fact and reason may often have been reported separately to Thucydides, who decided to connect them and knew where to insert them into the reconstructed course of the battle. The contrast between the apprehension of the "light-armed" before their first experience with the Lacedaemonians and their confidence afterward was doubtless important enough to be recorded; yet its importance would have escaped many historians, while others would have needed one or several sentences to explain it. Not so Thucydides (34.1). With a remarkable economy of words he has included whatever helps us to appreciate this change of morale, and yet has kept this topic subordinate to the main theme, the actual progress of the battle. The variety of syntactical structures available in his language was essential, and he has made full use of it. We may still note that some items, by occurring twice, provide links and create coherence. The poor visibility from which the Lacedaemonians suffer, where first referred to (34.2), is the result of missiles, stones, and ashes; the second time (34.3) it figures not as result but as cause, contributing to the helplessness of the Lacedaemonians, who simply no longer know what to do. A similar function is performed by the shouts of the "light-armed" fighters, which are mentioned three times. First (34.1) "shouting" is a concomitant of their attack as well as an expression of their newly won self-confidence. Next we read of the effect the shouts have on the Lacedaemonians. Being exposed to them and at the same time to an attack—Thucydides can hardly suggest in earnest that the shouts mattered more than the attack—they lost their nerve (34.2) since they were not used to this kind of fighting. Finally, when the desperate situation of the Lacedaemonians has reached its extreme, a more specific effect of the shouts has contributed to it; it was because of them that the Lacedaemonians could no longer hear the commands of their own leaders (34.3).

We have just seen how Thucydides, through his reconstruction and presentation, endows an episode of the war with a special function and thus enhances its significance. Extreme brevity and omission, too, may have a purpose, and to gain further insight into Thucydides' reconstruction, and composition, we turn to the first step that Athens took on the road to war.

In I 31 we have reached the point where a Corcyrean embassy appeals in Athens for help against the Corinthians, and, counteracting them, delegates of the Corinthians seek to prevent an alliance between Athens and Corcyra. The preceding eight chapters report with a concentration upon the essential which, as far as we know, no previous writer achieved, first the negotiations of Epidamnus with Corcyra and Corinth (24f.) and then the war resulting between the latter two as result of Corinth's intervention on the side of Epidamnus (chs. 26–31). So far, the Corcyreans have not needed aid from outside; they have defeated the Corinthians in a naval battle, crushed Epidamnus, and extended their own sway over large areas of the Ionian sea long considered a Corinthian preserve.[57] Now, however, on learning how extensive preparations the Corinthians are making to resume the war on a larger scale, Corcyra realizes the need to abandon its traditional

[57] See for these successes 29.5. For an illuminating reconstruction of the same developments by a present-day historian see Donald Kagan, *The Outbreak of the Peloponnesian War* (Ithaca, N. Y. and London, 1969) 205–250. Before the publication of this book, I had come to identical or similar conclusions on some of the political questions; I welcome the agreement and have shortened my draft; yet at the price of duplicating Kagan's arguments, I have set forth my own reasoning when I need it for the points I wish to make.

policy of isolation, and turns to Athens as an obvious potential ally (31.1–3).

In Chapter I we analyzed the contest of speeches and arguments between Corcyrean and Corinthian envoys in Athens; in Chapter IV we touched on noteworthy features in the wording of the speeches. What interests us at present is the effect of the arguments upon a fateful political decision. Far more effective than the debate about justice, expediency, etc., is that the envoys from Corcyra do not appear with empty hands. Corcyra's navy is one of the three strongest in Greece, and the Athenian response then and there will determine whether this navy will in the future war fight on the side of Athens or fall into the hands of Corinth, changing the balance of power to the detriment of Athens.[58] This argument is bound to influence the Athenians. At the same time they are under no illusions about the dangers of allying themselves with Corcyra at a point where it finds itself at war with an important member of the Peloponnesian League. After two days of meeting and debate, the Athenians decide upon concluding a "limited" alliance (44.1).

It is very instructive to see how Thucydides has handled questions of relative length and emphasis in these chapters. He allows the Corcyreans and Corinthians to present their cases in elaborate argumentation; both have weighty reasons in support of their appeal. Expediency as well as justice, the claims of past favors, and the bearing on future advantages are given their due.[59] The issue has thus been brought to the Athenians in its full gravity, and that they do not easily reach a decision is obvious from the necessity to hold a second meeting after opinions remained divided in the first. Yet a historian has every right to call Thucydides' account of their

[58] See 33.2 and esp. the strong trump card played off at the end 36.3.

[59] See for the former two esp. 32.1ff., 34.1ff., 35.4ff. (also 36f.), 40.1ff., 4ff., 42.1ff.; for the latter 33, 35.5, 36, 40.5, 41.2f.

deliberations "most unsatisfactory" and to complain about its brevity, since the arguments for and against an alliance have been compressed into a few short clauses. Surely "sharply differing attitudes" would have made "the situation ideal for a typically Thucydidean pair of speeches."[60] Thucydides' unwillingness to avail himself of this opportunity contrasts strongly with the readiness with which he allows the Corcyreans and Corinthians to argue at length for their respective interests. He "has deliberately ignored the factional conflict in Athens" and in particular—indeed "the most surprising of all the Thucydidean omissions"—has said nothing at all of Pericles' role in the debate. Failure to mention Pericles may seem excused by the impersonal tenor kept up throughout the account. Thucydides does not identify any individual Corinthian or Corcyrean and changes this method only when it comes to the appointment of commanders for the ten ships sent to the aid of Corcyra.[61]

Still the anomaly remains curious and is compounded when we later (50.5) become acquainted with an additional decision of the Athenians under circumstances that make it a complete surprise. Originally, only ten boats had been sent out from Athens, with instructions severely limiting any active assistance to the Corcyreans. Yet "fearing (what indeed came to pass) that the Corcyreans might be defeated and their own ten boats too few to defend them," the Athenians later decided to send twenty more boats. Quite evidently this decision involves the Athenians much more deeply in the war between Corinth and Corcyra. Even if we assume these ships to have been dispatched with the same instructions as the first ten, this cannot have happened without at least one

[60] See Kagan, p. 237.

[61] 45.2 (cf. Kagan's comments, p. 243). Correspondingly the commanders of the Corinthian forces are named (29.2; 46.2); those of the Corcyreans may not have been known to Thucydides.

other meeting of the Assembly, and this meeting would again produce a lively debate between conflicting opinions. Yet beyond the words just quoted, Thucydides tells nothing about the reasons and deliberations behind the sudden appearance of these twenty ships. Still more astonishingly, the words occur in a relative clause (50.5), interfering, though only for a moment, with the suspense with which we follow the naval operations in their most dramatic stage. When the boats appear on the scene of the battle, they are as much a surprise to the Corinthians as to the Athenians already present, not to mention the reader. The large Corinthian preparations having issued in an expedition, a decisive engagement between the two fleets is taking place. In the description of the battle (48f.) Thucydides has slowed the pace of his narrative and is less sparing of details, conceivably because these operations, even if not yet a part of his actual subject, are closer to it than the earlier developments. The Corcyreans are so thoroughly beaten that in the end (49.7) even the ten Athenian boats, when they join actively in the fighting, can no longer change the outcome. In short, the situation of the Corcyreans is desperate, and Corcyra itself seems to lie defenseless at the mercy of the Corinthians (50.3–5), when the arrival of the additional twenty Athenian ships prompts them to give up their attack (fear that still more Athenian ships might follow in the wake of these twenty is a further motive for not completing victory and conquest). The reversal of their plans is as dramatic as the completely unexpected appearance of the twenty additional boats; and since the facts themselves invited it, Thucydides has indulged his gift for creating a regular *peripeteia*.

Thucydides' reconstruction is surely not the only one conceivable. We have already expressed astonishment at his silence about the deliberations in Athens that must have preceded the dispatch of the twenty ships. It might not be easy to determine the best place for an account of these deliberations,[62] but some place could doubtless have been found. Once more—and even more radically than in the case of the two former assemblies—Thucydides has abstained from communicating to us what happened at these meetings, who spoke for and who spoke against the proposal, whether the apprehension that ten boats might not suffice was shared by everybody, and much else of the kind.

Again, what we miss most is mention of Pericles. There is no need to go over the ground covered by the investigations of eminent scholars. Arguing on the general basis of Pericles' dominating position and referring to the versions of these events in Diodorus and Plutarch, they give Pericles a major role in the debate. He must have had some, even if not the sole, responsibility for the decision to help the Corcyreans.[63] Thucydides, as we have seen, felt no obligation to bring out this responsibility; he preferred to treat the deliberations —i.e. the minimum he says about them—in a completely impersonal way. May we think of any reason for this preference?

We cannot help moving into the realm of speculation if we try to find this reason in Thucydides' over-all conception of Pericles and his statesmanship. A key motif of his policy for the entire Peloponnesian War is "no expansion" and "no additional enterprise."[64] It is well known with what fatal

[62] As it stands, the account of the Corinthian expedition (chs. 46-50) is very compact, and any interruption taking us to a setting as different as one or several assemblies in Athens would damage this compactness. So much must be admitted, but to think that Thucydides, whether or not it meant recasting the account, could not have informed us of what went on in Athens would be most unfair to his intellectual powers.

[63] In Plutarch, *Per.* 29, Pericles is the prime mover of both decisions. Of modern scholars, see besides Kagan, G. de Sanctis, *Storia dei Greci* (Florence, 3rd ed., 1942) II 260; F. E. Adcock, *CAH* V 181ff.; Ed. Meyer, *Gesch. d. Alt.* IV 282.

[64] See esp. I 144.1; II 65.6f.

results the Athenians departed from this wise course many years after his death. Moreover we have recently been warned not to associate him with any expansionist tendencies, particularly in Sicily and Italy, during the last ten or even more years preceding the war.[65] Well and good; still even the frustratingly brief report in I 44 about the motives for Athenian intervention on the side of Corcyra ends with the statement: ἅμα δὲ τῆς Ἰταλίας καὶ Σικελίας καλῶς ἐφαίνετο αὐτοῖς ἡ νῆσος ἐν παράπλῳ κεῖσθαι. Tantalizing words; yet they must reflect elaborate pleas made for Athenian interests in these two areas, no matter whether the pleas stressed economic, strategic, or political and, *sit venia verbo*, "expansionist" concerns—in fact I see no reason why all of them should not have figured in the debate. Even if Pericles, in keeping with a policy he had recently pursued, did not consider Corcyra as a steppingstone for expansion westward, if he resisted the extremists[66] and threw the force of his authority behind the relatively moderate proposal that in the end was adopted, any appearance of his name in association with "expansionist" tendencies would have damaged the conception of his political personality that is fundamental for Thucydides' understanding of the war.

[65] If Kagan 154–169 (cf. also 173, 235) has made a good case for his opinion, the views set forth by von Fritz (I 732ff.) a few years previously need qualification. Still the point of special concern to von Fritz—undue isolation of the great Sicilian expedition by Thucydides—would seem valid. How prone the Athenians remained to adventures in that direction is shown by their ready consent to the requests coming in 427 from Leontini. De Ste. Croix, pp. 220ff., is skeptical regarding expansionist policy in the West. It certainly is true that all theories about it are precarious.

[66] For divergent interpretations of Thuc. I 44.3 see again Kagan, 239ff., who also discusses Pericles' motives for advocating a moderate degree of help. Plut., *Per.* 29, gives us glimpses of the extremist party that attacks the ten ships as inadequate. Regardless of whether Pericles considered a war with the Peloponnesian League unlikely, likely, or inevitable, the future of Corcyra's fleet cannot have left him indifferent. Cf. de Sanctis, *op. cit.* 260.

At the time when the question of support for Corcyra came up in the Assembly, Pericles could still entertain hopes of averting the war. He may have favored support of Corcyra for reasons unrelated to "expansion" but related to the balance of naval power—and thereby even to the preservation of peace. Even so, the principles of "no new enterprise" and "no expansion of the Empire" as conditions for victory would have sounded mildly ironical if a new enterprise dangerously close to expansionist tendencies had led to the outbreak of the war. Worse than this, if he contributed to a decision related to—I put it vaguely, because Thucydides provides nothing concrete—Athenian interests in Italy and Sicily, the fatal expedition of 415 might have looked like a continuation of a policy promoted by Pericles. Surely Athenian policy before the war and during the war were two different subjects. A thoughtful reader might have regarded Pericles' attitude in response to the Corcyrean request as no less reasonable and justified than the policies formulated by him for a successful conduct of the war. But what makes the conception of his statesmanship so impressive is his firm determination. Inevitably the compactness and integrity of the picture would have suffered had it been necessary to make distinctions or to allow for something that looked like a deviation from the strict line.

The more we study the composition of larger units, the more we see how reconstruction may pass into "construction" that treats and organizes details with regard to their significance. Pylos has provided an illustration in the speech of the Lacedaemonian embassy, Corcyra in the peculiar selection of the material included and in the distribution of the accents. Since "reconstruction" is a modern term, we may as well define it as covering not only the discovery but also the organization of "facts." The subject of the work is the Peloponnesian War; Thucydides would consider his account of it as "true" if every part was treated in its relation to and significance for the whole (πρεπόντως τῷ ὅλῳ). Reconstruction, one of the novel manifestations of reason, could in these early days of exuberance be carried to such length.

The Sicilian expedition as narrated in Books VI and VII would do more than any other part of the work to substantiate this view; but since we cannot attempt the analysis of so large a complex, we must be content with looking at some of its last phases. The arrival of Gylippus (VII 1ff.) is the turning point after which Athenian fortunes move downhill. When Demosthenes appears with reinforcements for their side (42), prospects brighten somewhat, yet he himself takes a very realistic view of the situation. Not indulging in great hopes, he proposes to force the decision by one bold and imaginative action (42.4f.), and the attack upon Epipolae is planned by him in this spirit. If it succeeds, Syracuse will be conquered; in the opposite event, the Athenian forces should give up and return home. His plan for the attack is carried out, but instead of accepting its failure in the sense intended by him, the Athenians fight two more battles. How has Thucydides treated each of the three?

Although Demosthenes has decided to concentrate on an all-out attack, there are first some skirmishes. When they turn into attacks on the city walls and fail, the commanders agree to prepare everything for the one big attack at night.[67]

In tracing the course of this attack, Thucydides at first distinguishes several phases of Athenian success. The guards first encountered are overwhelmed (43.3), and when larger numbers of fighters are mobilized, the Athenians continue to keep the upper hand (4f.), a success that Thucydides explains as the result of having taken the enemy by surprise.[68]

[67] For Demosthenes' decision see 42.4f. (reading in 5 ἦ—καὶ MSS.—οἱ συντομωτάτην ἡγεῖτο διαπολέμησιν). For the skirmishes see 42.6; 43.1.

[68] 43.5. The capture of the Syracusan "counter-wall," one of the strategic objectives, is achieved (43.5; cf. 42.4).

It is only after they have moved farther that disorder in their ranks, combined with excessive confidence and eagerness, brings about a reversal, the Boeotians being the first to turn the Athenian victory into a rout.

At this point Thucydides changes the tenor of the description. He confesses himself unable to distinguish further stages of the battle. We have read of incipient disorder; now there is widespread ταραχή and ἀπορία. Thucydides knows what caused them and also what forms the confusion took.[69] In fact this diagnosis of causes and symptoms probably serves the dual purpose of explaining the thorough defeat of the Athenians and Thucydides' own inability to supply a step-by-step account of how it came about. Only at the end is he again in a position to report details, in particular why some men in the rout succeeded in saving their lives while others did not (44.8).

Chapter 45 contains the usual epilogue of a battle, the trophies set up by the victors and the losses suffered by the vanquished. The second battle begins in chapter 51. Between these chapters, Thucydides dwells on the morale in both camps. The Syracusans greatly encouraged ὡς ἐπ' ἀπροσδοκήτῳ εὐπραγίᾳ (46.1), use the changed situation to look for additional allies. On the Athenian side, everything, including health conditions, has developed to the worse. To give up the whole enterprise would be the logical conclusion—and Demosthenes insists on drawing it.[70] The reasons why his intention did not prevail require very careful explanation. Because Nicias' opposition was extremely important, Thucydides trusts himself to inform us both of Nicias' "secret" motivations and of the arguments he openly advanced in the deliberations.[71] This is an instance of the extraordinary con-

[69] See 44.1-7. Cf. J. de Romilly, *Histoire*, 168ff., and for a different opinion Delebecque, p. 64. Adam Parry, *YCS* 22 (1972) 47, n. 1, makes a good point on the "confusion."

[70] 47.3. Cf. the judgment formed by him on arrival (42.3ff.).

[71] 48-49.1; note esp. the first sentence of 48.3. May the astonishing

fidence with which Thucydides reconstructs motives. We shall presently come back to this subject.

Nicias prevails, even though Demosthenes meets him halfway with an alternative proposal (49.2). Yet when large reinforcements for the Syracusans arrive, the attitude in both camps changes again. The additional forces now present strengthen Syracusan readiness for the attack (50.3), while on the Athenian side even Nicias is now willing to give up. At this point the eclipse occurs, and Nicias with the majority of the Athenians regards it as an omen prohibiting departure (50.4). Thus the withdrawal is once more delayed. The chapter (50) containing these new developments is as dramatic as the preceding and following descriptions of battles. Although Thucydides allows himself a digression to report about battles fought in Africa by the reinforcements from Sparta, he is as brief as possible about each of their actions. At the end of one long sentence listing the stages of their journey, they have arrived in Sicily. We return to the mainline of the narrative, ready to learn with relief of an overdue decision finally taken. Yet immediately afterward we read that its implementation was postponed.

This delay proves fatal; for during the time thus gained the Syracusans, sufficiently aware of Athenian conditions and intentions and by now confident of their own superiority, move to the offensive. An attack on the Athenian fortification leads to no more than limited success (51.2). Yet on the following day, when the Sicilians attack simultaneously with their boats and on land, they score a definite naval victory. About the details of the naval battle Thucydides recounts

repetition of 48.2 be called a "long-winded recapitulation"? See K. J. Dover *ad loc.*; his hypothesis that further revision might have shortened the text is probably the best, although it does not remove all difficulties. As usual, we wonder how Thucydides could know so much even about secret thoughts. 48.3ff. incidentally shifts some of the responsibility to the *aura popularis* of Athenian democracy.

little (ch. 52),[72] but he specifies the fatal mistake made by one of the Athenian commanders, which makes it possible for the Sicilians and their allies to rout the Athenian ships in the center and cut off others. The Athenian fleet is decisively beaten. It is true that an attempt of Gylippus immediately afterward to destroy Athenian ships and sailors on land miscarries, that the Athenians save by far the greater number of ships and men, and that on the next day, too, a Syracusan device of setting the Athenian fleet on fire is frustrated (ch. 53). Still the victory of the Syracusans is λαμπρά (55.1). Thucydides, whose account of the battle is relatively short (ch. 52), suggests its importance by dwelling (in ch. 54) on the magnitude of the Athenian discouragement. No hope of producing a change for the better is left. By contrast the Syracusans are so elated that they now set themselves the objective of completely defeating the Athenians on land as well as on sea. They fancy themselves the liberators of Greece from the Athenian yoke, a supreme achievement and a claim to lasting glory.[73] Ἦν δὲ ἄξιος ὁ ἀγών (56.3): these words, reflecting as they must Thucydides' own judgment, may be read as prelude to the climax to which he is now building.

The climax as Thucydides has fashioned it is neither of the two earlier battles—although either could be justly regarded as the turning point in the fortunes of the war—but the final desperate attempt of the Athenians to break through the enemy's encirclement of the harbor. This is no longer a battle for their victory in the Sicilian war but merely a fight for rescue and survival. Defeat seals their doom. Realistically considered, there may have been not much hope of escape before, and some little hope even afterward;[74] nevertheless the "catastrophe" could be, and probably was, in Athens as-

[72] Cf. J. de Romilly, *Histoire*, 155 and n. 1.

[73] See 56.2 and, in fact, this entire chapter.

[74] VII 72; 73.1. Cf. below, p. 220. Note also II 65.12: the Sicilian disaster does not irrevocably decide the outcome of the entire war.

sociated with this battle; it had its special pathos, and this rather than its actual political or strategic significance prompted Thucydides[75] to marshal an unparalleled array of devices for building up this section.

In chapter 59 we find a statement that essentially repeats something already said in 56; another sentence is the complement, as it were, of a thought left incomplete in that earlier context.[76] These observations suggest that a sequence has been interrupted. What has been inserted between these chapters is a full "catalogue" listing in good epic tradition, and with a considerable amount of detail and thoughtful comment, the allies present on both sides. Their large number naturally magnifies the significance of the battle; and to ask whether the insertion of this catalogue would not have been equally or more justified at other junctures is to miss Thucydides' intention.[77] Thucydides has chosen this place because, in combination with other devices, it secured for the battle in the Harbor that unique tragic quality with which he wished to endow it.

The same purpose is served by no less than ten other chapters preceding the Great Battle. Chapter 60 reports how the Athenians, fully conscious of their extreme emer-

[75] From this point of view, something might favor the theory that Thucydides completed his account of the Sicilian expedition only after his return to Athens. It is difficult to imagine in what light the battle of the Harbor appeared to him before this return and how he would be able to describe the final phases so predominantly from the Athenian perspective. For the "enrichment" of sections preceding a decisive battle cf. J. de Romilly, *Histoire*, 160f.

[76] Compare καλὸν ἀγώνισμα in 56.2 and 59.2, as well as 56.1 and 59.3.

[77] In this question I side with Schadewaldt (*Die Geschichtsschreibung des Thukydides*, Berlin, 1929, 10ff.) against Schwartz (p. 202). Von Fritz (I 756f.) thinks the catalogues are in the right place but speaks of "mangelnde Ausarbeitung und Einfügung." Given the overriding purpose, the "Einfügung" 56.3f. is quite appropriate ("Ausarbeitung" under an originally different point of view seems conceivable). See also Regenbogen, *Kleine Schriften* (Munich, 1961) 212ff., 219.

gency, collect whatever resources are left to them, even the most unusual, in preparation for the breakthrough, the one and only rescue still open to them. Next (chs. 61–64, 66–68) follow the speeches the commanders on both sides address to their men before the beginning of the battle. They are the only pair of speeches preceding a battle in Books VI and VII, and, like all such speeches, must strike an optimistic note. Such a note is present in both, yet how differently it sounds. Nicias has to pull his men out of their despondency (ἀθυμία), whereas Gylippus and the Syracusan leaders inspire theirs with the prospect of crowning the successes already achieved by a final victory. In the one, the fate and future of Athens are at stake; in the other, survival and liberty are regarded as secured, and what remains is to punish those who dared to imperil them and at the same time to win resounding glory.[78] Normally such a pair of speeches would have fully sufficed to prepare the fighters (as well as the readers); but in this instance nervous consciousness of the impending final crisis causes Nicias once more to address each individual captain, reminding him how much depends on his conduct in this battle and on its outcome (69.2). We need not doubt that individual admonitions took place. Nicias' anguish while the decision moved closer would account for them, and they may have been more conspicuous on this occasion than on others. Yet, by mentioning them, Thucydides clearly furthers his intention of making his entire account of the Sicilian expedition culminate in this desperate battle.

The description of the battle begins in a very factual manner.[79] Demosthenes and two other commanders head for

[78] See esp. 66; 67.1; 68.2. See on the speeches J. de Romilly, *Histoire,* 157ff.

[79] In the preceding paragraphs we ought perhaps to have mentioned a few more facts recorded by Thucydides, e.g. the "ironhands" on the Athenian boats and the device used by the Syracusans against them (62.3; 65.2). But our point is how much Thucydides' reconstruction of the πραχθέντα goes beyond mere "facts."

their strategic objective (69.4). When we leave them in this enterprise, and remain in hopeful suspense, corresponding information is supplied about the strategic dispositions and plans of the Syracusans. Next we see the Athenian operation attain an initial success. The boats reach the "locks" of the enclosure and try to force them (70.2). Yet while they are thus engaged, not only this unit but the Athenian fleet everywhere in the harbor is attacked. The enemy rushes upon them from all sides. However, for some time the battle remains undecided, and Thucydides, having nothing new to report, avails himself of the time to change from the specific to the typical. He explains how the fighting men on board (ἐπιβάται) behaved (70.3, 5) and, more incidentally, for what the helmsmen had to watch out (6). He also describes what forms the collisions took and how these forms compared in frequency with one another (4–6). Soon, however, this factual approach to combat operations gives way to an entirely new tone. The section that follows must be left for a separate appreciation. When we finally return to the course of the actual battle, not many words are used to state its outcome (71.5). After a long duration, the Syracusans rout the Athenian fleet and immediately pursue the fleeing boats toward the land.

The section passed over deals with moral and emotional aspects of the battle. Here reference is made to noise and clamor, to the dismay caused by the unexpected turns of the battle, but more space is given to the encouraging shouts, admonitions, and appeals heard in both fleets, and still more to the anxieties and hopes of the Athenian soldiers who watch the battle from the shore.[80] The causes (71.2) as well as the

[80] See the admirable account of W. S. Ferguson in *CAH* V 308. The description in 71.1–4 is extraordinarily graphic (for psychological observation see 71.3 extr.; cf. above pp. 140f.) and most subtle. Beginning at a point where the battle is ἰσόρροπος, Thucydides follows the alternations between hope and fear and points out how largely they depended on impressions received from limited or even relatively unimportant phases of the battle. J. de Romilly (*Histoire,* 163f.) distinguishes two

manifestations (4) of their "fear" are included. The principal manifestation, lament, becomes general when, as the fleet is driven back to the land, the sailors "fall" into the camp of the land army.[81] So complete is their discouragement that the Athenians do not even think of asking for their own dead (72.2), and on the following day when Demosthenes favors one more attempt at a breakthrough—this time by surprise, the number of ships they could use being still larger than the enemy's—the sailors cannot be persuaded into a new fight (72.3f.). The only alternative is to depart, and this is now everybody's γνώμη (73.1).

Would it still have been possible to avert the catastrophe? Contradicting the impression that "everything" depended on the last battle, there is reference—oblique rather than direct—to hopes and plans in the Athenian camp, and there are corresponding fears in Syracuse.[82] Hermocrates finds it necessary to employ a ruse (73.2), and the Athenians, falling victim to it, fail to break camp early enough to find the roads free (73.3ff.). When after some further delay they finally leave, their escape is cut off (74.1f.). The pathetic element, so prominent in the account of the last battle, comes to the fore again, and perhaps even more powerfully, while Thucydides dwells on the depressing sights and experiences facing the army as it abandons the camp and departs (ch. 75); nor is it

---

main parts in the description of the emotions. 71.6 οὐκέτι διαφόρους (utterances) ἀλλ' ἀπὸ μιᾶς ὁρμῆς is certainly climactic; in 6f. emotion and action are no longer kept apart. J. H. Finley's comparison (pp. 321ff.) with battle descriptions in Euripides (*Supp., Heracl., Ph.*) is illuminating.

[81] 71.6; see *ibid.* for the immediate reactions of the army on land.

[82] In 71.2, 7, all remaining hope for the Athenians is tied to the outcome of the last sea battle; if this is not in agreement with 72.3 and 73.1, it yet reflects the feeling on that day and perhaps even the historian's own considered judgment. For Hermocrates' suspicions regarding the Athenian plans see 73.1; for hopes held out by Nicias to his soldiers, 77.4, 6.

absent later (e.g. 79.3, 80.3), although between the departure and the surrender[83] the facts themselves are so pathetic that any explicit emphasis on the concomitant emotions could only have weakened the effect.

In these final battles, length of treatment and, with it, distribution of weight are determined by the human and emotional significance attaching to the events rather than by a coolly realistic assessment of their factual importance. In the account of Pylos, we noticed the care taken to determine the function and significance of the "episode" in the entire war. The first step toward war is recounted with a view to a "higher truth," the correct appreciation of policies that in Thucydides' view are of paramount importance for the whole war; completeness or equality of coverage matter less. Does Thucydides by thus organizing his material depart from objectivity and lay himself open to criticism? Not necessarily, although it is of course unfortunate that among his contemporaries no one is engaged in reconstructions of a similar kind that could be compared with his. Still, if Thucydides used reason, i.e. *logos*, to recover facts and their causes, the *logos* would not be satisfied unless the right relationship, the right proportion, and, as far as possible, for each phase also its "meaning"—all of these being facets of *logos*—were established.

Samples for the reconstruction of thoughts and considerations have been presented in Chapter V on "Psychology." That, however, was not the place to deal with the chapters VIII 87f., which are unique, and therefore especially revealing. Thucydides here records three different versions of Tissaphernes' intentions when he went to Aspendos promising to fetch the Phoenician boats but failing to do so. The disquisition begins with an admission of discrepancies in the reports. Therefore οὐ ῥᾴδιον εἰδέναι (87.2). "Not easy to know";

[83] See for the surrender of Demosthenes ch. 82, of Nicias ch. 85.

for once (and this "once" is of course in the unfinished and unrevised Book) Thucydides has not come to a decision between the alternative explanations. Still, he strongly inclines to one of them; Tissaphernes did not wish to change the balance of naval strength in favor of either the Lacedaemonians or the Athenians but preferred a long war in which they would wear out one another (87.4). The argument in support of this explanation includes, logically enough a rational construction of what would have happened if Tissaphernes had actually put the Phoenician boats at the disposal of the Lacedaemonians; since, even without these, they equalled the Athenians in strength, he would κατὰ τὸ εἰκός have assured their victory. The next sentences supply an additional reason for choosing this explanation. The excuse offered by Tissaphernes as he returned without the boats is threadbare. Moreover, when he left for Aspendos, Alcibiades, to judge by his reaction, suggests, again ὡς εἰκός (88.1), that he knew "more" about the purpose behind the departure (and what he "probably" knew would—probably?—support the explanation that Thucydides favors).[84]

On other occasions Thucydides, as is his habit, has seen no need to let us know why he credits an individual with specific thoughts, considerations, or intentions. The thoughts of Cleon, Demosthenes, and Brasidas reported in Book IV have illustrated how sure he feels of his ground.[85] There is probably most "knowledge" in the account about Demosthenes and most guesswork in that about Brasidas; yet the tenor of the accounts scarcely varies, and there is not even any invocation of the εἰκός.

In the present chapter we have alluded to the thoughts that prompted Demosthenes immediately after his arrival in

[84] Brunt, p. 80, after examining the chapter decides that Alcibiades is Thucydides' source.

[85] See above pp. 164ff. Cf. also Kagan, 367f.

Sicily to plan an attack on Epipolae.[86] He realized the serious mistakes Nicias had made in the preceding year by wasting time and allowing the Syracusans to increase their forces from various quarters; he knows why his own attack has its best prospects "on the first day," and he perceives the special advantages inherent in the conquest of Epipolae. How could Thucydides be so accurately informed about these matters? He could learn from Demosthenes himself his opinion of the strategic situation in Pylos and in Aetolia,[87] for he probably had opportunities to talk to him after his return from these campaigns. But Demosthenes did not return from the Sicilian expedition. We may speculate whether one or two men who enjoyed his confidence did return and inform Thucydides.[88] Such possibilities cannot be dismissed, yet it is tempting to believe that Thucydides visualized the situation as it presented itself to Demosthenes on his arrival and, combining his own understanding of strategy with inferences from Demosthenes' actions, reconstructed his thoughts. He knew Demosthenes as a man ready to act and run risks, and this familiarity with his personality may also have aided him in the reconstruction.

Closely connected with this question is another. How could Thucydides know either the intimate thoughts or the openly stated reasons of Nicias when he opposed Demosthenes and,

[86] VII 42.3; see above p. 213. For observations suggesting that we read Thucydides' own views see G. Donini, *Hermes* 92 (1964) 116ff.; Dover, *ad loc.*

[87] IV 29.2ff.; 30.1; cf. III 97. That Demosthenes in pondering the chances for an attack had Aetolia in mind (30.1) is psychologically very probable. But did he himself analyze his considerations so closely when he was reminiscing? And did he refer so frankly to a disastrous campaign and his responsibility for the mistakes? Or is the probability in this instance due to Thucydides' reconstruction?

[88] D. H. Kelly, *CR* 20 (1970) 127ff. argues for the return of a larger number of Athenians than a reader of Thucydides would suppose.

after the attack on Epipolae had ended in failure,[89] was reluctant to break off the operations and return home. Probably, Thucydides reconstructed the thoughts of Nicias, guided by what he considered εἰκός or τὰ δέοντα in a given situation. Once we have made up our mind to take this view, we shall be ready to apply it in other instances, and may, if we need further encouragement, take note of VIII 46.5, where Tissaphernes' intention—here *one* intention only is allowed—to slacken his support of the Lacedaemonians is frankly inferred from his actions (ὅσα ἀπὸ τῶν ποιουμένων ἦν εἰκάσαι). First place among these goes to the position of trust he assigns to Alcibiades for the execution of his policies. Now whenever Alcibiades is involved, the hypothesis that Thucydides learned much from him directly (while both were exiled, living in Thrace, and had leisure to reminisce) has found strong support and is indeed attractive.[90] Thucydides, we would hope, would not succumb entirely to the spell of this brilliant mind. Keeping his critical faculty alert, he might realize that Alcibiades on occasion offered nothing better than guesses about a motive. We have noticed the admission of inference in VIII 46. The entire account in VIII 45–47.1 dealing with the influence of Alcibiades on Tissaphernes, the change of the latter to a less pro-Lacedaemonian policy, and Alcibiades' own plan is best regarded as a tissue of reconstructions. To separate a bedrock of solid information tidily from inference is not possible, but that both have contributed can hardly be doubted.

We need not continue this line of inquiry by speculating, for example, how far in the immediately following chapters

[89] VII 48. Reading how Demosthenes reacted to Nicias (ch. 49), we incline to think that something about the disagreement must have become known to others (including survivors of the disaster); but even on the most generous assumption of this kind, the formulation of the two positions in both its rational and (especially for Nicias) psychological aspects would be Thucydides' own.

[90] Cf. Brunt, pp. 59ff.

(50f.) Phrynichus' intentions are reported on the basis of his utterances that in some way or other had become known and how far Thucydides again used inference κατὰ τὸ εἰκός.[91] The hopes entertained by King Agis when he moved his army against Athens expecting the oligarchic revolution to have produced turmoil in the city (VIII 71.4) are intrinsically probable, and so are the desires of the oligarchs neatly arranged by Thucydides in a pattern of priorities (VIII 91.3); yet why should not the same probability that now recommends these explanations to us also have guided Thucydides in his reconstruction? As for brief statements about motives, Thucydides admits that his explanations why the Syracusans insisted on having Nicias put to death go back to hearsay or rumor; he claims no more than approximate correctness for them (VII 86.4, 5). The Lacedaemonians would have been more inclined to spare his life; certain obligations they have toward him are the reason for which he οὐχ ἥκιστα had handed himself over to Gylippus. The unfortunate Nicias had no way of letting anybody know his motive. Once again, the statement rests on a guess, even if a good and fairly safe one.[92]

Past History

Of necessity, Thucydides' reconstructions take on a different form when he deals with earlier Greek history and in particular where the very remote past is his subject. Four sections of his work treat phases earlier than the Peloponnesian War

91 Even the untangling of Phrynichus' correspondence with the enemy (chs. 50f.) must have created extraordinary difficulties. In this instance Alcibiades could have supplied much of the factual basis; see Delebecque, pp. 96ff.

92 Our discussion of λογισμοί makes no pretense of covering more than a few characteristic examples. Others would be easy to find. Striking agreements between the strategic plan and the actual unfolding of a battle have been stressed by J. de Romilly, *Histoire*, 124ff., 136ff., and *passim*; see above (Chapter V).

and its immediate causes. However, the "Sicilian archaeology"[93] is of a type so peculiar that we may as well omit it from our analysis. It is less a reconstruction than a record, not to say a chronicle, embodying primarily the founding yet also the later fate of numerous cities. Unlike other instances, Thucydides' intention is not to correct a specific opinion about facts of the past but to show the ignorance of his countrymen regarding the size of the country and the population against which they went to war. Moreover, Thucydides, according to the consensus of scholars, here for once follows a "source,"[94] and if there are occasions where he departs from his authority and trusts his own judgment, we have no way of determining them.

The other three sections are the so-called "Archaeology" of Greece in Book I, the less ambitious archaeology of Athens in an early chapter of Book II, and the "truth" about the Athenian tyrants presented in combination with a correction of the prevailing version concerning the deed of Harmodius and Aristogeiton. Certain methods are common to these sections, and, since they are hardly ever used in the bulk of the work, they deserve special attention. We best begin with the shortest, the "Athenian archaeology" of II 15. Its purpose is to explain why it was a special hardship for the people of Attica to leave their homesteads and move into the city when the Peloponnesian army invaded the country in the first year of the war. The reason was (in short) *τὸ αἰεὶ εἰωθέναι τοὺς πολλοὺς ἐν τοῖς ἀγροῖς διαιτᾶσθαι* (14.2). This in turn is traced to the political organization under which the smaller communities had lived.

The entire Athenian or Attic archaeology is constructed around one thesis: for a long time (and with effects lasting into the period of the Peloponnesian War) communities in

[93] VI 1–5.

[94] In a very acute study, K. J. Dover (*Maia* 6, 1953, 1ff.) identifies Antiochus of Syracuse as this source.

Attica had been to a very large degree independent and self-sufficient. This was changed through the *synoikismos* effected by Theseus (15.2). Having no doubt about the historicity of this *synoikismos*,[95] Thucydides feels entitled to use it as pivotal for his reconstruction. Another tradition relating to a war between Athens under Erechtheus and Eleusis under Eumolpus[96] confirms his conviction about the early conditions. While he does not go deeply into the communal life of the smaller units or into the changes effected by Theseus, we may yet notice a certain parallelism in his treatment of these two subjects: what before Theseus was done separately in each community was afterward done jointly for the entire city. However the other early communities do not interest Thucydides nearly as much as the first Athens, for which he has a special theory and in support of it special *tekmeria*. The original city was the Acropolis. Proofs (*tekmeria*) are the temples (or sanctuaries)[97] and in addition to them a ritual connected with the fountain Enneakrounos in this area (15.5).

The truth about the conspiracy against the Athenian tyrants and the end of this tyranny (VI 54–59) is something that Thucydides had reconstructed quite independently of his research about the Peloponnesian War. Here we need not discuss his excuse for incorporating his conclusions in the *History* but might record as peculiar that when in this instance he claims to have knowledge from ἀκοῄ and says spe-

[95] The festival of the *synoikia* (see on it L. Deubner, *Attische Feste*, Berlin, 1932, 36ff.), if meant to serve as a proof, is yet not actually formulated as one. On the historicity of the *synoikismos* see Gomme *ad loc.*, who is perhaps too positive in his statements and does not consider how much in 15.2 may be Thucydides' reconstruction. M. Cary in *CAH* III 578f., too, accepts a good deal. Reservations are expressed by U. Kahrstedt in *RE* s.v. "synoikismos" 1435f. H. Herter's treatment in *RhM* 88 (1939) 244 seems very sound.

[96] 15.1 extr. See on the tradition about this war F. Jacoby, *Atthis* (Oxford, 1949), 124.

[97] On problems connected with their identification see Gomme *ad loc.*

cifically εἰδὼς μὲν καὶ ἀκοῇ ἀκριβέστερον τῶν πολλῶν (55.1), this cannot mean "tradition" in the sense of the "Archaeology," where it is the version he opposes; rather what the word here suggests is oral information passed on in Athenian circles. We may imagine that individuals whom he considered reliable and in a position to know provided him with a clue, whereafter he continued making inquiries until he felt assured. In this way Thucydides has learned to regard not Hipparchus, as was commonly believed, but Hippias as the oldest son of Peisistratus who succeeded his father as tyrant. To support the knowledge thus acquired he again adduces *tekmeria,* in this case evidence nowadays called epigraphical (55.1).[98] When a well-known document mentions children of Hippias, yet not of his two brothers, this is a *tekmerion,* though to become conclusive—even by what we should consider rather lax standards—it needs the support of an argument: "it was likely for the eldest to marry first" (55.1). And finally after ἀκοή, τεκμήρια, and τεκμήρια used in combination with arguments, there is an argument pure and simple: if Hipparchus had been the tyrant, it would have been difficult for Hippias to maintain himself in the tyranny, which he had so suddenly taken over (55.3). The truth being thus established, Thucydides still thinks it necessary to explain the origin of the erroneous opinion and its prevalence among the Athenians of his day: Hipparchus was the victim of the conspiracy; his name would therefore be remembered, and he rather than Hippias would be thought of as the tyrant (55.4).

Thucydides argues so energetically and with such a variety of methods for the seniority and the rule of Hippias because they are the only items in the reconstruction that he regards in need of such support. Everything else is simply narrated, and we are left to guess whether his version as a whole goes back to the "more exact knowledge" that he claims to possess

[98] On the altar here mentioned see also 54.6; see Dover *ad loc.* Epigraphical evidence is used also 59.3.

or whether he acquired only some of his facts in this manner and then pieced the whole together in accordance with *to eikos.*[99]

By far the largest reconstruction of developments for which there were no witnesses is the Greek "Archaeology" in I 2-19. Although ostensibly written to prove that the Peloponnesian War was the κίνησις μεγίστη for the Greeks and not only for them (I 1.2), it embodies much thought that originally need not have been connected with that purpose. A skeptical attitude to Homer and to the conventional picture of the past is likely to have formed in Thucydides' mind even before he began to write his own historical work in a critical spirit unknown to former generations. And since it was not his way to acquiesce in a purely negative reaction, he welcomed the opportunity of putting something different in the place of what he repudiated. We should keep his "thesis" in mind, but not insist on a very close relation to it for every item in these chapters.[100]

Despite his critical attitude, Thucydides cannot dispense with tradition, ἀκοή. When in chapter 4 he introduces Minos' thalassocracy—a subject central for the entire reconstruction—he explicitly invokes ἀκοή as his authority. The word need not refer solely to hearsay but may as well include the epics that were as often "heard" as read. In any case, Thucydides makes ample use of the epic, especially the Homeric poetry,[101] even if he feels free to treat it as a quarry from which he takes whatever fits his over-all conception and interprets even that with the utmost freedom. Besides the *tekmeria* supplied by Homer there are also *semeia, martyria, paradeig-*

[99] 56.3 is a passage for which this alternative becomes particularly acute. Did Thucydides really know what the few conspirators "hoped" would happen?

[100] It may suffice to refer to the arguments of 8.1 concerning the Carians as early inhabitants of islands in the Aegean sea.

[101] See e.g. 3.3; 5.2; 9.4; 10.3 (the last two items suggest some hesitation in using Homer as evidence).

mata[102] (if these words indicate different types of evidence, it is hard for us to find the difference). Finally, there is frequent recourse to the *eikos*, that favorite concept of Thucydides and his progressive contemporaries. As we know, Thucydides' thinking is guided by the *eikos* even where the word as such does not occur. In particular the psychological *eikos* is indispensable for his reconstructions, and the realistic psychology known to us from his entire work is apparent in many phases of this section.

To analyze the Greek Archaeology, step by step and thought by thought, is not necessary for our purpose.[103] It will suffice to look at some representative samples of his procedure.

To begin with a relatively short unit, the Corinthians, as we read in chapter 13 (2–5), were the first to have a fleet approximating the modern type as well as the first to build triremes. As in Book VI, when he argues for the seniority of Hippias, Thucydides begins by referring to "tradition," which here, however, need not (as in VI 55) be the minority opinion. And, again as in VI, he supports this tradition by others that, slightly manipulated, yield evidence of the *tekmeria* type. There is first of all the employment of a Corinthian shipbuilder by the Samians; the time when this happened, even if not precisely known, lies sufficiently far back to support the primacy of the Corinthians (13.3). Next there is the "oldest sea-battle" on record, which was fought between the Corinthians and the Corcyreans; its date is fairly certain and again fits in with the thesis (13.4). Furthermore, much may be inferred from the geographical position of Corinth. Oc-

[102] *Tekmerion* occurs 1.1.3; 3.3; (cf. 20.1; 21.1); *paradeigma* 2.6; *semeion* 6.2. The actual use of the words however does not indicate the extent to which Thucydides thinks in such terms. For some historical background of these concepts and methods see my book *Die Entwicklung der aristotel. Logik und Rhetorik* (Berlin, 1929) 26f. Cf. George Kennedy, 99ff.

[103] Still less can it be our task to offer a reasoned judgment about the validity of the conclusions in the light of modern historical methods.

cupying a site where people from every direction would pass by, it was bound to develop a flourishing trade. Intrinsically probable as this inference is, it is borne out by the word ἀφνειόν ("wealthy," 13.5) used by the early poets as epithet of Corinth. Finally if Corinth had even at an early time been so successfully active in trade, its leading position would inevitably be strengthened as soon as the sea had been made generally accessible. This was accomplished through the destruction of piracy, a point, we shall presently see, of great importance in Thucydides' scheme.[104]

The development of a fleet and sea power, as Thucydides traces it through its successive stages, appears to be the backbone of the entire reconstruction.[105] Minos was the first to have a fleet (ch. 4), which caused a profound change in the living conditions of Greece. Due to it, later generations had a far safer and more settled mode of life. Thucydides reasons thus and, encouraged by what he considers *eikos*, links the building of the first fleet to another event of hardly less consequence, the extermination of piracy (*ibid.*). By its removal, Minos hoped to secure the increase of his own revenues from the islands he had conquered by his fleet and on which, as Thucydides again seems to know from tradition,

104 I cannot find the later chapters of the Archaeology as desultory as von Fritz, 591 ff. Granted that some topics might have been treated more fully or with more causal links, Thucydides, whose aim was to show the limited extent of earlier organizations, enterprises, etc., could nonetheless be satisfied (note esp. chs. 15f.). Why he ignored the power created by Pheidon of Argos I do not know but should not from the sketchy treatment of some subjects infer that Thucydides planned some rewriting. Nothing in chs. 20f. suggests such intention. Incidentally the subject of ch. 12 is not "Machtzerfall" (von Fritz, 590, 591) but the unsettled and limited conditions even after the first common enterprise (cf. 11.2; it took long before this changed, 12.4). For causality patterns in the Archaeology see Adam Parry, *YCS* 22 (1972) 52ff.

105 For Athenian connotations of "thalassocracy" see de Romilly, *Histoire*, 276. Thucydides' special interest in this topic throughout the body of his work has been studied by her in "Thucydide et l'idée de progrès," *ASNP* 35 (1966) 167ff.

he established his sons as rulers. This motive—the only one specified by Thucydides—provides the *eikos* he needs to connect the decrease of piracy with the creation of Minos' thalassocracy. For as long as piracy flourished, there was no safety, and no possibility of commerce; no settlement near the coast could be attempted.[106]

Whence did Thucydides derive his knowledge about the prevalence of piracy? Two impressions seem to have converged. In the epics, piracy was treated as a respectable profession, and in his own days he knew it to be practiced by the inhabitants of some regions (5.2)[107] where success in this profession enhanced a man's reputation. The same people were in the habit of carrying arms, a testimony for the one-time prevalence of robbery not only on sea but on land. He himself has noticed this habit among several Greek tribes who maintain the "old custom" (5.3). If in his own days something is practiced in the more backward regions, this is a σημεῖον (6.2) of a practice at one time common throughout Greece. When in addition the bearing of arms among non-Greek people (5.1 *init.*; cf. 6.1, 6) is taken into account, the final conclusion approximates an original identity of customs everywhere.[108]

After Minos had cleared out the pirates, especially from the islands, there was an increase of property; life in general became safer, and after a while there were differences of wealth and *pari passu* of power. For wealth is a prior con-

[106] See also ch. 7 and 8.2f.

[107] The meaning of ἠπειρῶται is not settled (see Gomme *ad loc.*). I incline to take it as equivalent of οἱ ἐν τῇ ἠπείρῳ παραθαλάσσιοι (5.1) but do not feel sure. On the section dealing with piracy cf. W. Schadewaldt, *Thukydides*, 73ff.

[108] The original conditions of human beings in general is not the subject of the "Archaeology," but it was of great interest at the time (cf. H. Herter, *Maia*, N. S. 4, 1963, 464ff.; Guthrie, II 473), and if Thucydides sees his way to make an incidental contribution to it, he does not let the opportunity go by. Cf. again J. de Romilly, "Progrès" 143ff.

dition for conquest; the weaker see "gain" or advantage (κέρδος 8.3)—a typically Thucydidean explanation—in accepting the wealthier and stronger as their masters. It should, however, be said that, for Thucydides, piracy is not the only cause of the unsettled living conditions and the frequent migrations of the early period. Another cause is the ever-present danger of stronger groups' arriving and ousting the weaker from their land (2.1; cf. 12.1-3).

The Trojan War (8.4ff.) is not epoch-making in the same sense as the thalassocracy of Minos.[109] Still, as the first common enterprise of the Greeks, and because of its unparalleled fame, it demanded a place in the revolutionary new construction of past history. Moreover tradition presented the Trojan War in such dimensions that Thucydides has to explain how it relates to his thesis about the smallness of everything that happened before the Peloponnesian War. Supported by the prevailing chronology in which the Trojan War was later than Minos' rule, Thucydides assigned it to the stage where the rule of the stronger over the weaker had become a familiar feature of Greek life. The great power wielded by Agamemnon is an extreme instance and represents an advanced step of this condition. Nevertheless, it has its specific causes, and to identify them Thucydides once more makes the largest and most sovereign use of the mythical tradition. If "memory" about historical events in the Peloponnesus has preserved the fact of Peleus' arrival, this is welcome, but what matters most about it is that he is said to have come as a rich man to a poor native population (9.2). Once more wealth results in power.[110] An increase of this power in the generation of his children may also be extracted from the myth; what remains for Thucydides himself—be-

[109] See however 3.1 and cf. de Romilly, *Histoire,* 252ff., 264 and *passim,* 288.

[110] See in general on the importance of the economic motif in the Archaeology de Romilly, *Histoire,* 263ff. and "Progrès" *passim.*

sides selecting events that suit him from the myth—is to supply realistic psychological motives, such as fear, hope for protection, and demagogic talent.[111] Looked upon in this spirit, the command of Agamemnon over the other kings and his relatively large army are due not so much to the high-minded attitude of χάρις (9.3), a willingness to be of help and do favors, or to the oaths sworn by the suitors of Helen, as to power and the normal human reaction to it, fear.[112] On this point, where psychological understanding helps to make a new version convincing, the mythical tradition is discarded without hesitation.

Such arguments put the Trojan War in its true historical context. Still why was it, like other early enterprises, small by comparison with the Peloponnesian War, Thucydides' own subject? Thucydides proves this by a very realistic, almost statistical computation of the number of men participating on the Greek side. Homer supplies the total number of ships. To find from this the number of fighters, Thucydides combines observations, assumptions, and a subtle piece of reckoning. The basis is again furnished by the *Iliad*. If the rowers of some boats are also called "archers" (the observation), the same men must have done the rowing and the fighting; the presence of many other persons for service on the boats is unlikely in view of the type of ships then in use (10.4, an assumption κατὰ τὸ εἰκός). Finally, Homer also specifies the number of men on each boat for the Boeotian contingent and that of Philoctetes (again an observation). The considerable discrepancy between the two figures is best explained if Homer selected the smallest and the largest

[111] The clause τὸ πλῆθος τεθεραπευκότα τῶν Μυκηναίων is curious. How could Thucydides know this? The phrase has a somewhat anachronistic ring ("comme un démocrate," de Romilly, *Histoire*, 277).

[112] Δύναμις 9.1; φόβος 9.3. However Thucydides discovers (9.4) in *Iliad* 2.108 and 612 further evidence for Agamemnon's supereminent power, esp. on sea.

contingent.[113] This makes it possible to determine the size of an average contingent, and this average size multiplied by the number of boats yields the total Greek manpower before Troy. For an effort made by all of Greece, the final verdict on the number of fighters is: "not many" (*οὐ πολλοί*, 10.5).

If the use here (10.4) made of the literary evidence strikes us as bold, it is tame by comparison with the pattern constructed for the actual warfare (ch. 11). At any time only a fraction of the Greek army would be actively engaged before Troy, the others being employed in provisioning the army through agriculture and robbery. This, in Thucydides' view, is a necessary assumption, because if the entire Greek army had been engaged before Troy, the city would not have been able to resist ten years. To prove a theory by arguing that its alternative would lead to results at variance with the "facts" is a method not peculiar to Thucydides.[114] The theory itself is in this instance necessary because without it an accepted "historical" fact would no longer be possible.

Quite different in "methodological" respects is the use of a hypothesis in 10.1, where Thucydides anticipates an objection and defends his position against it. The small size of present-day Mycenae should not be played off against its great power in early days. If either Athens or Sparta would be abandoned by its present inhabitants and later generations would form a judgment as to its one-time importance by looking at the remains, such judgment would in either case be far off the mark.

A few words about the conditions Thucydides assumed as

113 Astonishing as this hypothesis may seem to us, Thucydides must have thought it probable (*ὡς ἐμοὶ δοκεῖ*). Homer must have had some rational motive for selecting these two. On the other hand Thucydides (10.3) is not altogether happy about accepting Homer's figures, since he knows the habits of poets.

114 See for arguing *e contrario* (even if with different intent) e.g. Antiphon 5.34 f., 68, *al.*; "X," *Ath.* 1.4, 6, 10, *al.*

his starting point may still be appropriate. To begin at a very low point and to construct a gradual progress from it was in accord with an intellectual trend of the time.[115] Normally, however, the subject was human life in general, not Greek political life. Thucydides begins with a composite picture, whose units (if we discount some as being more or less identical with others) would be: no firm settlement, but frequent migrations; no cultivation of the ground beyond what was needed for a very short time; no commerce or other mutual contact either by sea or land on account of fear. No large possession and no existence of larger well-equipped towns are propositions easily deduced from such initial assumptions. If we ask what justification Thucydides had for these assumptions, two answers may account for every item. Migrations and changes of possession were a part of the mythical as well as of the historical tradition, and Thucydides had already convinced himself of widespread robbery existing at the time on sea as well as on land. Given the degree of imagination with which we may credit him, he would easily from these data find a way to the slightly more specific assumptions made in chapter 2.[116]

For his reconstruction Thucydides could consult no witness. His material consisted of the epics and perhaps here and there of other traditions as well. In addition, he could draw on observation and on information of the most varied character —the carrying of arms in certain regions, the Carians found buried in the graves of Delos; yet each item became useful to him only after it had passed through a process of reasoning and served as basis for inferences. Other matters included in the reconstruction, such as the commercial advantages inherent in the location of Corinth, are the result of intelligent reflection. On the whole, speculation of the boldest type holds

115 See above p. 232 n. 108.

116 On the use of Attica as *παράδειγμα* (2.5f.) see the analysis of von Fritz, pp. 577ff.

sway in these chapters; yet, as though to make up for this boldness, Thucydides everywhere lets us know how he arrived at his conclusion. The one feature as well as the other sets the Archaeology apart from the bulk of the work. We have said that Thucydides normally in the *History* acquaints us only with the results of his investigations, not allowing us to know how he arrived at them. Very often we wonder how much he learned from trustworthy sources, what he filled out through his own reasoning, how he chose between conflicting reports, etc. The peculiar subject matter of the Archaeology made it necessary for him to depart from his normal procedure. It would be a serious mistake to think that in the account of the Peloponnesian War there is the same degree of imagination, speculation, and over-confidence in the powers of human intelligence that characterizes the Archaeology. Still Thucydides feels sure about almost everything he reports and presents facts as well as causal connections in an apodictic and authoritative fashion. Against the persuasive effect of this presentation we must be on our guard.

"Reconstruction of the past" may not be the heading under which to discuss the "Pentecontaeteia" (I 98–118.2); nor is this section simply the proof of a thesis. For it does not show us a continuous growth and expansion of Athenian power, and Thucydides, although telling us how this power increased and how the Empire became consolidated, never maintains that these developments reached their peak in 431 or were bound to continue thereafter.[117] Relatively the best description of the Pentecontaeteia is found in a passage

[117] Cf. von Fritz, 612; Thucydides does not suggest an uninterrupted upward trend, and in view of 113, 115.1 such a thesis would have been difficult to uphold. P. K. Walker's theory (*CQ* 7, 1957, 28ff.) with which Kagan, 371, expresses some degree of sympathy, needs qualification. (In I 23.6 the phrasing *τοὺς 'Αθηναίους μεγάλους γιγνομένους*—not *γενομένους*!—deserves attention; what according to this passage the Lacedaemonians fear is a new increase materializing just then, *scil.* by the alliance with Corcyra etc.)

leading up to it I 97.1: ἡγούμενοι δὲ αὐτονόμων τὸ πρῶτον τῶν ξυμμάχων καὶ ἀπὸ κοινῶν ξυνόδων βουλευόντων τοσάδε ἐπῆλθον πολέμῳ τε καὶ διαχειρίσει πραγμάτων μεταξὺ τοῦδε τοῦ πολέμου καὶ τοῦ Μηδικοῦ, ἃ ἐγένετο πρός τε τὸν βάρβαρον αὐτοῖς καὶ πρὸς τοὺς σφετέρους ξυμμάχους νεωτερίζοντας καὶ Πελοποννησίων τοὺς αἰεὶ προστυγχάνοντας ἐν ἑκάστῳ. At the same time we learn how "the Athenian empire came into being" (I 97.2) but not everything in the Pentecontaeteia is written with this purpose in mind. Defeats in Egypt and in Boeotia contribute nothing, the changing relations to Sparta at best indirectly something to this topic.

If present-day historians shake their heads about the omission of highly important events in the Pentecontaeteia,[118] they should think twice before they relate such omissions to the unfinished condition of the entire work. Thucydides is patently selective, and his ideas as to what was essential need not have coincided with those held today. Still, I hesitate to fall back on this explanation for all of the truly awkward problems, and since I do not consider the Pentecontaeteia a reconstruction in the same sense as, e.g., the Archaeology, I may be excused for not coming forward with suggestions in which my own confidence would be at best half-hearted. Thus, to choose the most controversial item on the list of omissions, Thucydides' failure to mention the transfer of the "League's" treasury to Athens in 454/3, after he has recorded its original establishment in Delos, is certainly astonishing.[119]

[118] See the formidable lists of omissions in Gomme, I 365ff., 370ff., 385ff. As he includes even matters of Athenian "internal" and "cultural" history, he in effect presents the blueprint for an alternative historical sketch. Gomme admits that Thucydides may have "thought" some items "irrelevant to his theme" but is sure about what "even the briefest summary," if finished, would have included. See n. 120. I should not commit myself about relevance and irrelevance nor maintain that the blueprint misses Thucydides' intentions. This would probably be true for some items, but for how many? Indifference, even inadvertence should not be ruled out.

[119] Gomme, 370; von Fritz, 608ff., with whom I often agree, although I wonder whether the impression of restless Athenian activity in many

Explanations are not lacking. At that point of his account Athens' relation to the members of the League is no longer his main concern; a few energetic sentences in chapter 99 set forth how this relation changed and told us all we need to know about the reasons. Whether he considered the transfer of the treasury as significant, revealing, or symbolic for this change is a question that we cannot answer for him. Where he deals with the period around 454/3, his mind seems focused on military matters—expeditions, conquests, defeats, etc.—to a degree that even the peace of Callias remains unmentioned.[120] No "solution" of the kind can be dismissed out of hand; yet may any of them be proffered with genuine conviction? No more, I should say, than the assumption that Thucydides *must* have felt dissatisfied and *must* have intended to improve whatever strikes modern readers as a serious shortcoming.

Style and tone of the Pentecontaeteia are predominantly factual, and the *post hoc* relation appears to prevail over the *propter hoc*. Still, in many instances causality is given its due, if only by way of a participle. And even very tangled cause-and-effect relationships connecting developments in distant territories are brought out with all desirable clarity. We see the inhabitants of Thasos, besieged by Athenian forces, call upon the Lacedaemonians for help against Athens, and we learn why Sparta, having promised this help, is unable to supply it. The revolt of the helots keeps the Spartans occupied at home, and when the helots hold out in Ithome, their

areas is really one of Thucydides' intentions. I do not discuss I 128-138 (exile and death of Pausanias and Themistocles).

[120] Chs. 109-111. In ch. 112, however, we read of the three years' truce between Athens and the Peloponnesians as well as of Cimon's last expedition against the Persians and his death, events which preceded the peace of Callias. We tend to assume that if Thucydides had finished his work, it would in every respect be perfect and in particular satisfy all our demands. Not to share this view involves no lack of respect for his eminence.

resistance is so tenacious that Thasos must in the meantime surrender. As another effect of the resistance, the Lacedaemonians, unable to handle the siege, apply to the Athenians for assistance. Athens does send troops, yet among the Lacedaemonians suspicions develop against them—nor does Thucydides fail to tell us what kind of fear aroused this suspicion—and the Athenians are bidden to go home; this in turn causes indignation on the Athenian side, and the result of this bad feeling is the renunciation by Athens of its alliance with Sparta and in its place a rapprochement with Argos and Thessaly (chs. 101f.). Thus the Pentecontaeteia, incomplete in content and jejune in form, nevertheless, where its author sees fit, brings out complete interrelations of several developments, each of them important in its way.

CONCLUSION

In a "Conclusion" it is usual to pull the threads together, and if the same threads have run from chapter to chapter, the Conclusion is expected to tie them into a firm knot. We have warned our readers in the Introduction not to expect anything of this kind. For in this monograph, chapter has not been built upon chapter; each has its individual subject, and, in each, one manifestation yet always a different one of the same basic tendency is discussed and illustrated. The chapters are parallel. Moreover we have, again in the Introduction, given away our thesis, and all that we could now do would be to repeat this thesis and insist that the promise has been fulfilled, the thesis proved, and that the Greek Enlightenment is not properly appreciated as long as its achievement is confined to the propagation of new studies and revolutionary theories and to the corresponding criticism of traditional habits, beliefs, and institutions. A just appraisal of it ought to include also the forms and uses of reason that had not been known previously, or if known had not been brought into play so often, so readily, and with such delight in experimentation.

However, no reader who is not yet convinced will be converted by one more assertion. We may do ourselves a greater service if we look ahead, trying to discover the later fate of the intellectual devices and experiments that we have come to know in their early stages. How far did they become a permanent equipment of the Greek mind? A large question, and we have earlier in this book called attempts to answer it premature. We do not now retract this statement, which would doubtless be true of any account offered with a pretense to completeness. However, as throughout the bulk of this monograph, we have proceeded selectively, so we may now, becoming even more selective, suggest a few perspectives, in the hope thus to convey a roughly correct idea of developments in a later period.

One impression we report with a high degree of confidence is that there is a general calming down. No author is as indefatigable again in daring and ruthless manipulations of the Greek language as Thucydides. No character (as far as I can see) uses persuasion so craftily, so successfully, and at the same time with such frankly admitted dishonesty as Medea. The "reform projects" and speculations about a better world order that belong to the inventory of New Comedy are, ever since the fundamental investigations of Friedrich Leo, considered a legacy of Euripides; yet none of them envisages so radical a reorientation of human life as either Theseus or Hippolytus in the play from which we have culled so many examples. Of the passions whose emancipation we have studied in Euripides' "earlier" tragedies, *eros* became the favorite in Hellenistic poetry; in the Third Book of Apollonius' *Argonautica* its phases, symptoms, and crises are analyzed with profound and most sympathetic understanding. Phylarchus and a few other historians who arouse their readers' pity (ἔλεος, cf. Polyb. II 56) made it the fashion for a time to speak of "tragic historiography." Shall we venture to add that, while many later historians made ample use of their reason as well as of their imagination, none employed them as keenly and yet in the service of truth as Thucydides, and that none perhaps or at the most one or two had as profound a conception of truth? However, a Polybius and a Posidonius must be appreciated on their own terms.

It also seems to be the case that experiments that we treated separately in different chapters because they lacked mutual contact begin to develop such contact. A noteworthy development of this kind has been mentioned. Plato's *Phaedrus* includes the program for a scientific *psycha-*

gogia based on psychology. The rational soul needs its specific type of persuasion, while each part of the irrational soul requires its own form of persuasive speech adjusted to its predominant emotion. What Plato here has in mind is entire speeches, not "parts of speeches" such as proem and epilogue to which professional rhetoricians usually confined their instructions for the treatment of the emotions. Aristotle, too, must be thinking of entire speeches when in the Second Book of his *Rhetoric* he implements Plato's scheme, defining with a certain amount of explanation the kind of people liable to feel hatred, fear, anger, etc., the conditions apt to create such a state of mind, and thirdly the kind of people likely to be the objects of such emotions. The alternative approach to the emotions that was favored, as we just said, by professional teachers of rhetoric survived side by side with this broader and more philosophical treatment. There need not have been much active competition nor need we think of budding orators as being faced with the choice between clear-cut alternatives. True masters of oratory would not lose their grip on the hearers' feelings when, after the proem, they set forth the facts and argued their case; and if in the *peroratio* they added more fuel to the fire, this does not mean that the fire was on the point of dying. Demosthenes surely knew to keep the flames alive though he may never have paid attention to Plato's demands or heard of Aristotle's scientific *psychagogia*. And even before him Lysias, though less impassioned, secures the jury's sympathy through his *ethos*. In the *narratio* of the speech (12) in his own cause—the only speech we are still permitted to regard as certainly authentic—we see him at every turn make sure of pity for himself and indignation at the accused. The arguments no longer stick out but are embedded in the even flow of the presentation.

It must be admitted that Antiphon, who represents fifth-century oratory, does not keep his appeal to pity, good will, etc., within the limits of the proem. He, too, is aware of pleading his case before human beings. Still there is something rigidly self-conscious about many of his enthymemes and arguments; even if he casts them in the form of antitheses, one senses his eagerness to comply with the "rules." In the fourth century, the fusion of argumentative techniques and devices for persuasion goes farther. Demosthenes' periods leave the hearer's mind convinced and his feelings swayed, figures of speech contributing unobtrusively to both effects; for figures are what survived of the heterogeneous and more numerous manipulations to which the Greek language had been subjected in the fifth century. Thucydides' mannerism had no following; other drawbacks apart, it turned the attention of listener or reader from the content to the puzzling expression.

In the chapter on Argumentation (I) we have given our principal attention to the *in utramque partem disputare*. The capacity for it is declared by Aristotle a characteristic trait of dialectic (*Rhet.* A1, 1355a29-36; cf. *Top.* A1, 100a18ff.; 2, 101a34ff.). We can easily verify this for his own dialectical as well as his rhetorical treatise. His rhetorical τόποι (*Rhet.* B23) are constitutive for enthymeme, his dialectical for his peculiar kind of dialectical syllogism, and in the *Topics* where he sets forth the τόποι of dialectic, he frequently indicates how to use them for proving, and how for refuting a thesis. We need not think of him as reviving a tradition that in the meantime had been abandoned. For although Plato's dialectic sets itself higher goals and moves along new paths, the arguing *in utramque partem* retains a modest place in it. Quite apart from the *Parmenides*, an extreme case to be sure, since it is an adaptation of Zeno's method for a special purpose, the speeches of Socrates in the *Phaedrus* for and against the claims of the true lover may, cruel as it must seem, be mentioned as an example of this method. So may, with less cruelty, arguments like those in the *Sophist* for Movement and for Rest, for Being and for Not-being, for the materialists' conception of Being and for that of the "Friends of Forms" (237a-249d). This aspect of dialectic in Plato still needs closer study. In the later history of the Academy, reactions against a dogmatic Platonism lead to a revival of the Socratic search and questioning, which creates propitious conditions for an *in utramque partem disputare*. Arcesilaus practiced it (cf. D. L. IV 28) but the best example is Carneades' disputation in Rome for and against justice, especially the justice of Rome's conquests and empire (*Lact. inst.* V 14.3ff.; cf. 16.2ff. = Cic. *de re p.* III 9, 21). In Cicero's dialogues, the form is used to provide a hearing for the diverse schools of Hellenistic philosophy.

However, we have repeatedly said that the Age of Enlightenment produced far more arguments than we could identify and analyze. Thus, to focus on the *in utramque partem disputare* in Plato means to select one kind of argumentation while ignoring a large number of others. Unfortunately, we have to ignore them here, although it should today be possible to trace some lines of continuity between them and the argumentative methods employed in the Age of Enlightenment. Richard Robinson, through his analyses in *Plato's Earlier Dialectic* (Oxford, 2nd ed., 1953), has greatly facilitated this task. As far as I can see, there are instances where continuity can be established, others where the continuity, though present, is overshadowed by the special turn that Plato gives the argumentation, and finally not a few where the almost complete loss of the original works of the sophists forces us to end in a *non liquet*. Whenever Plato is moving in the tracks of Socrates' *inductio*, we are, of course, on new ground.

Still, more important than matters of detail are two intellectual traits of the fifth century that survive into the fourth. One is the increased interest in arguing as such and, with it, the greater skill in using carefully chosen, at times subtly wrought arguments; the other is the speculation about "concepts" and their mutual relations. We have seen this emerge in the Eleatics and then again, with a difference, in Thucydides, who theorizes about the relation of courage, daring, experience, and fear, not about that of infinity, eternity, and oneness (cf. Melissus B3ff.). The difference between courage and daring (τόλμα) and the interdependence of knowledge and courage are problems that Thucydides shares with early Platonic dialogues (*Lach.* 192c ff., 197a ff., *Protag.* 330a ff., 349a ff.).

Among such conceptual relations, even syllogisms approximating the first figure have come to light. We have noticed them in Thucydides, yet might with equal right identify them in Gorgias (B3.70 fin.): "if Being is eternal it is infinite, if infinite it is nowhere, if it is nowhere, it is not. Thus if Being is infinite it is not at all." Nevertheless, it seems best to regard such passages as accidental and to take the view that, where much arguing takes place, the syllogism is hard to avoid. Even if it is not as inevitable as the *reductio ad absurdum*, experiments, once they are given the relation of concepts as field of operation, will sooner or later produce syllogisms. Naturally enough, the peculiar dignity and importance of this form is not realized at the time; nor indeed could it be realized before logical cogency had become an issue and not only the content but the form of arguments were subjected to scrutiny. No single step in this process may have been as dramatic as the final answer, which Aristotle provided through the discovery and definition of valid syllogisms. That the preparatory stages are reflected in Plato's dialogues is known today, and some effort is made to identify them.

With as much right as "Socrates" and Plato, the orators call for comments. Here, continuity between the argumentation of the late fifth and of the fourth century is certain; a break would be *a priori* improbable. What we may expect—and indeed find—is refinement. Analyses of the arguments employed by orators later than Antiphon have been undertaken in dissertations and articles; these prove helpful in separating the typical from the accidental. When reading a paper of the kind, for example, John J. Bateman's on Lysias (*Phoenix* 16, 1962, 157ff.), we find little in the types of argument, as distinct from what Bateman calls "subtle use," that would not have its parallel in Antiphon—or elsewhere in the fifth century, but we hardly need go beyond Antiphon. On the other hand if we study Aristotle's rhetorical *topoi* (*Rhet.* B23), a classification of arguments according to form and logical structure, we have reason to doubt whether all of them could be illustrated by examples prior to the fourth century. However, such doubt need not prompt conclusions about an enriched equipment or the like. For Aristotle's classification is not the only one conceivable (the *topoi* being, as Kant said of the Categories, "aufgerafft," not deduced), nor should we ever in this connection forget the limited amount of material preserved from earlier times. We do not read a single political speech (*demegoria*) of the fifth century in its authentic form—whether Aristotle read any is highly dubious; a few "winged words" of Pericles are typical of his information.

Fortunately we can again perceive "trends" of the development. When Attic oratory reached its height, the reasoning, whether moving in old or new grooves, runs far more smoothly. Without effort, the orator is in control of the entire instrumentation. Enthymemes have become more sophisticated—at least in the orators; with Thucydides, who represents the *non plus ultra* of sophistication, we need not compare them. Even more impressive is their progress in style and diction. Compared with the struggle for unusual phrasing so often conspicuous in Thucydides, everything in Demosthenes and Aeschines looks natural, and if "natural" is not the best description of Isocrates' periods, we may yet admit that they are smooth and true to type.

We have said a few words about utopian speculations early in this "Conclusion" and in the chapter devoted to this topic have gone beyond our normally observed time-limits for a brief consideration of Plato's *Republic* and of the *Cyropaedia*. We need not here point out that designs for an ideal commonwealth did not end with the *Republic*; they rather begin with it, and we should in particular like to know more about Zeno's scheme for a *cosmopolis* that was said to have been written "on the tail of the (Cynic) dog." Alexander's conquests of the Orient opened up a world where even in earlier days Ionian explorers had become acquainted with numerous customs different from but not on that account worse than the Greek. Now it is not so much the foreign *nomoi* that claim attention as the Indian sages who fascinate by their ideally simple life—not that the Greeks would not build up their own saints' lives around the figures of a Pythagoras, a Diogenes, etc. Strange seas inspire miracle stories about voyages to paradisical islands. Alexander's life and deed and all that happened or could be seen in the East during his reign and later under the diadochs was fantastic enough but imagination refused to acquiesce in it. Plato's "Atlantis" and Theopompus' "Meropis" were bound to have a literary progeny. More and more, the purpose of fantastic stories was entertainment; there is no reason to think that Euhemerus aimed at anything else.

The exotic is a picturesque rather than a serious answer to the demands for reforms. The "ought to" of the critical speculations was met by the Hellenistic philosophers. Arguing the case for the gods, they offered assurance that the gods were better than popular beliefs made them out to be and that human beings were wrong to complain about the absence of Providence. If there was a right to expect it—a point not all schools would concede—it was man's own fault that he did not discover its evidence throughout the world. In the area of human conduct, the ethical norms set up by Reason demanded more than could reasonably be expected of human frailty. The Stoic sage was close enough to utopia. He alone was king, was rich and was beautiful (*St. V. F.* III 589ff.). There was no point in going beyond these paradoxes.

Little need be said on the later fate of "rational reconstruction." Every historian dealing with military, political, or other developments practices it in some way and with some degree of freedom but there would never be another Thucydides. It is possible to speak of a "Thucydidean tradition" in ancient historiography and to sympathize with the tendency (initiated by H. Strasburger and recently carried forward by Oswyn Murray, *CQ* 22, 1972, 200ff.), of distinguishing between a Herodotean and a Thucydidean approach to history. The criteria for qualifying as a Thucydidean approach would be a special interest in wars, politics, and altogether in developments rather than static conditions, a judicious selection of the material, the "pragmatic" attitude or some affinity to it, attention given not only to the actions but also to the sufferings, *pathe*, but no rhetorical or melodramatic treatment of them. Still, whatever they may be and however many or few later historians may pass the tests, coordination of events and construction of larger, meaningful units is something very personal. It is bound to reflect a historian's individual outlook, interests, the measure of his penetration to the core of things, and at times, of course, also his bias and partisanship. The possibility that future studies will discover Thucydidean influence in, say, Polybius' composition of historical units must be admitted but for the time being there is nothing to record.

Should we still summarize the findings of this Conclusion? As we might have expected, the intellectual experiments are a transitional stage in the history of Greek thought. Except for some types of argumentation and the psychological dichotomy that pits reason against the irrational impulses, hardly any experiment survived in the form that we have come to know. But if transitional, they also are preparatory, representing a ferment that precedes the consolidation needed to build solid structures on firm ground. Moreover this period of ferment, transition, and experimentation has its peculiar charm and is characterized by a very remarkable productivity.

SUBJECT INDEX

INDEX

AUTHORS AND PASSAGES

Library of Congress Cataloging in Publication Data

Solmsen, Friedrich, 1904-
Intellectual experiments of the Greek enlightenment.

Includes bibliographical references and index.
1. Philosophy, Ancient. 2. Reason. 3. Sophists
(Greek philosophy) I. Title.
B187.R35S64 180 74-25629
ISBN 0-691-07201-9